THE ESSENTIAL GUIDE TO
WOODWORK

THE ESSENTIAL GUIDE TO
WOODWORK

Chris Simpson

Thunder Bay
P·R·E·S·S

San Diego, California

CONTENTS

Introduction

Working with a natural material such as wood is both a rewarding and satisfying pastime. Wood has a special quality that is like no other material—it is a pleasure to touch and a delight to look at.

Every piece of lumber is unique, with a diversity of color, texture, and strength. Its versatility and unique qualities are a source of constant inspiration to the creative woodworker. It is an appreciation of these qualities, combined with good function and design, that will give you many years of enjoyment in fine furniture making.

To gain the most pleasure from your woodworking experience, it is important to give yourself a firm skill base that will allow your interest and enthusiasm to develop fully. To help you achieve this, this book has been divided into four sections.

The opening chapter, "Wood and Other Materials," gives general information on the foundations of woodworking, including an introduction to the natural resource of timber and its unique qualities and challenges. This will help you to make the right choices when you come to choose, buy, and store wood for yourself.

The second chapter, "Design and Construction," concentrates on the importance of design and shows how every piece that you make needs to be both functional and aesthetically pleasing. There are useful tips that will help you to achieve a harmonious balance between the two.

The third chapter, "Tools and Techniques," moves onto the practicalities of woodworking. It opens with advice about workshop design, and the accessories and tools that you will need to begin your woodworking experience. All the basic skills needed to produce fine woodwork are clearly and succinctly explained with illustrations and photographs to help wherever relevant. From straightforward common processes, such as sawing and planing, and to more specialized aspects of woodworking, such as carving and turning, this section will enable you to master and develop your skills.

Above: Much of the joy of working with wood is derived from the fact that it is a natural living product.

Opposite: Sori Yanagi's "Butterfly" stools (1956) show how lumber can be converted into fine pieces.

*Opposite: An elegant
linen chest—just one of
the challenging projects
that lies ahead in
this book.*

Project rating

Basic

Simple woodworking
exercises that are suitable
for beginners.

Intermediate

Moderately difficult
projects for those
woodworkers who have
some previous experience.

Advanced

Complex, challenging
projects for more
advanced woodworkers.

The fourth chapter features stylish projects
that will enable you to put your skills into
practice. Divided into basic, intermediate,
and advanced, you will be able to go straight
to a project that is suitable for your level of
expertise. From a simple letter rack, to a
challenging workbench, to a complex linen
chest, these pieces will make stunning
additions to your home.

Each project contains a materials list,
a tools list, and step-by-step instructions.
Illustrations and photographs are included
to help you complete each project, and
drawings show the sizes of components and
how they fit together. Measurements are
given in imperial—feet, inches, and fractions
of an inch. When beginning the projects,
do not cut all the lumber to the size given

in the materials list. Work through the
steps and always check measurements as
you progress.

This book provides a sound foundation
for the acquisition and development of
your woodworking knowledge and skills.
It also provides you with the opportunity
to develop your skills through a wide range
of interesting, creative, and useful projects.
The importance of precision and accuracy
are emphasized, as is the need to develop
a sense of, and an ability to, appreciate and
produce quality work. Producing quality
work requires much effort and skill, but
the sense of achievement and the pleasure
of working with the unique natural resource
of wood are what makes woodworking such
a popular and rewarding experience.

*Right: Coming to grips
with basic woodworking
skills is a fundamental
part of your
woodworking adventure.*

*Far right: Make sure
that you have all the
necessary tools that you
need for each project
before you start.*

WOOD AND OTHER MATERIALS

A NATURAL RESOURCE

Timber is a natural product, unlike so many of the materials we use for everyday living. So the woodworker could be said to renew the essential bond between man and nature that has, to some extent, been lost in our modern world.

The range of different timber species – both hardwoods and softwoods – offers an extremely wide choice of materials. Each species has its own properties and characteristics. Even when using the same species of timber, each piece will present different challenges. They will also differ in appearance, giving variations in color, pattern, texture, and finish.

The beauty of a growing tree contributes to the pleasure of woodwork.

In order to gain the best results from working with timber, it is important to be aware of some basic facts about the material – for example, how trees grow, how they are converted for use, and how we can utilize these characteristics.

Ecological concerns

The issue of ecological matters is an important concern, and it has rightly become difficult to source endangered species. It is now recognized that forests must be maintained to ensure a continuous supply of quality trees. In a well-run forest, mature timber is extracted with care and new planting is constantly taking place.

The science of forestry has greatly improved in the developed world and pressure is also being put on developing countries to ensure forests are carefully managed so that the disastrous effects of deforestation are avoided in the future. Many nations are also seeking to help sustain their economies by not exporting the logs they produce, but carrying out conversion nearer the source.

How a tree grows

To appreciate the various properties of timber, it is useful to understand how a tree grows and to learn about its structure. A tree is an extremely efficient organism. The trunk is the main conduit for transferring water and minerals, which are absorbed from the soil through the roots. The leaves of the tree take in carbon dioxide, give off oxygen, and harness the energy of light, which, through the process of photosynthesis, produces all the nutrients that the tree requires to thrive.

Tree structure

The trunk's structure consists of tubular cells, which are held together with a chemical known as lignin. The direction of these cells determines the nature of the timber's grain. The cells tend to be long and thin, running lengthwise along the trunk and branches.

Food storage and the sap circulation take place through the cells of a tree. In a softwood tree the cells have a simple structure of hollow, spindle-like cells, while hardwood trees have long and needle-like cells. This difference in cell structure is what distinguishes a softwood from a hardwood.

A section through the tree's trunk shows the pith at the center. This is formed from the original sapling, is often weak and can suffer from

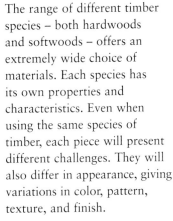

A cross-section of a tree trunk shows the various layers of growth.

This annual growth can be seen in concentric rings, or growth rings, through the timber and can be used to determine a tree's age. Each growth ring contains large earlywood and smaller latewood cells. Earlywood is the part of the annual growth rings that grows at the beginning of the season. Latewood is produced toward the end of the season, and has a different texture. It is usually denser and darker than the earlywood.

The growth rings in hardwood timber can be categorized as either ring porous or diffuse porous. Ring-porous timber shows a difference in cellular structure between timber laid down in the different growth periods of the tree – open cells when the tree is growing in spring and summer, and tighter grouped cells when growth slows in autumn and winter. Diffuse-porous timber is found in trees where there are no marked seasonal changes and the cells are much more regular in size. This relatively even distribution and regularity of fibers make diffuse-porous hardwoods, such as beech, easier to plane and sand to a finish than ring-porous hardwoods, such as ash or oak.

fungal attack. The heartwood, which surrounds the pith, is the mature timber that forms the structure of the tree as well as providing some food transference. Sapwood surrounds the heartwood, and is where most of the transference and storage of nutrients takes place. Sapwood from most timbers is not used for furniture making since it offers little resistance to fungal and insect attack.

A tree trunk has medullary rays, or ray cells, which conduct nutrients through the sapwood. These medullary rays are usually quite visible in hardwoods, but can be difficult to see in softwoods.

Growth rings
Each year, the tree grows because the living cells in the cambium layer, which lies immediately behind the bark, sub-divide. As the tree grows, the cells in the cambium layer develop into specialized sapwood cells, and a new sapwood ring is formed around the growth from the previous year. At the same time, the oldest sapwood converts into heartwood. This means that, with each period of annual growth, the heartwood becomes larger, while the size of the sapwood does not vary much during the lifecycle of a tree.

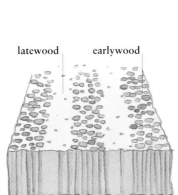

Earlywood and latewood

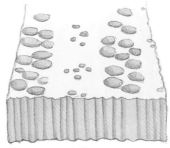

Ring-porous timber

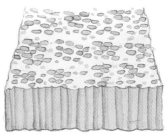

Diffuse-porous timber

HARDWOODS AND SOFTWOODS

The terms "hardwood" and "softwood" do not refer to the hardness or softness

of a specific tree species. They are biological divisions and not a description

of the wood's durability.

Even though most hardwoods are hard and most softwoods are soft, hardness cannot be used to classify different woods. Balsa is a hardwood and some softwoods can be very hard.

Hardwoods grow in most parts of the world, and are generally preferred by furniture makers. Although they are often more expensive than softwoods, they are usually more durable and come in a larger range of colors with widely varying characteristics.

They can, however, be difficult to obtain and a few of the more expensive, exotic hardwoods are cut into veneer sheets to make better use of the lumber. Most countries have indigenous species, even though fashion has, in the past, led to the importation of particular types for specific uses, such as teak for outdoor furniture and boats and mahogany for fine furniture.

Softwoods are usually light in color, ranging from an off-white to a mid-brown. They can be easily identified by looking at the growth rings where the contrasting grain pattern of the earlywood and latewood is found—these two differ in color and density. Softwoods often have a more open grain, are easier to work, and are generally used for building and carpentry work. Fashion has intervened, however, and there is a strong market in many countries for pine furniture.

Hardwood trees growing in their natural habitat.

Softwood trees growing in their natural habitat.

Species of hardwood

The term "hardwood" generally refers to trees that have broad leaves. Hardwoods are found in both temperate and tropical climates and can be either deciduous or evergreen. They are generally preferred by furniture makers because they have a wider range of colors and textures. Below and overleaf are some examples of the most commonly used hardwoods.

Pericopsis elata
AFRORMOSIA

Origin: West Africa
Characteristics: Durable type of wood, with a grain that varies from straight to interlocked. Yellow-brown in color, which darkens over time when exposed to light. It is similar to teak but is less oily and often used as a teak substitute in furniture making (as is Iroko, see page 16).

Fraxinus spp.
ASH

Origin: Europe (right), North America (left)
Characteristics: Heartwood and sapwood of similar color in pink, gray, and cream. Prominent growth rings best highlighted using back-cut of live-sawn board with a tangential cut. Quarter-sawn boards produce straight grain. Suitable for laminating and steam-bending. Sands and finishes well.

Fagus spp.
BEECH

Origin: All over Europe, best from Baltic regions
Characteristics: This type of wood is whitish in color with little variation between sapwood and heartwood. Growth rings visible with distinctive fleck produced by medullary rays. Easily worked and commonly used in furniture for bent wood pieces. Cracking and warping can occur if seasoning is not carefully controlled.

Buxus sempervirens
BOXWOOD

Origin: Southern Europe and parts of West Asia
Characteristics: Boxwood is a fine and even-textured wood; straight grain and dense. Often found as a hedgerow tree and therefore seldom available to buy in lumber form. It is most commonly used for making small items of furniture, such as those produced by turning or carving.

Liriodendron tulipifera
AMERICAN TULIP TREE

Origin: Central and South America
Characteristics: Dense and fairly hard. Texture can vary but it usually has irregular grain. The wood has very attractive color in the grain, ranging from pink to red stripes over a yellow base. Difficult to work and, due to limited availability, it is usually just used for smaller items or veneering.

Toona Australis
AUSTRALIAN CEDAR

Origin: East coast of Australia
Characteristics: Rich red color in heartwood; sapwood pale cream to pink. Medium-density with tendency to be a little soft—requires careful handling. Good grain pattern in back-cut boards; quarter-sawn boards produce straight, even grain. Scarce and expensive in large section sizes. Sands well and can be polished to mirror finish.

Acacia melanoxylon
BLACKWOOD

Origin: Tasmania and east coast of Australia
Characteristics: Medium-weight hardwood. Sometimes called Tasmanian blackwood, the resins can stain your hands black. Fairly straight grain, some interlocking can give fiddleback appearance. Pinkish-yellow to mud-brown tones with dark-brown growth rings. Works well with sharp tools. Sands well, finishing to a high polish.

Guilbourtia demensei
BUBINGA

Also known as African rosewood

Origin: West Africa
Characteristics: Coarse but even-textured wood; grain varies from straight to interlocked and irregular; relatively durable. Bubinga is red-brown in color with a purple hue. It can be used in fine furniture making when crafted and finished.

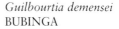

Cedrela
CEDRELA

Origin: Brazil and Mexico
Characteristics: Cedrela is a prized wood from Brazil that is used extensively in furniture manufacturing throughout Europe. White-colored sapwood, tending to pink; heartwood pinkish brown with purplish highlights. Works particularly well and has a fine texture, allowing you to achieve a high-quality finish with minimal effort. Sands, glues, and polishes well.

Ceratopetalum apetalem
COACHWOOD

Also known as satinwood

Origin: Australian east-coast rain forests
Characteristics: Pink to light brown color with good grain pattern when tangentially cut and straight grain when quarter-sawn. Easily machined with distinctive odor when cut or sanded. Finishes well with hand tools, sands well, and accepts most polishes. Becoming hard to get and relatively expensive.

Ulmus spp.
ELM

Also known as nave or red elm

Origin: Central and Southern Europe, Scandinavia, and North America
Characteristics: Sapwood yellow to white, contrasting with brownish red heartwood. Medullary rays are not prominent and pores are fine, giving a fine texture. Used in carpentry and cabinetmaking. Difficult to achieve fine finish.

Milicia spp.
IROKO

Origin: West Africa
Characteristics: Medium yellow-brown in color and can be difficult to work because of occasional stone deposits. It has an interlocked grain and is strong and durable. Like Afrormosia (see page 15) it is used as a teak substitute because it is very durable but less oily. It is good for outdoor use as well as for indoor furniture.

Dyera costulata
JELUTONG

Origin: Malaysia and Indonesia
Characteristics: Classified as hardwood though soft in texture. Exercise care in handling. Close, even grain in a pale color range. Grain has tendency to crush when chiseling, so sharp tools are important. Easily workable by machine and used extensively for pattern making. Sands and polishes well.

Prunus spp.
CHERRY

Origin: Europe (left), Asia Minor, and the United States (right)
Characteristics: Open grain with dark, open pores and pink-to-brown heartwood; often used as decorative veneer. Susceptible to insect attack and shrinkage. Can be machined easily, but warps badly if not seasoned properly. Sands well and holds a finish very well—it is particularly good to use for cabinetmaking.

Diospyros spp.
EBONY

Origin: Parts of Africa and India
Characteristics: Very dark to black heartwood with black grain structure. Sapwood lightish pink. Extremely hard but works well with sharp tools. Available in very small sizes and quantities, hence used only as inlays and on musical instruments. Density means it can be difficult to polish. Sanding dust can stain pale lumber.

Astronium fraxinifolium
GONÇALO ALVES

Also known as tiger wood (USA) or zebrawood (UK)

Origin: South America
Characteristics: Difficult to work because of its irregular grain, which varies in hardness; medium-textured and durable. Its character is given by its dark streaks and it can be very attractive when used in furniture either as solid or veneer.

Eucalyptus marginata
JARRAH

Origin: Southwestern Australia
Characteristics: Hard, heavy wood. Heartwood varies from pink to dark red. Fairly coarse texture and generally straight grain. Back-cut boards can show pleasant grain pattern, but gum veins and pockets sometimes spoil finish. Can be difficult to work because of hardness. Sands well and finishes to a high polish.

Dalbergia cearensis
KINGWOOD

Also known as violet wood and violetta (USA)

Origin: South America
Characteristics: Lustrous and even-textured wood, which has very attractive coloring and is fairly good to work. Kingwood is usually straight-grained and durable. Due to its limited availability, it is often used as veneer, inlay, or in marquetry. Also used in turning.

Guaiacum officinale
LIGNUM VITAE

Origin: West Indies
Characteristics: Known as the heaviest of all hardwoods. Even grain and texture, with greasy feel. Brown coloring with a green tinge. Density and oil content makes it very durable. Mainly used as decorative trim pieces in fine furniture. Density makes it hard to work and gluing is difficult because of high oil content.

Swietenia spp.
MAHOGANY

Origin: Honduras, the Caribbean islands, and Mexico
Characteristics: Medium-weight of varying density. Yellow sapwood and pink to reddish-brown heartwood. Revered cabinet lumber for several centuries now. Grain pattern can range from plain to magnificent. Works very easily and stain highlights the grain patterns tremendously.

Quercus spp.
OAK

Origin: Europe (right), North Africa, North America (left), and Asia
Characteristics: This type of wood is strong and durable with pronounced pores. Can be extremely heavy. European variety generally yellow and North American pink to reddish. Commonly used in furniture, boatbuilding, and kitchen cabinet work.

Platanus spp.
PLANE
Also known as lacewood

Origin: Europe, except far north, and Asia Minor
Characteristics: Yellowish sapwood and copper-colored heartwood. Strong, close-linked medullary rays. Used in wood turning, fine cabinetmaking, and inlay work. Sands well but can be difficult to finish.

Gonystylus spp.
RAMIN

Origin: Borneo, Indonesia, and the Philippines **Characteristics:** Medium-density tropical rain-forest wood prone to infestation of insects and fungi. Pale yellow to white in both sapwood and heartwood. Straight, even grain, making it easy to work in all directions. Glues well and can be easily polished.

Tilia vulgaris
LIME

Origin: Europe
Characteristics: Straight-grained wood with uniform texture. Fairly soft and light in color, which darkens to light brown with exposure—it is best to treat it with a preservative. Lime is good to work and is often used in carving, turning, and for making some musical instruments.

Shorea spp.
MERANTI
Also known as Pacific maple and lauan

Origin: Malaysia, Indonesia, and the Philippines
Characteristics: Color ranges from pale brown to pink and dark red. Susceptible to insect attack. Weight and density varies greatly. Plain grain pattern with occasional interlocking grain. Not ideal for outdoor work. Best used as base product for veneering over, or it can be easily stained.

Pterocarpus spp.
PADAUK
Also known as African coralwood and Andaman redwood

Origin: Africa and South-East Asia
Characteristics: Medium density with striking red colour—ideal highlight or contrast wood in marquetry or inlay work. Straight grain and even texture; can have fiddleback feature. Unfortunately the very strong color on recently worked wood darkens with time.

Peltogyne spp.
PURPLEHEART
Also known as amaranth (USA)

Origin: Central and South America
Characteristics: Fine- to medium-textured wood, which is strong and durable. Generally straight-grained and attractive purple color when freshly worked but darkens over time. Purpleheart is commonly used for furniture making, veneer work, and turning.

Dalbergia spp.
ROSEWOOD

Origin: Brazil, India, Honduras
Characteristics: These trees are short so sawn lumber is often not of great length or width. Very dense and hard to work. Sapwood off-white and heartwood yellow to pale pink, with dark brown to purplish veins. Best suited for small decorative projects such as jewelry boxes and inlays.

Castanea sativa
SWEET CHESTNUT

Also known as European Chestnut and
Spanish Chestnut

Origin: Mediterranean, Switzerland, and Germany
Characteristics: Similar appearance to oak.
Sapwood is much whiter than heartwood.
Used for handles, shutters, in wood turning,
and for kitchen-cupboard door making,
rather than actual cabinetmaking. Sands
and polishes well. Slight acidity can corrode
metals and stain wood.

Tectonais grandis
TEAK

Origin: India, Burma, and Southeast Asia
Characteristics: Whitish sapwood and heartwood
brown to ocher with dark growth rings. Oily
and waxy to the touch. Natural oils make it
very durable, and water and fungus resistant.
Sands well; gluing may cause problems. Ideal for
outdoor furniture. Machines well. Recommended
finish of teak oil. Expensive and hard to find.

Millettia laurentii
WENGE

Origin: Central and East Africa
Characteristics: Very hard and heavy timber.
Difficult to work and be aware of painful
splinters when working. However, wenge has
a superb black color with either fine grain or
an elaborate figure. It can be used to
make interesting furniture and is also used
in turning. When finishing, use black wax.

Acer pseudoplatnus
SYCAMORE

Origin: Europe and West Europe
Characteristics: Sycamore has a fine
texture, often straight-grained but
boards with quarter-sawn fiddleback
grain are very sought after for some
musical instruments. Sycamore is
one of the whitest types of woods
but its grain darkens over time.
Good to work and makes attractive,
light-colored furniture.

Juglans spp.
WALNUT

Origin: Eastern United States (right) and
Canada, and mild regions of Europe (left)
Characteristics: Dark brown with
occasional purplish tinge. Used for high-
quality cabinetmaking. Mostly straight
grained but can exhibit fiddleback grain.
Walnut is a generic term often applied
to many species of dark brown wood.

Microberlinia brazzavillensis
ZEBRANO

Also known as Zingana and sometimes zebrawood
(not to be confused with Gonçalo Alves, see page 16)

Origin: West Africa
Characteristics: Coarse and open-textured
wood, which is light in color with interlocking grain.
Expensive to buy and so generally used
as veneer or inlay, though it is sometimes used
in fine furniture or cabinetmaking.

Species of softwood

"Softwood" refers to types of trees that grow in cold regions, primarily in the northern

hemisphere. Softwoods tend to have needles instead of leaves and are usually evergreen.

Pseudotsuga menziesii
DOUGLAS FIR

Origin: North America, Canada, and Europe
Characteristics: Straight, pronounced grain; clear
definition between earlywood and latewood.
Yellow with prominent orange growth rings.
Tough and water resistant. Used as building
lumber, but prone to splitting so should be
coated with preservative to improve external
durability. Nails tend to follow grain direction.

Tsuga spp.
HEMLOCK

Origin: North America, Himalayas to North
Burma, West Vietnam, China, and Japan.
Characteristics: Pale yellow with distinctive
growth rings. Even textured with good, straight
grain. Easy to work, but predrill for nailing near
end sections. Poor seasoning can cause surface
checking. Not very durable for exposed work
and does not accept preservative treatment well.

Larix spp.
LARCH

Origin: All over Europe and North America
Characteristics: Straight-grained, uniform texture tougher than many other softwoods. Heartwood pale to rich red. Dries fairly rapidly, which can result in shrinkage and distortion and cause knots to fall out. Not particularly durable and resists preserving treatments. Slightly difficult to work and should be predrilled for nailing and screwing.

Araucaria angustifolia
PINE, PARANA

Origin: South America
Characteristics: Mid-weight and straight-grained with an even texture, its growth rings are not very conspicuous. Heartwood light brown with occasional red streaks. Can distort during the seasoning process and end splits are conspicuous. Treat with preservative when using externally. Tendency to twist and jam on blade when sawed.

Pinus strobus
PINE, YELLOW

Origin: North America and Canada
Characteristics: Quite soft, but with straight grain and mild texture. Pale yellow to brown; can show resin-duct marks. Easily dented so protect when being worked. External use not recommended; treat with preservative. Works easily but blades must be sharp to avoid furry finish. Nails well; screws can strip thread if inserted with a screw gun.

Picea abies
SPRUCE, EUROPEAN

Origin: All over Europe
Characteristics: The "Christmas tree." Pale with little color difference between sapwood and heartwood. Straight-grained, even-textured and visible growth rings. Can be very knotty. Not a durable wood so treatment with preservatives is recommended for outdoor use. Easily worked and glues quite well, but staining can be patchy.

Thuja plicata
WESTERN RED CEDAR

Origin: North America
Characteristics: This wood is used outdoors because it is very durable. Light pink to reddish-brown, changing on exposure to silver/gray. Extremely light and not particularly strong; avoid structural use. Larger sections suffer from collapse during seasoning, but can be reconditioned. Works well, glues easily, and accepts all finishes.

Pinus sylvestris
PINE, HARD
Also known as Scots Pine

Origin: Western Europe and Great Britain
Characteristics: Tall tree of up to 130 ft.; plantation planted in many countries. Light yellow to reddish-brown color and can have much resin present, particularly in sapwood. Distinct figure and matures to beautiful color over time. Can suffer distortion and resins may bleed through a finish.

Pinus Ponderosa
PINE, PONDEROSA
Also known as British Columbia soft pine (Canada), Western yellow pine, and California white pine (USA)

Origin: Western USA and Canada
Characteristics: The sapwood is soft and even-textured, while the heartwood is darker, striped and resinous. It is used widely in furniture making and carpentry.

Sequoia sempervirens
SEQUOIA

Origin: North America
Characteristics: Texture can vary but generally straight-grained, colored reddish brown with a contrast between earlywood and latewood. Generally nonresinous. Owing to its properties, it can be used for exterior work such as shingles, exterior sidings, and posts, but it can also be used effectively for interior carpentry.

Picea sitchensis
SPRUCE, SITKA
Also known as Menzies Spruce and Western Spruce

Origin: Northwestern United States
Characteristics: Tree grows up to 245 ft. Straight-grained with even texture, nonresinous and creamy white with occasional pink tone. Treat with preservative for outdoor use. Works well with sharp tools, but knots can bleed resin. Relatively high strength-to-weight property.

Taxus baccata
YEW
Also known as Common, Irish, or European Yew

Origin: Europe, North Africa, Middle East, India
Characteristics: Tough and very hard. Heartwood orange-red to purple-brown; sapwood light. Decorative interlocked grain patterns. Durable but can be difficult to work. Gluing difficult due to oily nature. Stains well and finishes to a high-quality polish. Burr pieces often used in veneers.

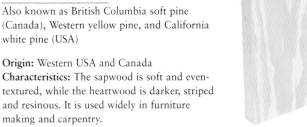

LUMBER MILLING AND SEASONING

Once the tree has been felled the wood is converted into workable pieces of lumber, which are then dried out or "seasoned" in the open air or in kilns.

Milling the logs

Felled trees are cut into logs, which are then sent to sawmills to be converted into planks or boards on large bandsaws or circular-saw machines.

Usually only the trunks or very major limbs are milled. Branches help to support the foliage, hence wood from branches has a high degree of movement and contains reaction wood that is prone to splitting, making it economically unviable for use in a piece. Instead it is used for chipping in certain manufactured boards.

Through-and-through sawn lumber at the sawmill.

Methods of milling

When lumber dries it shrinks and, because this shrinkage can cause distortion, the annual growth rings always try to straighten out. Therefore, wood cut from different parts of the trunk will move in different ways—for example, planks cut horizontally across the top of the trunk will be more prone to distortion than those cut across the center.

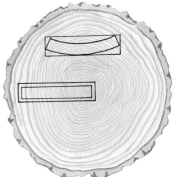

The orientation of growth rings determines the degree of distortion.

Through-and-through sawing

Lumber is very often milled "through and through," which means the log is sawed into planks in a series of slices. As a result, planks cut from the edge have different properties to those cut across the center. This is also known as plain-sawing, and although it produces lumber at its widest, it is prone to uneven shrinkage and distortion. These boards can show a highly figured grain pattern because they are cut across the growth rings.

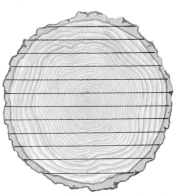

Through-and-through sawn lumber.

Quarter-sawing

Where minimum timber movement is required, the log can be quarter-sawn. True quarter-sawing would mean the boards were tapered, but this is uneconomic and less wasteful methods of sawing are used. Quarter-sawn lumber shrinks more evenly and produces a more stable plank because a smaller amount of growth ring is available to shrink. Quarter-sawn boards have much straighter grain patterns.

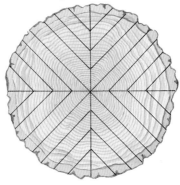

Quarter-sawn lumber.

Methods of seasoning

All newly cut lumber contains a high percentage of water, which must be removed by a process of drying out called "seasoning." This water is present either as free water or as moisture, the latter being present in the cell walls. The first stage of seasoning is to remove the free water and then, as seasoning continues and moisture is lost from the cell walls, movement and shrinkage will start to occur within the lumber. If, however, seasoning takes place too quickly, stresses are created within the lumber. The whole process therefore needs to be very carefully controlled.

There are two main methods of seasoning lumber—air drying and kiln drying.

Air drying lumber

Planks that are seasoned by the air-drying method are stacked on spacer battens at least 18 in. apart—the air spaces between each plank are essential to avoid mold and fungal attack.

Lumber drying naturally in the open air, with spacer battens in between the planks.

The stack is built in a dry, sheltered spot and protected from rain and direct sunlight. It takes approximately one year to dry every 1 in. of board thickness for hardwoods and slightly less for drying softwoods. With this method, lumber can only dry to the ambient humidity—the humidity of the atmosphere it is drying in—which is generally about 15 percent. If the lumber is meant for interior use, the humidity needs to be reduced in a kiln where the extraction of moisture is carefully controlled.

Kiln drying lumber

A kiln for drying lumber is like a large oven in which temperature and humidity can be carefully controlled, so that moisture content is reduced to 8 percent or less. Planks are fed into the kiln on racks, a mixture of hot air and steam is introduced, then the humidity is slowly reduced to the required moisture content. Kiln-dried lumber needs to be stored in a controlled environment. If it is dried to below the air's moisture level and then placed outside, it will take up moisture again.

An industrial kiln for drying large quantities of lumber.

PROPERTIES AND DEFECTS OF LUMBER

When choosing a lumber for woodwork our choices are often influenced by the look of the grain, figure, and texture, and whether the wood is free of any defects.

Properties of lumber

Since lumber comes from a living tree, the characteristics and properties of each species will vary greatly. Differences can also occur within a species or even within an individual tree. Some lumbers will be easy to work, others less so; some will be strong, others weaker. The color and appearance of the grain, the figure, and the texture of the wood will also vary. All of these characteristics are determined by cell structure.

Grain

In lumber where growth has been even and the cell structure is in line with the main axis of the tree, the wood will be straight-grained and easy to work. However, in some trees growth will not be so even and this may result in grain that is not straight. Grain that is not straight is called interlocked grain, wavy grain, and curvy grain.

Lumber with wavy grain.

A fiddleback grain is wavy with regular light and dark streaks and is used to make violin backs. These irregular grained woods are often difficult to work, but can have attractive patterns. The term "grain" is also used to describe the way wood is worked. Sawing and planing can be done with the grain—that is, in the direction of the wood fibers. Sometimes sawing, chiseling, and planing are done across the grain—at right angles to the grain direction. In wood with irregular grain, where the grain is random, planing may have to be done both against and across the grain.

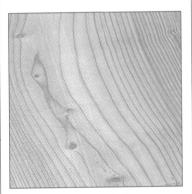

Lumber with interlocked grain.

Figure

Figure is another term for grain pattern. Figure can be caused by grain direction, but also marked differences between earlywood and latewood, size of the growth rings, method of milling, and color distribution. "Imperfections" also contribute to the figure. These might include curls—which occur at the fork between a branch and the trunk—and burls, which are abnormal growths of some sort, usually as the result of an injury the tree has sustained.

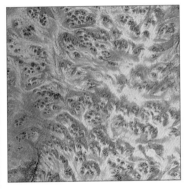

Lumber with burls.

Texture

Fine-textured woods have densely spaced cells, while coarse-textured woods have large, open-spaced cells.

Even-textured lumber has only a slight variation between early and latewood. Uneven-textured lumber, as the name suggests has much greater contrast between the seasonal growth rings.

Common lumber defects

Some lumber defects can arise from felling, some from careless kilning and some from incorrect storage. For example, if lumber has not been dried correctly, stresses are introduced, which make the wood hard to work. If the lumber has not been dried sufficiently, shrinkage, warping, and splitting can occur. Defects such as these will be marked at a good lumberyard and are best avoided because they are harder to work with.

Shakes

Shakes are splits in the wood that are caused by poor felling or stresses incurred during shrinkages.

Lumber with shakes.

Honeycombing

The problem of honeycombing occurs in a board if the outer fibers of the board or log dry out faster than the inside. When this happens the wood inside shrinks more than that outside, which leads to checking, or splits, within the lumber.

Honeycombing.

End splits

End splits are caused by the ends of the boards drying too rapidly. This can often be prevented by sealing the ends during the air-drying process.

An end split.

Distortion

Bowing, warping, twisting, winding, or springing can be caused by poor stacking of the boards, or from stresses that have built up during poor seasoning. These stresses make the wood difficult to cut.

Warping and end splits.

Ingrown bark

Ingrown bark is unattractive and weakens the structure of the lumber.

Knots

Knots form where the stumps of dead branches have

been overgrown with new growth rings. This makes the grain pattern around the knot very irregular and difficult to plane.

A knot.

Insect or fungal attack

Defects in wood caused by insect or fungal attack are most often found in furniture in old buildings, where systems of ventilation and heating are often antiquated and inadequate. Damp environmental conditions allow pests and fungi to attack. Any sapwood left on the lumber will suffer the worst. New lumber is less likely to suffer, because much greater care is now taken in harvesting, milling, and seasoning, although it may occur when proper care is not taken at source. Remember, however, that if damp conditions are present there is always a risk of infection.

Lumber suffering from fungal attack.

BUYING AND STORING LUMBER

When buying wood, it is best to visit a lumberyard personally in order to examine the boards for defects and to select the best pieces to suit your needs.

Buying hardwoods

Hardwoods are cut from the tree into planks and the stated thickness of the board is the sawn size. However, the maximum dimensions you have to work with must allow for planing the plank all around so it is flat and square. For example, a sawn plank purchased at 1 in. will finish between $^{13}/_{16}$ and $^{7}/_{8}$ in.

depending on how much has to be removed in order to make it flat, straight, and square. In order to arrive at a specific dimension of 1 in., a thicker board would have to be purchased, thus giving more waste. You also need to consider how much width you will get out of a plank.

When buying hardwoods in planks, there may be some resistance to turning

over too many boards in a stack to find the best grain characteristics or color, especially if you require only a small amount. However, if you are reasonable generally lumber dealers will be happy to oblige.

Buying softwoods

You will encounter a similar situation regarding measurements of sawn softwoods, but the dealer will normally allow you to pick out the pieces yourself. Sometimes softwoods can be purchased "planed all around" (PAR) or "dressed all around" (DAR)—that is, planed or dressed on all four sides. But the size given would be expressed in the original sawn size—for example, a board labeled 2 x 1 in. will actually be about $1^{13}/_{16}$ x $^{7}/_{8}$ in., but it will not be to an exact measurement. It will be to the nearest size that the lumberyard can plane in order to achieve a reasonable finish on all faces. As a result, a purchase made on one occasion may differ on another.

General pointers

Finished sizes also vary according to the country of origin and the milling standards in that country. Some countries have standard

When buying lumber, examine any defects that are marked on the wood.

thicknesses and widths, allowing for a consistency of product from one yard to another. This tends to be the case particularly with common building and carpentry grade lumber and milled sections such as moldings and baseboards.

The more exotic lumber for fine cabinet work is generally supplied rough sawn. If it needs to be planed, then the maximum thickness and width will be provided.

When purchasing lumber in large quantities the cost is often calculated by its cubic content, although in smaller volumes it may be sold by the length or piece. Be aware of how the dealer makes the calculations. Some dealers may want to charge you by the cubic foot, which can become quite confusing, particularly if you are used to dealing in cubic meters. Remember there are 424 cubic feet in a cubic meter. So ask the dealer for the cubic meter rate in addition to the cubic foot rate and then make sure they both add up correctly.

If you live a long way from a dealer there are mail-order companies that will supply a large range of lumber of varying sizes. The product is obviously more expensive but often there is no alternative, especially if you need a specific species. Generally, however, suppliers have a reputation to maintain and give a good service.

Storage in the workshop

Once you have obtained your lumber, you must ensure that it is stored under suitable conditions. Hardwood planks are best stored in a similar way to that found in a good lumberyard—horizontally with spacers in between each board and away from sunlight and direct heat sources. It is sometimes the case that softwoods are stored vertically at the suppliers, but this is best avoided unless it is absolutely necessary as a result of space constraints. In general, make sure that your workshop is dry and well ventilated.

You will find that as you undertake more projects there will be material left over. Not all of this will be waste and you should store any scraps that may be useful to use in later projects. Ensure, however, that this is undertaken methodically so that you know where to find different types.

Lumber is best stored horizontally.

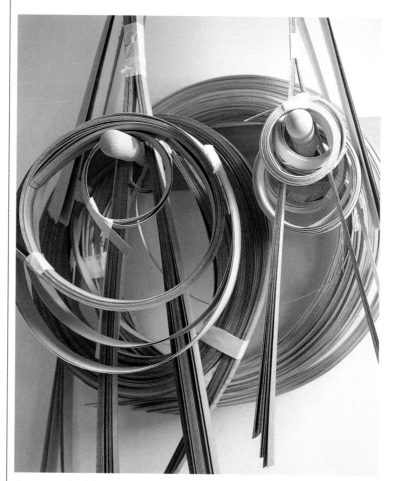

Store wood safely out of the way on a wall, away from direct heat and light.

MANUFACTURED BOARDS

Even though the natural characteristics of wood are a major part of its attraction,

they also tend to cause problems including shrinkage during mass manufacturing.

Therefore, the industry has developed a number of ways of using lumber to make

board materials that are much more dimensionally stable than natural lumber and

are readily available to the home woodworker.

Board sizes

Manufactured boards are usually produced to standard thicknesses, which are precise and expressed either in imperial or metric sizes. The sheet size is generally made to a standard 8 x 4 ft. Larger sheets can be made available to special order—that is, approximately 10 x 5 ft. Some of the thinner thicknesses may be sold at a different size—for example, $1/16$ in. aeroply may be found 5 ft. square. Many outlets, however, will cut standard sheets into smaller sizes, normally increments of the standard sheets—for example, 4 x 4 ft. or 4 x 2 ft. When tackling the projects in this book, you may decide to amend the sizes that are given in the accompanying drawings (see pages 52–3). If you do so, it is always important to consider how easily the required size can be cut from the standard sheet with the minimum of waste.

Types of manufactured board

There are various types of manufactured board available on the market today. These include plywood, particleboard or chipboard, fiberboard, and blockboard. Manufactured board can be used on its own, but also often forms a base for wood veneer (see pages 30–3).

Modular storage cubes made of preveneered MDF (see pages 228–33).

Plywood

Plywood is made from constructional veneers, which are laminated and glued together, with the grain alternating along and across the board. Usually there is an uneven number of layers so that the outside grain directions on the faces of the finished boards are the same. Plywood is available in a range of different thicknesses—from a flexible 1/8 in. sheet to a hefty 1 3/16 in. board.

Plywood can have various numbers of layers—the thinnest, three-ply, has three layers. As its name suggests, three-ply is made from just three laminates—two face veneers and a core that is sometimes the same thickness.

Thicker boards, or multi-plies, are made of more sheets of laminates—always an odd number finished to the standard board thicknesses. The performance of plywood is determined by the quality of the laminates and the type of adhesive used in the manufacturing process. Interior grade plywood is normally bonded with a urea-formaldehyde adhesive. These are suitable for most interior work, but other types should be chosen if they are to be used for kitchens or bathrooms. Exterior grade plywood— termed weather and boil proof or WBP—is bonded with phenolic adhesives, which are highly resistant to weather, wet and dry heat, insects and fungi. Marine plywood has laminates that are selected so that they are fault-free. For very special applications resorcinol adhesive can be used.

Particleboard or chipboard

Particleboard, also known as chipboard, is made from small wood chips, which are glued together under pressure. It is stable but can be affected by moisture if a waterproof adhesive has not been used. Some boards are made from similar-sized particles, but often you will find boards with outside layers of high-density particles sandwiching a coarser core, such as in graded-density chipboard. Decorative chipboard is also available with faces of wood veneer or plastic laminates.

Other boards with greater tensile strength are available, but more for building work than furniture making. Oriented-strand board is made from long strands of wood. Flakeboard or waferboard is made from big chips of wood, bonded in layers with random grain direction.

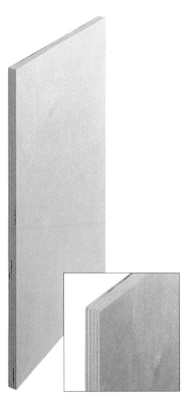

Three-ply plywood

Nine-ply multi-ply

Particleboard

Fiberboards

Fiberboard is made out of tiny particles of wood (finer than sawdust) that are fixed together with a tough resin. For many years, the best-known material was standard hardboard, which normally has one smooth and one textured face. Standard hardboard is available in a large variety of thicknesses—from $1/16$–$1/2$ in. Fiberboard is often used for making cabinet backs and childrens' toys.

One problem with hardboard, as well as chipboard and other particleboard, is that lippings, either solid or veneer, have to be applied to the edges. To overcome this problem, medium density fiberboard (MDF) was developed. MDF has a dense, smooth surface texture that is ideal for routing or painting. The edges can be polished so that there is no need to use

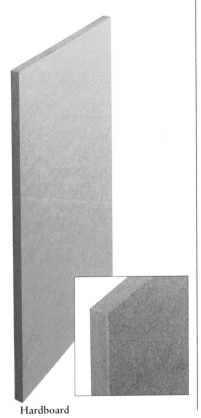

Hardboard

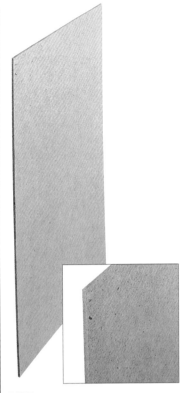

MDF

lippings. It has now become a standard material for much furniture making and also has certain applications for some interior trim. MDF comes in thicknesses ranging from $1/4$–$1\ 1/4$ in.

Blockboard

Blockboard is constructed of solid wood strips between laminates. They are particularly suited for worktops and shelves. Boards are normally sold in full $4\ 1/2$ x 4 ft. boards, with thicknesses ranging from $1/2$–1 in.

Laminboard is a top quality block construction board. The core strips of solid wood are quite narrow—approximately $3/16$ in. wide. It is usually edge-glued with two laminates on either side of the core, commonly with the grain of the outside in line with the direction of the core

strips. This is probably the most stable manufactured board available.

Standard blockboard has core strips that are wider than laminboard—approximately $3/4$ in. The core strips are not necessarily glued, and are sandwiched between outside laminate faces in one or two layers on each side. A problem with this board is that the strips can show through the outside veneers, particularly if there is only one on each face.

Battenboard is a cheaper blockboard where the interior strips are much wider—from $1\ 1/4$–$1\ 1/2$ in. Obviously show-through is much more likely.

In addition to these boards, solid boards made from wood strips, joined end to end and glued together to make a wide board, have been used in the furniture industry and are

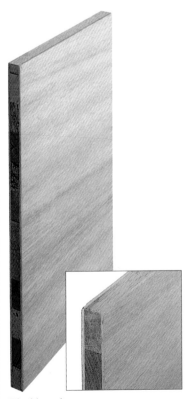

Blockboard

available in many do-it-yourself outlets. If you can visually accept the pattern of the board's strips, they are stable and are a useful alternative to other boards and solid wood.

Buying and storing manufactured board

When you wish to depart from the sizes of the projects as given or want to develop your own designs, always remember at the planning stage to reduce waste as much as possible by checking that the components needed can be economically cut from the standard-size sheets.

Unless you are purchasing from a company that carries a large range, the selection available from local outlets may be limited. When buying plywood, birch ply is best for making furniture because of its quality and birch veneer faces. Often the plywood available locally uses low-quality veneers. With blockboard and particleboard, the local quality can also be variable. There are several grades of specialized boards that use different adhesives or resins as bonding agents. The best can be entirely waterproof if required; if you need a high-performance variety, you will need to order from a company that specializes in high-grade board.

Manufactured boards can be stored vertically as long as they are well supported to ensure that they do not bend or warp. Support the boards in a strong shelf rack along one side of the workshop. They must also be stored under dry conditions because they can soak up moisture.

Dining chair back made of plywood (see pages 276–81).

Birdhouse made of exterior-grade plywood (see pages 246–9).

VENEERS

A veneer is a thin sheet of wood that is used for structural or decorative purposes. With many types of wood now hard to find in solid form, the use of veneer for decorative purposes is becoming more common.

Many types of wood have such interesting and unique characteristics that, in order to conserve and extend their use, they are made into veneer.

There is a vast range of veneer available to the wood-worker today. This is the case with woods that exhibit highly decorative grain patterns, such as curly mahogany.

For structural use they tend to be known as constructional veneers and they are usually cut to thicknesses of between $\frac{1}{32}$ and $\frac{1}{8}$ in.

How veneers are produced

In early times, veneers were produced by sawing, which resulted in thick veneer—as much as $\frac{1}{8}$ in.—and a very high waste element from the sawdust. Veneer-slicing machines were developed in the 18th century to produce thin veneers.

Sliced veneers

Flat slicing is where the log is supported on a carrier and a series of slices is produced. This can be standard flat slicing, quarter-cut slicing, or flat-sliced quartered. Quarter-cut slicing is used to produce veneer with a more varied grain pattern than flat slicing. Flat-sliced quartered veneer is produced when quartered logs are cut across the log. Sometimes when slicing, fine cracks, known as knife checks, can occur on the back face of the veneer. This is called the open or loose face. If possible lay this face down, although when using book-matched veneers this will not be possible.

Rotary-cut veneers

The rotary cut is used for constructional veneers and some decorative veneers. The trunk of the tree, after the bark has been removed and softened by steaming, is set on a machine similar to a huge lathe. As the machine revolves, a continuous sheet is cut from the log. The cutting knife reduces in radius to give a sheet of even thickness.

Veneers range in thickness from $\frac{1}{32}$–$\frac{1}{8}$ in.

SLICED VENEERS

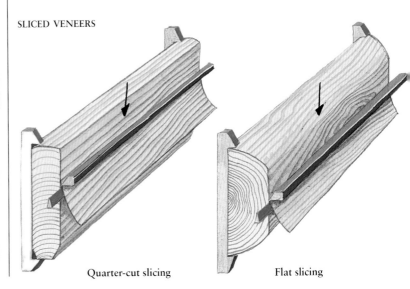

Quarter-cut slicing   Flat slicing

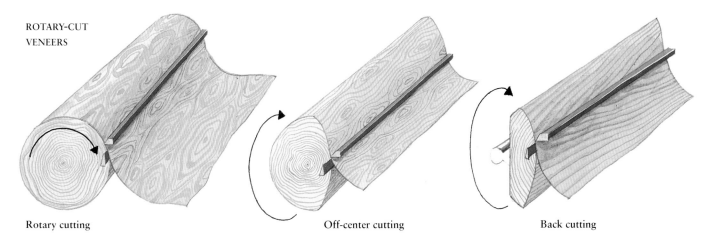

ROTARY-CUT
VENEERS

Rotary cutting   Off-center cutting   Back cutting

For decorative veneers, the log can be positioned in different ways so that various grains and figures are emphasized. Rotary cutting can be off-center, half-round, or back cutting. Both off-centre cutting and half-round cutting produce a figure similar to flat-slicing. The back-cutting method is often used to make the most of curly and burl veneers.

The surface of this tray is made with oak veneer on manufactured board—the handle and lipped edge are solid oak.

Veneer types

Many types of veneer are available today and have been made from a wide range of hardwoods, with varying colors, grains, figures, and textures. The specific type of veneer is obtained by slicing the log in various ways, as described on pages 30–1. The part of the tree that the veneer comes from—for example, the main trunk, burls or the fork—will also determine the type of veneer that is produced.

Some of the most common types of veneer that you will come across are described below.

Crown-cut veneers are the most common veneers used to decorate tables and other traditional furniture. They are produced using the flat-sliced quartered method of veneer slicing.

Curly veneers are produced from the fork of a tree where the trunk divides. They are produced using the back-cutting rotary method. The figure that is found on curly veneers is called a feather figure. Striped veneers are produced using the quarter-cut flat slicing method. This results in a radial cut being made across the width of the tree's growth rings.

Burl, or burr, veneers are often used for smaller pieces such as jewelry boxes or as a decorative focal point on larger pieces.

Some types of burl veneers are highly figured. They are produced using the back-cutting rotary method.

Some interesting veneers are created from hardwood lumber with irregular grain. These are called freak-figured veneers and are rotary cut.

Artificial dyes are also used to make veneers in various different colors.

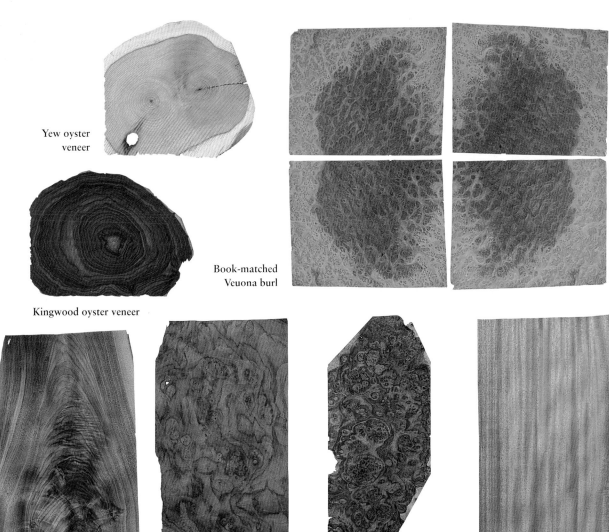

Yew oyster veneer

Kingwood oyster veneer

Book-matched Veuona burl

African walnut curly

American walnut burl

American walnut burl

Mahogany African striped

Buying and storing veneer

Veneers are available from specialized suppliers who normally carry large stocks of many species. The most common types are normally to be found in fairly long lengths—12 ft. or more—and between 10 and 14 in. wide. Thicknesses vary, depending on the intended use. Where exotic veneers are needed, the size will be much smaller and will depend on the log or the side of the log from which they are cut. Calculate how much veneer you require and allow around 15 percent for waste. Every veneer is different, so finding a matching veneer may be tricky.

Veneers are fairly brittle so take care when opening your rolled up sheet or it may crack. If the veneer has end splits, then repair it immediately with paper veneer tape, which is available from veneer suppliers.

Veneers should be stored flat, in a cool and dry environment. They should be stored away from bright light as the colors can deteriorate. If using matched veneers, the leaves should be numbered.

A veneer hammer and animal glue are used in traditional veneering. Modern adhesives can also be used.

Store veneer in a cool, dry place, away from direct light.

A utility knife and straightedge can be used to cut veneers to size.

OTHER MATERIALS

Even though most of the materials used by furniture makers are wood-based,

there are other furniture materials that you will sometimes wish to use. Most of

these are listed below and are included in some of the projects in this book.

Glass

If you want to use transparent panels in your furniture, then you have the choice between glass and plastic (see opposite). Glass has been used by man for many centuries, is readily available in sheet form and adds an interesting quality to many furniture pieces. Glass is available not only in flat and clear types but in frosted and patterned varieties that can add interesting effects.

Even though it is possible to learn how to cut glass in your own workshop, unless you plan to use it frequently it is easier to have it cut by a professional.

Glass is generally available in most areas by suppliers of windows and glazing materials. When ordering glass, especially if it has to fit into a frame, cut a sheet of board material to the exact size needed, try it in place and then give that pattern to the glazier, asking for it to be cut to that precise size. Whenever glass is to be used without a frame, as in the feature table project (see below and pages 196–9), it is essential to have the edges either finished or polished, and to have the sheet hardened so that it will not harm anyone if an unfortunate mishap does occur. These processes can normally be carried out by your glass supplier.

Store glass upright on edge, ensuring that the sheets cannot fall or be knocked over.

Metal

You will often use different types of metal in furniture making, particularly when using screws or other hardware. The projects in this book make frequent use of bolts, machine screws, and threaded studs. Metals include iron and steel, brass, aluminum and other alloys, and precious metals. While there is a large range of different metals, the most usual type in the workshop will be brass, aluminum, or steel.

Brass and aluminum are fairly easy to work and a small metal vice with some basic metalworking tools will suffice for most purposes—the most common are hacksaws, drills, and files (see pages 146–7). Steel requires more effort, but since the work is largely simple fabrication it is easily achievable. Even though adhesives can be used to join metals, it is easier to undertake the fabrication yourself and to take these components to a local metalworker to have them soldered, brazed or welded.

Metals are available in home-improvement stores or from hardware stores, engineering firms and metal fabricators. Metals can be purchased in many sections or in lengths of rod, bar, or tube.

It is best to store metals in a rack or vertically in cardboard tubes.

Hardware, such as this unusual lock, are usually made of metal.

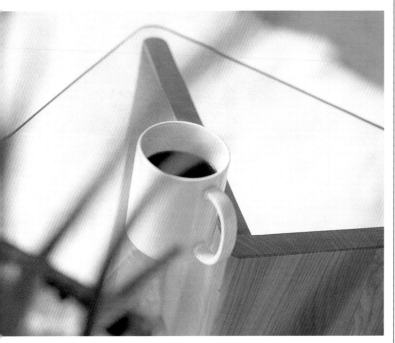

Where glass is used without a frame the sharp edges must be polished.

Aluminum offers a lightweight and sturdy option for chair legs.

Fabric

Fabric can be derived from chemicals, plants such as cotton, or animals. In woodworking, fabric is normally used as upholstery or as a decorative feature on a piece of furniture.

Ceramics

Ceramics can provide additional interest to furniture. A large range of tiles are readily available from local suppliers and can add interest, color, and a very durable surface to horizontal work areas.

Leather

Leather works well in furniture making. It is not only used as an upholstery material but also as straps for chair arms, such as on the easy chair project (see pages 250–6), and on the tops of desks. Leather is available from saddlers and leather merchants. To store leather, roll the hides.

Plastics

Plastics, which are manufactured from chemicals, are generally used and fabricated in factory conditions. A vast range of plastics is available in many forms: sheet, powder/granules, liquids, and both flexible and rigid foams. There is a huge variety of plastics and many are chemically formulated for specific uses. They are very useful in the workshop since many of the modern plastic-based adhesives and finishes can be applied to them.

As a material, however, plastic is most likely to be used in two applications. First, as a cushion for a chair—polyurethane flexible foam—and second, for drilling and shaping a transparent panel. For example, when making the CD rack project (see pages 200–5), plastic sheets need to be cut to size and drilled. For the sheets, use either acrylic or polycarbonate, which can be worked easily using a combination of wood- and metalworking tools.

Plastic sheets are sometimes available from home-improvement stores or plastics suppliers. It is best to store plastic upright on edge, ensuring that the sheets cannot fall or be knocked over.

Leather upholstery is here combined with wood to luxurious effect.

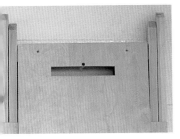

DESIGNING FOR YOURSELF

Once you understand the basics of construction and have explored the

possibilities of design, you may feel ready to try designing your own furniture

and will need to know how to turn your ideas into practical drawings.

Tools for drawing

If you have developed your skills to the point of wanting to design your own furniture, you will need to invest in some drawing equipment—including a flat, square-cut drawing board, a large set square for drawing vertical lines, a T-square for drawing horizontal lines, a compass, a protractor for drawing angles, French curves for drawing curved lines, and a scale rule.

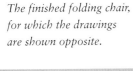

The finished folding chair, for which the drawings are shown opposite.

Working drawings

Working drawings show how a piece is made and are critical in furniture making. The drawings in this book are more decorative than standard working drawings, with color, grain, as well as shadow added.

Views

Working drawings follow a convention that is understood worldwide. A working drawing presents a piece in a series of different views. The plan presents the view from the top, the front elevation presents the view from the front, and the side elevation presents the view from the side. Sections show the internal structure, such as the details of joints, by showing the piece as though it has been cut through on a particular axis. It is sometimes easier to combine an elevation with a section.

Perspective drawings and details

The drawings for each project also include a perspective drawing, which attempts to show how the piece will appear visually.

Perspectives are useful in showing how things fit together, particularly if they are either exploded to show the parts separately or sectioned, when some parts are removed to make a construction clearer. Details of important joints or particular features of a piece are also given where relevant.

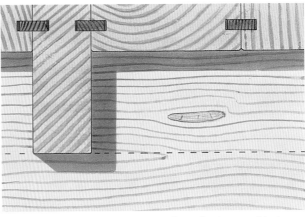

Detail of tongue-and-groove joints from the dining table (see pages 218–22).

FRONT ELEVATION

SECTIONAL SIDE ELEVATION

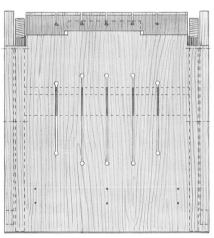

PLAN

SINGLE-POINT
PERSPECTIVE

Scale

For a working drawing to be really useful, it needs to be drawn to scale. It may be drawn full size (or 1:1). Usually, however, the piece itself is of such a size that the drawing must be smaller, in which case you must scale it down. For example, the most common scale is 1:4, where $\frac{1}{2}$ in. represents 2 in. When using a scaled drawing, a special rule called a scale rule is used so that the dimensions of the actual piece can be read from the drawing.

A scale is not given on the drawings that are featured in this book, but annotated dimensions are given throughout. These accurate, full-size dimensions will remove the possibility of doubt and mistakes if you attempt to make the piece yourself.

Models and mock-ups

Once you have designed your piece it is a worthwhile idea to try out the design before you start to build it. This can be done by making either a scale model—for example, using balsawood—or a full-sized mock-up using fiberboard. By making a scale model or mock-up, you can check all he dimensions and proportions of the piece.

TOOLS AND
TECHNIQUES

THE WORKSHOP

If you are new to woodworking and furniture making, it is important to spend time planning the design of your work space. Initially, you may use any extra space—in your garage, for instance—so that you can try constructing some basic projects before you commit to a long-term workshop and equipment. It is worth temporarily adapting a sturdy table as a workbench and obtaining some basic tools.

When you are sure that you want to develop your skills you will need to set up a dedicated workshop, which will include a good quality workbench, a range of vices and various hand, power, and machine tools.

Planning a workshop

A clean, well-planned, dedicated workshop will provide a safe, effective, and pleasurable environment in which to develop and

refine your woodworking skills. To have a fully dedicated space for woodworking may not be feasible, unless at some time you graduate from hobby to professional work. However, it is possible to adapt and dedicate spaces

A well-designed and fully equipped workshop is essential for a woodwork enthusiast.

such as basements and garages. Circumstances will dictate the size that will be available to you, but with due consideration, and accepting that you will need to move machinery, most spaces can be made to accommodate a workshop area.

Whether you decide to adapt or dedicate space for your workshop, all of the principles of workshop design described here need to be considered.

The floor surface

The floor needs to have a finish that will enable you to keep it clean and even—a concrete floor painted with floor paint will serve well. The place where you stand at your workbench benefits from having a slightly less hard surface. Industrial-type rubber flooring works well for this.

Power sources

Almost all mechanical equipment is powered by electricity, and so it is essential that the power supply meets all of the necessary regulations and that its distribution is suitable and safe to run your power and machine tools.

Avoid the temptation of buying secondhand industrial machines. While cheap, they may require more power than your home is wired for.

Lighting

It is best to have as much natural lighting as you can. North-facing is preferable, but if this is not possible and you have direct light, you may need blinds to stop the sun's glare. This will no

doubt have to be supplemented by artificial light. Fluorescent lights can give an even illumination, but spotlights can be very useful over the workbench and your machinery.

Heating and humidity

Heating and air conditioning may be necessary, depending upon the climate. Furniture makers are always concerned about the fact that wood moves. Ideally the workshop should be at the same temperature, and definitely the same humidity, as the environment where the completed work will stand.

Access

As long as the pieces made are small scale, access might not be a problem. However, larger pieces will need to be moved out of the space when completed and inaccessible places can give rise to severe problems. Try to select a place where materials and equipment can be moved in and completed furniture moved out. Attic or basement areas therefore may not be suitable.

Security

As your facilities grow, be sure that your valuable tools are secure because they will be very expensive to replace.

Storage requirements

It is convenient to have many tools, particularly hand tools, hung on the walls near the bench. However, hand power tools should always be stored in cupboards for safety reasons, and drawers are needed for many of the smaller tools to keep them tidy.

Ensure that you have the necessary power supplies and a heat source, such as this wood burner.

You will collect many types of materials. Hardwood planks are best stored in a similar way to that found in a good lumberyard—horizontally with spacers in between each board and away from sunlight or direct heat sources. Softwoods can often be found at the suppliers stored vertically, but this is best avoided unless it is absolutely

It is best to store tools safely near your workbench.

Use a bench shelf for the most useful and commonly used items.

Wherever possible, store tools safely out of the way on a wall.

necessary. In general, ensure that the workshop is dry and well ventilated so the wood does not soak up moisture. Manufactured boards should be stored in a vertical stack against a wall or partition.

As you work, you will find some material will be waste but other, particularly exotic, lumber may be worth retaining for future jobs. It is useful to have some boxes or bins where you can keep small pieces of wood for

this purpose. Make sure, however, that this is undertaken methodically so that you know where to find different wood types quickly and easily.

Sundries such as hardware, adhesives, and polishes can be stored on open shelving or in cupboards. Remember, however, that if you are going to have large quantities of finish, it should really be stored outside the workshop in order to reduce the risk of fire.

Power tools will soon become covered in dust if left on a bench. Store them in boxes under or near the bench.

Label and store containers safely.

Health and safety

Always be aware of the possible problems, but work with caution and confidence. Make sure that you have a first-aid box available.

Fire

Your workshop should have fire-safety measures built into it. A fire extinguisher or fire blanket should be on hand; install a smoke detector. Prevention is better than cure, and so ensure that dust and shavings are removed daily and that you do not smoke. Also make sure that there are no sparks from electrical or other equipment.

Some materials may be flammable, so store large amounts of such material outside in a metal fireproof box, and bring only enough material into the workshop to complete the current job. When using finishing oils applied by cloth, always unfold the cloth and leave it outside to prevent spontaneous combustion.

Fine dust and chemical fumes

When work is generating fine dust or chemical fumes, ensure that you wear a face mask or respirator, and use safety goggles whenever your eyes may be vulnerable. Some form of exhaust system or extractor is needed when you progress to machine tools and this is also useful for many of the hand power tools. With machines such as table saws and combination planes, exhaust is very important.

Most of your finishing may well utilize oils and waxes, but if

For your health and safety, always use a dust extractor of some kind when working with power tools.

you are working with solvent-based finishes that generate noxious fumes it is better to have a part of the workshop specifically dedicated as a small finishing or spray booth. Then you can fit a ventilation system to remove fumes. In this situation you should always wear a suitable mask.

Noise

When using machines or processes that generate high noise levels always wear ear protectors or plugs.

Hand tool safety

Accidents can happen, and so be aware when procedures could be dangerous and take special care.

Dust mask   Ear protectors

Machinery safety

With any woodworking machinery safety is paramount. Follow these guidelines:

• Never make adjustments without turning off the power.

• Always follow the manufacturer's instructions for the specific machine.

• Inspect the machine before you switch it on and always check the machine after making adjustments.

• Always use the guards supplied.

• Never attempt to machine small items without adequate jigs.

• If anything happens to your piece of work, switch off the machine before attempting to rectify the situation.

• Most important, when using any cutting machine, be it a table saw, portable power saw or router, wear safety glasses. Safety glasses are also recommended for drilling operations and nailing, particularly when using large nails.

THE WORKBENCH

A good, sturdy workbench is an essential element of a woodworker's

workshop. A thick, hardwood top is best to use as a work surface, and

the underframe should also be of a sturdy hardwood.

Make sure the worktop is level. The usual height for a workbench is between 32 in. and 34 in., although different heights can be made to order.

Workbench fittings

The workbench should be fitted with well-machined vices. Many workbenches have both side and end vices already installed. However, if you need to purchase and fit vices separately, the most important vice is the main woodworker's vice. Buy as large a capacity as you can afford, and fit the vice as close as possible to one of the legs of the underframe; this will prevent any flexing of the worktop when the working lumber is clamped in the jaws of the vice. It should also be properly set into the bench so that when the wooden vice cheeks are applied, no metal shows and the top of the vice is perfectly flush with the top.

A large woodworking vice is useful for holding work securely.

You will need to drill large holes or cut mortises in the worktop so that a bench stop can be fitted. These are normally used with an end vice, which can be useful for clamping small jobs as well as holding the work.

Most workbenches are made with a tool well, which enables a large work piece to be moved across the worktop without sweeping hand tools onto the floor. Many workbenches also come with a drawer or cupboards for the storage of tools or materials underneath.

The workbench project featured later in this book (see pages 188–92) would be a good investment. It has a strong underframe with some substantial lumber for the main working area, a ply well for tools, and a deep backboard to make the structure rigid.

Try to make a workbench one of your first major projects (see pages 188–92).

Folding bench

Sawhorse

Other types of benches

Proprietary folding benches can also be bought. Although not substantial enough to be your main bench, they can be useful in the workshop if you need to undertake work such as fitting away from your base.

Sawhorses, or trestles, are also useful when initially cutting sheets of manufactured board.

Maintaining your bench

A workbench needs to be well-maintained to provide good, long-lasting service. Here are a few tips for good maintenance:

• Support the work piece away from the work surface, using padded strips of lumber. This will protect the work surface as well as the piece that you are working on. Specialized rubber mats are available that allow nails, screws, and working debris to fall through the mats to the work surface. As an alternative to these mats, a layer of hardboard can be placed on the worktop surface and changed when it becomes damaged.

• Clean the work surface down regularly with a brush to remove debris.
• Avoid using carpet as a surface protector; it can trap and hide nasty abrasive materials, such as glass fragments, small nails, and screws, in its surface.
• Avoid nailing anything into the surface of the workbench if possible. Try to use a clamp or screws instead.
• When drilling, always make sure that you use a piece of scrap material between the work piece and the worktop.
• Check that the surface of the worktop is straight and without twist. This can be achieved with winding sticks, which are parallel pieces of lumber. Set the wood edge-up at either end of the workbench and sight across the top edges to test. Or you could use a level and a straightedge to test for level. Adjust the workbench with chocks to set the worktop true and flat.

A temporary workbench

If you have just started woodworking, you may want to make a temporary workbench initially rather than investing in a permanent one right away.

In this case, you will need to find an existing table that has a strong structure, and make a temporary top.

Take a sheet of manufactured board, 1 in. thick, and cut it to a size that is 6 in. larger than the existing table all the way around. Fit some baize—a soft, usually green, woolen fabric resembling felt—to the underside and make four corner blocks so that the surface will not move out of position. On the edge where you wish to work, fit another strip of board 12–16 in.—the same length as the base board—and glue this board into position.

You should have enough room to fit a small vice and it would be advisable to use a couple of C-clamps to hold it in place and ensure that it is stable. This should give you a surface that enables you to start work.

Ideally, the workbench should be level with your waist, and so you may have to make some chocks for the legs.

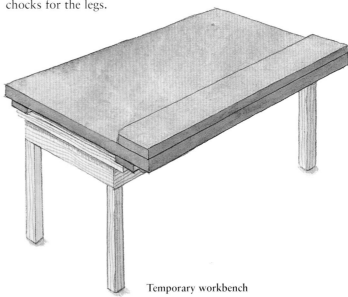

Temporary workbench

THE ESSENTIAL TOOL KIT

If you are a woodworker with experience you will already have a set of tools, but if you are starting this pleasurable journey you will need to begin by purchasing some basic tools. The list below is a reasonable starting point.

It is good practice to extend your tool kit by purchasing reasonably priced tools as they are needed for a particular job, and also to have a long-term plan for expensive tools, power tools, and machine tools. Within your budget always purchase the highest quality that you can afford since they will last longer and will be easier to use. A good list of hand power tools would include a power drill, jigsaw, orbital sander, and router. Machine tools would include a pillar drill (drill press), a table saw, a bandsaw, and a combination plane.

Below is a summary of the tools that you will need as you begin your woodworking journey.

Measuring and marking tools

The importance of accurate measuring and marking is stressed often throughout this book, and it is advisable to obtain the best-quality tools available on the list. The most important are:

Beginner's tool kit

A jack plane
B beech mallet
C try square
D marking pencils
E sliding bevel
F screwdrivers
G tack hammer

H file
I coping saw
J C-clamp
K basic cabinet scraper
L gooseneck cabinet
   scraper
M chisel

N marking knife
O marking gauge
P tenon saw
Q panel saw
R folding plastic
   ruler
S steel ruler

• For workshop-based furniture making, a folding ruler is useful, but if you need to do a lot of site work a steel tape can be more useful.

• A good-quality, accurate steel ruler—12 in. long—is essential for measuring and marking work.

• Pencils need to be hard enough to give a precise fine line, but soft enough to be seen. A 2H grade will be adequate.

• Some people use a marking knife that is ground on one face only, but a more traditionally sharpened blade is usually preferable.

• A good-quality try square or combination square is essential. A combination square is a more expensive option, but is preferable since a good-quality tool will give much better results and will last longer if cared for. If money is tight, however, a good-quality try square will suffice.

• A traditional sliding bevel will suit well.

• You will need other gauges later, but a good marking gauge will suffice at first. If you buy a mortise gauge as well, be sure that it is the type with a screw adjustment for setting the space between the points rather than a simple slide.

Sawing tools

• A good-quality panel saw cuts both solid lumber and manufactured boards.

• A backsaw, a small tenon saw, or large dovetail saw will be needed for fine work—8 in. will be suitable.

• For curved cuts, a coping saw is essential.

• Even though most power tools will be added to your kit at a later date, if you wish to undertake large-scale or a large amount of work, then a jigsaw will be a welcome addition. The jigsaw removes much hard work, and can cut both solid lumber—up to 2 in. plus—and manufactured board, and also helps with some fine work. Metal blades are also available.

Surfacing tools

• A jack plane is the most useful to start with.

• A cabinet scraper, for fine finishing on difficult wood, is a must.

Cutting tools

A range of bevel-edged chisels— $\frac{1}{4}$ in., $\frac{1}{2}$ in., and 1 in.—will suffice at first.

General tools

• Small cordless electric drills are now so reasonably priced that they are the best tool for early drilling jobs. You will need a range of drill bits: twist drills from $\frac{1}{32}$–$\frac{1}{2}$ in. or dowel bits from $\frac{1}{8}$–$\frac{1}{2}$ in. There may be a need to drill holes larger than $\frac{1}{2}$ in. and a set of spade bits from $\frac{1}{2}$–$1\frac{1}{2}$ in. will tide you over until you can afford more expensive bits.

• Buy a small power router with basic bits.

• For initial shaping work, rasps will suffice until spokeshaves are needed.

• A tack hammer is good for fine work. Heavier hammers will be needed later.

• A beech mallet is essential for both joints and assembly.

• Both Phillips and slot screws are now used, so buy a screwdriver that accepts different-size heads—or use screw bits in your power drill.

• A hacksaw and a range of small files will cover jobs where some modification to metal parts is necessary.

• Holding and assembly tools, including sash clamps and C-clamps, are essential. Purchase a small set of four light sash clamps—30 in.—as a start, and two 10-in. and four 6-in. C-clamps.

More advanced tools

Once you have the basic tool kit, the following are worth considering:

• An orbital sander will help you with finishing large surfaces.

• A floor or bench-mounted drill press (or a large electric drill and a drill stand) is a very useful addition to the workshop.

• A table saw is useful for many precise operations.

• A belt sander is also useful, but it is essential that you get this bench mounted.

• A bandsaw will enable you to cut curved components and thick pieces of lumber.

• A combination plane means that you can purchase sawn wood, and ensure that work is straight, flat, and to the correct thickness.

A selection of chisels is an essential part of your tool kit.

MEASURING AND MARKING

Accurate measuring and marking are vital in achieving quality work. Even the slightest inaccuracies in the early stages will inevitably lead to complications later. There is an old craftworkers' saying: "measure twice, cut once."

Tools

As with any aspect of woodworking, the range of equipment available for measuring and marking is vast. However, some tools are more useful and adaptable than others, and so it is worth finding the best ones that can be trusted for the job. A rough measurement is adequate for converting planks into slightly oversized pieces, but precise measuring and marking are essential in tasks such as preparing to cut specific lengths of wood or waste from a joint.

Rulers and measures

A **folding wooden** or **plastic ruler** or a **retractable steel tape measure** are equally suitable for the initial measuring of length, but are not accurate enough for precise marking. A **steel ruler** is best for precision marking. A 12-in. ruler is essential and a longer one in excess of 24 in. is also useful. Buy a quality ruler that has accurately marked measurements. A **steel straightedge**, at least 24 in. but preferably 32 in. long, is useful for marking straight lines or checking the flatness of a surface. A **vernier gauge** is useful for measuring small dimensions. A small plastic one that will measure to $^3/_{200}$ in. is adequate.

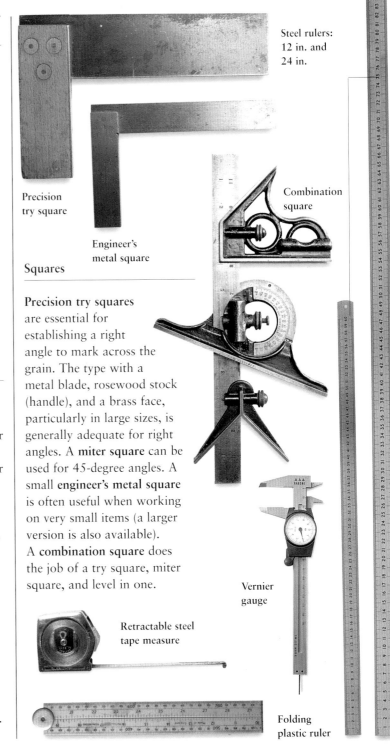

Steel rulers: 12 in. and 24 in.

Precision try square

Engineer's metal square

Combination square

Squares

Precision try squares are essential for establishing a right angle to mark across the grain. The type with a metal blade, rosewood stock (handle), and a brass face, particularly in large sizes, is generally adequate for right angles. A **miter square** can be used for 45-degree angles. A small **engineer's metal square** is often useful when working on very small items (a larger version is also available). A **combination square** does the job of a try square, miter square, and level in one.

Retractable steel tape measure

Vernier gauge

Folding plastic ruler

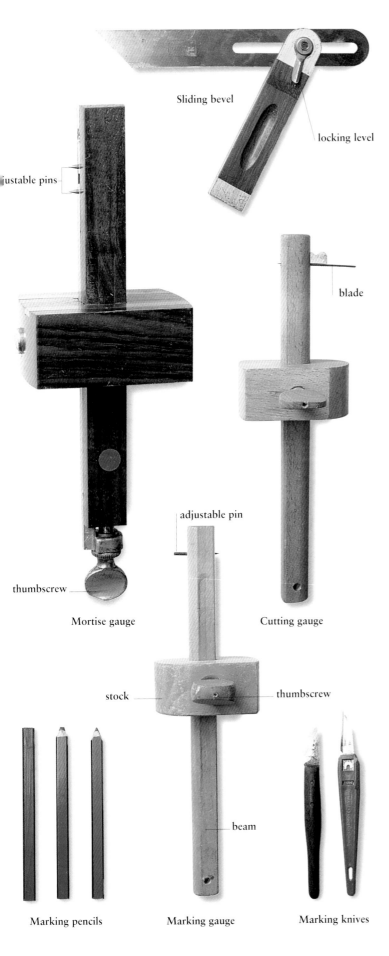

Sliding bevel

locking level

justable pins

blade

thumbscrew

Mortise gauge

adjustable pin

Cutting gauge

stock

thumbscrew

beam

Marking pencils

Marking gauge

Marking knives

Sliding bevels

A **sliding bevel** is necessary for marking dovetail joints and for other angled work. They are available with a wooden handle or all in steel, the engineer's version. The screw allows the sliding bevel to be set at the required angle with the aid of an accurate protractor.

Pencils

Pencils can be used for precision marking if they are fairly hard and can be sharpened to a good point or chisel edge that will last. It is best to use a pencil mark for rough guidance and for setting out; use a marking knife to make a cut line when greater accuracy is required, such as when marking joints, or for sawing or chiseling.

Marking knives

Marking knives are much more accurate than pencils and provide a slight indentation for saw teeth. Always use a knife for marking across the grain, running the blade along the waste side of the desired line.

Gauges

A gauge is the best tool for marking along the grain and there are several types available. Each has an adjustable marking device that can be set at the required measurement and used to score a line. A **marking gauge** has one steel pin, whereas a **mortise gauge** has two independently adjustable pins for marking the position of mortise-and-tenon joints. A **cutting gauge** has a small blade that is most suitable for cutting lines across the grain.

Measuring equal divisions

You can divide a piece of lumber or board into equal divisions, where the actual width of the divisions is not vital, without using mathematics. Lay a ruler at an angle across the surface so that clear increments mark exactly the required number of divisions.

Using a bevel to determine a ratio

Bevels can also be used to determine a ratio—for example, on dovetail joints. For a ratio of 1:4, square a line across from the edge, measure up four units—say, 2 in.; on the edge of the board measure one unit—say, ½ in. Then join the two points with the blade while the stock is against the edge.

Preparing the tools

All measuring and marking tools should be used with care or their accuracy can be affected.

Checking a try square

1 To check if a try square is accurate, lay it on a piece of board that has a straight edge. Position the metal-edged stock along the straight edge.

2 Mark a line on the board face against the try square blade, at right angles to the edge. Turn the square over and mark another line a short distance from the first. If the lines are parallel, the square is accurate. If not, repair can be difficult so it is best to replace the tool.

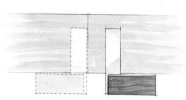

Check with a try square.

Adjusting a sliding bevel

1 Make a mark on the edge of a board and use a protractor to make a second mark at the desired angle. Join the marks to give a line on the face of the board that is at the correct angle to the edge.

2 Loosen the screw on the sliding bevel and align the outer edge of the bevel along the angled line. Retighten the screw to set the bevel.

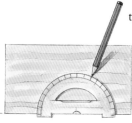

Adjusting a sliding bevel.

Preparing the lumber

Before measuring and marking the lumber for a project, it is important that it is perfectly flat, square and straight.

Checking lumber

1 Check to see if the surface is free of pits or bumps by running a straightedge across it. If the surface is not flat, it should be planed true—perfectly flat—before the wood is measured and marked (see Planing, pages 74–81).

Use a straightedge to check for flatness.

2 You can check if the board is straight by positioning two steel rulers across each end. Now sight along the board and, if the two rulers appear parallel, the wood is straight.

Check that the board is straight.

Marking the faces of timber

1 Make the face-side mark (usually a scroll shape) on the timber surface, toward the edge to be planed next.

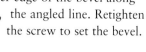

Face-side mark.

2 Plane the edge straight and at right angles to the face side. Check with a straightedge and try square.

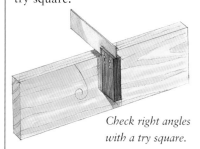

Check right angles with a try square.

3 Apply the edge mark, conventionally a "V" shape, on the face edge.

Apply edge marks.

Taking measurements

Measurements of lumber and the accessible parts of projects can easily be made with a steel ruler. Simply position the end of the ruler on one edge of the surface and read the required dimension at the other.

Measuring awkward spaces
Some measurements can be difficult to make because a ruler cannot be held in the best position for accuracy. For example, measuring across the internal diagonal of a frame or cabinet, in order to check for squareness, can be a tricky task.

1 Cut two strips of wood that, when overlapped, will span the distance to be measured. Cut a bevel at one end of each strip.

2 Hold the strips together, positioning the beveled ends in each corner. Mark a line on each strip to show where they meet.

Use beveled strips across diagonal.

3 Place the strips on a flat surface, match up the lines and measure from point to point. Alternately, measure from the line to the point on one strip and add it to the total length of the other strip.

Marking rough measurements

For approximate measurements parallel to the edge of the lumber, you can make the marks with a pencil and improvise a gauge by using a finger or rule.

Gauging with a finger
1 Hold the pencil between your thumb and index finger. Rest another finger on the edge of the board so that the pencil is at the required distance from the edge.

2 Keeping the hand and pencil steady, run the pencil along the board to make a line parallel to the edge.

Gauge a line with your finger.

Gauging with a ruler
1 You can also use a ruler as a gauge. Place the ruler on the wood's surface so the end is the required distance from the edge.

2 Hold a pencil against the end of the ruler and use your other hand to keep the ruler at the correct distance from the edge. Run the ruler and pencil along the board's length to make a line parallel to the edge.

Marking precise measurements

Precision is best achieved with a marking knife or a gauge, which will give a clean indentation for positioning a chisel or saw.

Using a marking knife
1 Hold a ruler or try square firmly in place and position yourself so that you can see where the edge meets the board.

2 Position the knife blade flat against the edge of the ruler or square and mark the board by pulling the knife along the edge with care.

Using a marking gauge
1 Use a ruler to set the position of the stock at the correct distance from the pin or blade and lightly tighten the thumbscrew. Check this against the board and make any required adjustments by tapping the gauge on the workbench. To increase the gap, tap the base of the beam; to decrease it, tap the beam at the head. When the pin is in position, tighten the thumbscrew.

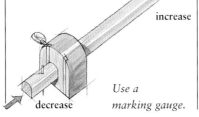

increase

Use a marking gauge.

decrease

2 Position the stock against the face edge, with the pin just touching the surface of the face side. Slightly rotate the marking gauge and run the stock along the edge.

Using a cutting gauge
You can use a cutting gauge in place of a marking gauge in order to achieve a cut line. This tool is used in the same way, but the blade must be very sharp and firmly inserted in the beam.

Gauge a line with a marking gauge.

Using a mortise gauge
One pin is fixed in position while the other is attached to an adjustable metal bar. The pins must first be set at the correct distance apart—that of your chosen mortise chisel. Then, the stock may be adjusted along the stem and tightened with the thumbscrew. The gauge is then ready to mark two parallel lines along the board.

Set the pins at the correct position.

Finding the center point

Marking gauges can also be used to find the center point on a piece of lumber. Set the pin to approximately half the surface width. From each side, make a small mark with the point. Keep adjusting the stock by tapping the beam, as described at left, and repeat the operation until the marks line up from each side, at which point the mark is perfectly centered.

BASIC SAWING

Some saws can be used to cut timber into manageable sizes, and others to cut intricate joints and shapes. It is useful to separate the skills into basic sawing, which is discussed here, and fine sawing, which is discussed on pages 82–5.

Saw teeth

The teeth on saws differ to suit the type of sawing that is to be undertaken. However, all but the smallest saws are sharpened and set in a specific way. Each tooth has a leading edge, which makes the cut, and a less upright side known as the trailing edge. The shape produced is known as the pitch. The teeth are also set—that is, bent first to one side, then to the other—so that the cutting is more effective and the blade does not bind in the cut. The cut that the saw makes is called a kerf.

Hand saws

There are three main types of hand saw—the **ripsaw**, the **crosscut saw,** and the **panel saw**—and all taper in length to assist the blade's movement. The main difference between each of the saws lies in tooth size. Large teeth remove a lot of material, whereas smaller teeth make smaller, finer cuts. Tooth size is generally measured by the number of teeth per 1in., and is expressed as teeth per inch (tpi). This applies where teeth are measured from the base of one tooth to another, but if you are calculating from point to point instead, the measurement is described as points per inch (ppi).

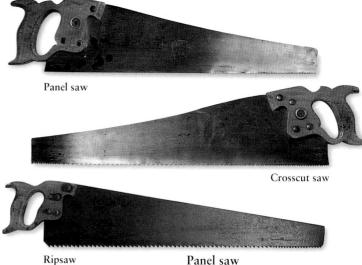

Panel saw

Crosscut saw

Ripsaw   Panel saw

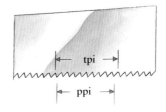

Saw teeth are measured as tpi or ppi (teeth or points per inch).

Panel saw

Panel saws have much finer teeth than ripsaws and crosscut saws, with a tpi of 10 to 12. They can be used on solid timber, and are also more suitable than the other saws for cutting manufactured board because of the finer teeth.

Crosscut saw

The crosscut saw is designed for cutting solid lumber across the grain. The leading edge has a greater pitch than a ripsaw's and the teeth are sharpened at an angle so that each tooth has a knife-like cutting edge. These saws have more tpi (8 to 9) than ripsaws, and while many experienced craftworkers will use both types, most enthusiasts find that possessing one crosscut saw is adequate.

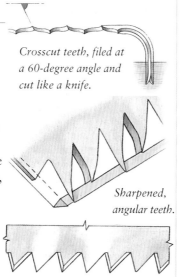

Crosscut teeth, filed at a 60-degree angle and cut like a knife.

Sharpened, angular teeth.

Ripsaw

The ripsaw is normally the largest of the hand saws. It is sharpened for cutting wood along the grain and thus has few tpi (4 to 5). Each tooth has an upright leading edge, which is filed to a chiseled point at 90 degrees to its face.

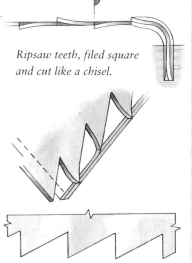

Ripsaw teeth, filed square and cut like a chisel.

The teeth of the ripsaw are squared off.

Using a hand saw

All of the saws described at left are generally used for cutting material to an approximate size. For this reason, an allowance of about ⅛ in. for planing is needed. Bear this in mind when marking the cut lines, both along and across the grain. Always hold the saw firmly, with the index finger pointing in the direction of the cut. This will help to keep the handle from twisting with the movement of the blade.

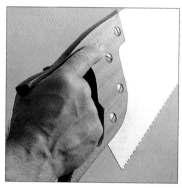

The correct grip for a hand saw.

1 Mark the lines to be cut, both along and across the grain. Cuts along the grain or in manufactured board are generally easier if the material is supported horizontally on sawhorses or trestles.

For cutting along the grain, support the board horizontally on trestles.

For cutting short pieces of lumber along the grain, it may be possible to put the wood in a vice, so that it can be cut vertically.

Cut short pieces of wood along the grain in a vice.

For cutting across the grain, it may be more convenient if the board is cramped to a workbench.

Cramp the timber to a bench to make cuts across the grain.

2 Use your thumb in order to locate and steady the saw on the waste side of the cut line and make some short strokes to begin the cut. Take care to keep your thumb away from the teeth of the saw.

Use your thumb to steady the saw as you start the cut.

3 Remove your thumb once the saw has started a small kerf in the wood. Continue to apply pressure to the handle so that you guide the saw along the cut.

4 Gradually increase the length of the strokes that you take and build up a steady rhythm, ensuring that each forward cut stays on the waste side of the line.

5 On some wood, the cut can begin to close as you work farther down the length of the board. This may cause the blade to bind and interrupt the flow of movement. Insert a small wedge in the kerf, so that the cut edges remain separated. You could also add a little wax or even soap to the side of the saw to act as a lubricant and help it slip through the cut.

Cut along the grain with a wedge in the kerf to separate the wood.

Cutting cleanly

Generally, sawing along the grain of the wood should not present too many problems with splintering or splitting. However, sawing across the grain can cause the grain to fracture and break out on the underside. This should not be a cause for concern when you are sawing prior to planing, because the damage will be removed later as the wood is refined. However, precautions need to be taken when you are cutting after the wood has been planed true and to size.

If breakout is a particular problem, you could use a finer toothed saw and/or lower the angle of the saw as you work—especially when you are working on veneered boards such as plywood.

Sharpening a saw

Saws should be sharpened regularly to ensure that they cut smoothly and accurately. While traditional craftworkers used to sharpen their own saws, many modern woodworkers take their tools to "saw doctors." These people specialize in saw sharpening, and work with machines or, for very fine saws, by hand. Some modern saws, especially cheap ones, may have hardened teeth that can be sharpened only by machine, while others must simply be replaced when the teeth become too blunt. It is, therefore, more economical in the long run to buy quality tools that can be serviced regularly, rather than constantly replacing them.

Sawing manufactured board

Use a panel saw to cut manufactured board. Hold the saw at a low angle to prevent breakout on the bottom face, especially on veneer-faced boards. Steady the work with a cramp or your knee.

Power saws

There are two main types of power saw – the hand-held saw and the machine saw. Although these tools are unlikely to remove the need for hand tools and careful, skilled craftwork, they are versatile and can be useful for some woodworking tasks. For example, power saws are ideal for cutting heavy or large pieces of wood, which would need a lot of effort if sawed by hand. The jigsaw is also good for intricate work, helping to ensure accurate and precise cuts.

Hand-held power saws

The **jigsaw** is particularly useful for initial rough cutting wood both along and across the grain, as well as manufactured board. It can also be used for fine work, giving accurate and precise cuts. The tool can be used with a variety of blades, all of which are designed for cutting different materials and producing different results. Most blades cut with a vertical—or reciprocating—motion, although some advanced saws can have an orbital action. The blade always cuts on the upstroke and can saw solid wood up to 2 in. thick. Some varieties have different speeds so that they can be used on plastics and soft metals.

Many woodworkers also use a **circular saw** for cutting solid wood and manufactured boards. Light and portable, the saw is suitable for site work, but a hand saw or jigsaw is usually an adequate alternative in the workshop and is much safer to use. However, the circular saw can be useful if it is mounted in a stand as a first table saw. The saw consists of a sole plate that will rest on the work, a saw guard to prevent accidents, a fence for parallel cuts and a tilt mechanism for angled cuts. Unlike jigsaws, circular saws are always used for straight cuts, though the blade can be set to cut through the material, or work to a set depth.

Using a jigsaw

Jigsaws can be used to cut freehand straight or curved lines, or in conjunction with fences and guides that direct the cut. However, always ensure that there is nothing in its path that is likely to foul the blade.

1 Hold the jigsaw firmly by the handle with one hand. Use the other hand to support the weight of the lumber or board, or cramp the work down.

2 Start the saw and bring the blade up to the edge of the work, resting the sole plate on the work; ease it through the board. Always saw on the waste side of the cut lines—the blade cuts on

the upstroke, which can cause grain breakout that will need to be cleaned up later.

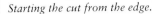

Starting the cut from the edge.

3 Work slowly, firmly, and smoothly, avoiding any sudden changes in direction that may cause the saw not to cut true or the blade to break.

Making internal cuts

1 Measure and mark the shape on the wood.

2 Drill (see Drilling, pages 96–100) a starting hole in the waste area that is large enough to accommodate the blade of the jigsaw.

3 Insert the jigsaw blade through the hole and use the tool to cut the shape in the normal way.

Use a jigsaw to make a neat internal cut.

Machine power saws

Like hand-held power saws, machine power saws can make light work of large pieces of lumber and board. They can also be set to levels of accuracy for repetitive work that can be hard to achieve with hand-held tools.

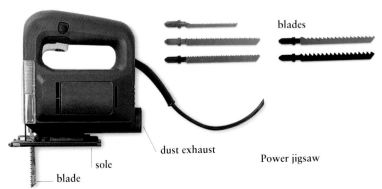

blades

dust exhaust

sole

blade

Power jigsaw

The **table saw** is the most popular kind of machine tool. This is basically a machine with a rigid, flat table through which a circular saw blade projects. Behind the blade is a riving knife. The blade can be set to produce different depths of cuts and in most models can also be angled. The machine has a secure fence against which parallel cuts can be made, and adjustable fence slides, set in grooves, for crosscutting. There are many types of saw blades, which means that the machine can be used to make both quick cuts as well as precise saw cuts. Always operate the saw with extreme care, checking that it is set correctly, with all the necessary guards in place, before beginning any work.

Table saw

Radial-arm saws can be used to perform many tasks in woodwork, including crosscutting and jointmaking. They can also be used for ripping lumber, although this can be hazardous so always use extreme care. Some machines may also be set up with a sanding disk. Specialized machines that are dedicated to a specific task often perform better than ones that do multi-tasks.

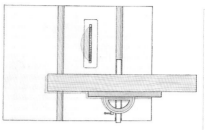

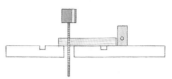

Radial-arm saw

A **bandsaw** (see page 85) is another useful machine for cutting, especially shaped work.

A **miter saw** is used for precision cutting of angles and square ends. It is used for cutting miter joints for baseboards, moldings, and picture frames. The saw assembly and motor are hinged on an arm, which is lowered to cut the wood. The arm is spring-loaded to return the saw to the "up" position. The saw has a fixed top guard that covers the blade and a lower guard that retracts as the arm is lowered onto the work. The miter saw can be turned to make angle cuts. Most saws turn at 45 degrees to each side, and some turn up to 60 degrees.

Other types of miter saws include **compound** and **compound slide saws**. These allow the motor assembly to turn both vertically and horizontally.

Using a table saw

1 Check that the table saw is set to the correct adjustments before turning it on. To cut wood into parallel pieces, set the fence to the required distance from the blade; be sure the blade is at the correct height.

Set the fence securely so that it is at the right distance from the blade.

Saw the wood into parallel pieces.

2 To crosscut, set the adjustable fence to the required angle. Miters and specific angles can also be cut by setting this fence, or by canting the blade. Hold the timber against the crosscut fence. Slide the work towards the blade and cut steadily. Once cut, slide the work away from the blade before bringing the crosscut fence in front of it.

Make angles and miters with the fence.

3 Use push sticks, spare battens, to feed timber through the blade, so that you can keep hands clear of the blade. This should have a notch cut in the leading end to hold the timber down while pushing it forward.

Use push sticks as a safety measure when using a table saw.

Miter saw safety

- Check that the guard is working correctly.

- Use the vice at the base of the saw to hold your work.

- Ensure the tilt adjustments are tight.

- Never 'cross hands' when operating the saw.

- Always use the correct saw blade.

SHARPENING

Effective woodworking relies on tools that have sharp cutting edges. This is particularly important for hand tools, such as planes, chisels, and gouges, as well as the blades and cutters in machine tools.

The following description of sharpening uses a wide chisel to demonstrate the process, but exactly the same methods are used for plane blades and narrow chisels, although the grinding angle for narrow chisels is smaller: for wide chisels and plane blades, the angle is 25 to 30 degrees, and for narrow chisels the angle is 20 to 25 degrees.

Sharpening is carried out in two stages: the blade is first ground to an angle and then it is honed in order to achieve the sharpest edge.

High-speed grinder

tool rest

Strops

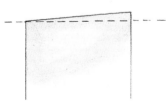

stone disk

Motorized whetstone

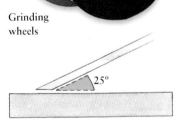

grinding wheel

Grinding wheels

Grinding

Chisel and plane blades can be ground to an angle using a high-speed bench grinder or a slow-speed motorized whetstone.

High-speed grinder

High-speed grinders are a quick means of grinding an angle. The blade is held against the rotating wheel. The wheels are usually made from aluminum-oxide and rotate very fast, at around 3000 rpm or more. Make sure that heat does not build up; otherwise the temper of the blade will be removed, rendering the tool useless. If this happens, the metal will change color. Cool the blade frequently in water.

Flattening the back of a new blade

New blades will need to have their backs flattened on an oilstone. To do this, lubricate a coarse or medium stone with oil and rub the back of the blade along it. Ensure that the surface is flat by regularly checking it against a straightedge.

Sharpening a plane blade

When sharpening plane blades, hold the blade at a slight angle to the stone. This will help to ensure that the whole of the cutting edge makes contact with the stone.

1 Always wear safety goggles when using a grinder even though the tool has protective spark deflectors. Before grinding a bevel, check that the cutting edge on the blade is square by holding it against an accurate try square. If it is not square, sharpen the edge on the grinder, before moving onto the bevel.

Ensure that the cutting edge is square before you start on the bevel.

2 Hold the tool at the correct angle to ensure that you will achieve the correct bevel. For a wide chisel, this is about 25 degrees. Then, adjust the tool rest to match.

25°

Ensure that the grinding angle is correct before you start.

3 Switch on the grinder, and hold the blade between your index finger and thumb. Position the blade on the rest, ensuring your fingers are well clear of the wheel. Move the bevel forward until it just starts to grind. Move the tool from side to side over the face of the wheel to sharpen the full width.

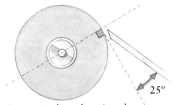

25°

Start grinding, keeping the angle steady at 25 degrees.

4 Inspect the sharpened edge often to check that it remains square and at the required angle.

Motorized whetstone

Use a motorized whetstone for the same job. This has a horizontally or vertically mounted whetstone, turning at under 500 rpm, which is lubricated by a stream of water or oil. The slower speed and built-in lubrication help to ensure good control, while removing the risk of drawing the temper.

1 Check that the cutting edge of the blade is square. Bring the tool down firmly onto the stone at a 25-degree angle.

Grind the chisel on the whetstone at an approximate angle of 25 degrees.

2 Inspect the bevel often to ensure that it remains square and at the required angle. The grinding process generates a burr, which will be removed by honing.

Honing

Honing produces the final cutting edge on the tool blade. It is achieved by rubbing the ground tool edge up and down a stone that is lubricated with oil. This produces a second bevel, which will give the sharp, cutting edge.

Oilstones

Most people starting out in woodwork use an oilstone made from synthetic materials such as aluminum oxide or silicon carbide. These are available in coarse, medium, and fine grades and are the cheapest varieties on the market. However, as you develop your woodworking skills there are some suitable alternatives. For example, natural stones such as Arkansas have a range of hardnesses, while some woodworkers prefer to use Japanese waterstones. There are also manufactured sharpening stones that have hardened particles bonded into them.

Japanese waterstone

Oilstone housing tray

Honing sequence

The grinding of the chisel blade will have produced a bevel of 25 degrees. To ensure the tool is ready for use, this bevel now needs to be sharpened or honed to an angle of 30 degrees.

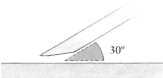

The honing angle must be 30 degrees.

1 Place the edge of the blade flat on the stone, bevel side down. Hold the blade firmly in one hand and place your other hand on the top of the blade. Lift the tool slightly to give the correct honing angle—5 degrees more than the grinding angle.

2 Work the bevel by rubbing the blade firmly up and down the stone, ensuring that the whole cutting edge is in contact with the stone.

Make the bevel by honing the chisel at an angle of 30 degrees.

3 When you have produced a bevel of about $1/32$ in., continue the same process on a finer stone. The rubbing action will cause a burr to form on the back of the blade. To remove it, turn the tool over and make a few light strokes, holding the blade perfectly flat. This removes the burr and leaves a sharp edge.

Create a sharp edge by removing the burr.

Honing a narrow chisel blade

Use a zigzag or figure-eight action. Move the chisel along the stone to ensure that its surface does not become unevenly worn. If you find this process difficult, honing aids that hold the blade in a given position are available, but it is worth persevering to develop this skill yourself.

Truing stones

After a great deal of use, an oilstone will become hollow. This makes it difficult to keep a square edge on chisels or blades; therefore, it needs to be flattened. Grind the surface with carborundum powder and oil or water, on a sheet of glass. Continue to rub the face of the stone until it is flat.

Using a leather strop

A leather strop helps to remove any trace of a burr and leaves an extremely sharp blade. Hold the blade, and swipe the honed bevel away from the sharp edge. Then turn the tool over and do the same to the back. You should now have a razor-sharp edge. If a fine, shiny line along the cutting edge appears on the blade, continue sharpening.

PLANING

Planing is one of the most satisfying woodworking skills to master. It is also one of the key processes; precision and accuracy are vital for achieving a perfectly flat and straight surface with an exact square edge.

Hand planes

There is a range of planes available—each developed to carry out a specific function or job. The most familiar is the bench plane, and we will use this to examine the basic structure of all planes, together with the planing process.

Bench planes

The **try** or **jointer plane** is the longest bench plane. It is used to ensure that the board surface is as level as possible, and removes warps or irregularities that may have occurred during seasoning, or may not have been rectified during the sawing and milling processes. The length of the plane, 2 ft., helps to ensure that this first surface is as level as possible.

The **jack plane** is a bench plane of medium length and can be used after the try plane, or to accomplish the same result on a shorter piece of material.

The **smoothing plane** is the shortest of the bench planes and, as its name infers, it is used for final finishing. It is also an ideal tool for dealing with wood that has a difficult grain.

Once bench planing is complete, most boards will require finishing with sandpaper.

Try or jointer plane

Jack plane

Smoothing plane

Bull-nose plane

Bench rabbet plane

Wooden rabbet plane

Side rabbet plane

Shoulder plane

Rabbet planes

A rabbet is a recess cut into the edge of a piece of wood—and is mostly used for fitting panel boards.

A **bench rabbet plane** is used for cutting large rabbets and is basically a version of the jack or smoothing plane—the blade extends across the whole width of the sole. In order to cut the rabbet accurately, a fence, along which the plane can run, should be cramped in position.

A **rabbet and fillister plane** has both a guide fence and a depth gauge, and is suitable for cutting small rabbets. With careful use, it will also cut a rabbet that is square and true. In some models, the cutter can be mounted in two positions; the front position is used when planing a stopped rabbet. Some types of this plane can be fitted with a spur that cuts the wood fibers, so that a rabbet can be made across the grain.

The **shoulder plane** was developed as a means of trimming the shoulders of large joints; although smaller, it can also be used in a similar way to the bench rabbet plane.

A **side rabbet plane** is used for easing the width of a groove because it cuts the vertical edge of grooves, or rabbets.

A **bull-nose plane** is similar to a shoulder plane but the blade is very near the front, facilitating the trimming of stopped rabbets.

Plow and combination planes

A simple **plow plane** is designed to cut grooves. It has a range of cutters, usually from ⅛–½ in., and has both a guide fence and depth gauge.

A **combination plane**, or molding plane, is similar but it has a wider range of cutters and is able to make tongues, beads, and other special shapes.

Specialized planes

There are a number of specialized planes available.

Compass planes, as the name implies, are special planes that can be adjusted to cope with both concave and convex curves. Set the flexible sole to the curve that you want to plane and generally try to work with the grain.

Block planes are general-purpose, lightweight planes that can be used with one hand.

A **hand router plane** is very useful for fine work and for special applications such as making small recesses.

Traditional planes

The planes described here are the traditional ones found in the cabinetmaker's tool chest. However, it must be remembered that, with recent technical developments, much rabbeting, routing, and molding can be carried out by a small, electrically powered hand router (see pages 90–3).

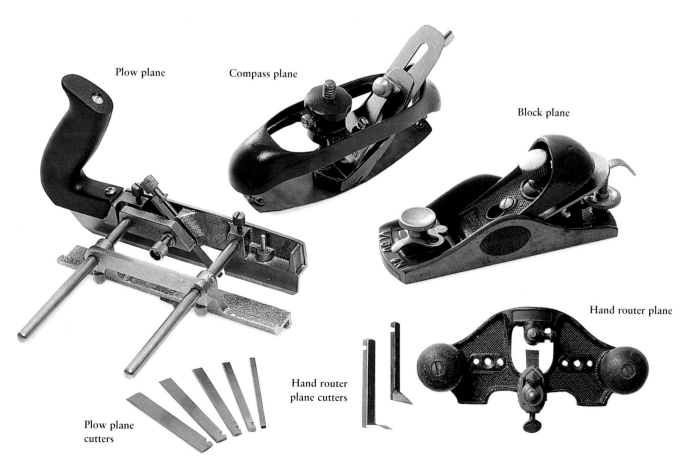

Plow plane

Compass plane

Block plane

Hand router plane cutters

Hand router plane

Plow plane cutters

All-metal bench plane

A   sole
B   mouth
C   frog casting
D   frog-locking screws
E   frog-adjusting screw
F   lever-cap screw
G   lateral-adjustment lever
H   cap iron
I   cap iron screw
J   lever cap
K   depth-adjustment wheel
L   depth-control lever
M   Y-lever
N   handle
O   blade
P   knob

Preparing a plane for use

Most new planes, apart from the most expensive, hand-finished varieties, need a few adjustments before they are ready to use. Like many tools, the plane needs to be fettled, or "tuned," to make it fit for precision work. Old planes should be checked and refettled occasionally, as required.

The main part of the plane is the sole (A). This needs to be machined perfectly so that the underneath is totally flat. Unfortunately, mass-produced castings are often not left long enough to "settle" or normalize, before the process of machining takes place, and this can result in a less than flat surface.

Fettling the sole

If a sole is badly deformed it may be easier to find a machine shop that can surface, machine, or grind the sole face flat. If there is not much to be done, though, you can do it yourself.

1 Spread some carborundum powder over a perfectly flat sheet of glass. Alternately, tape some wet-and-dry emery paper to the glass surface. Use different grades of powder or paper, working from coarse through to very fine.

2 Hold the plane at the front and rear, and push the tool over the surface. Rub the sole firmly over the surface, using an oil lubricant to enable the powder or paper to cut efficiently. This tends to be an extremely messy job!

3 As the rubbing continues, any high points become increasingly polished. Check the sole frequently to ensure that the whole face slowly develops an even polish and, therefore, an overall flatness.

4 Use increasingly fine powder or paper to polish the sole to the finest finish.

The two tables, fence, and guard.

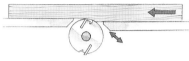

Change the thickness of the cut by adjusting the infeed table.

2 Position the board on the infeed table and raise the guard so that the wood can pass beneath. Stand to the side of the infeed table and, with the machine switched on and at operating speed, apply pressure on the board so that it does not rock. Slowly feed the wood through the planer. As the piece passes under the guard, transfer pressure to the outfeed table so that the cut will give the flattest possible surface.

3 Continue to apply pressure until the whole of the piece of wood has passed through the planer. Then lead the piece through again and continue doing so until the surface is flat. If the board is cupped or bowed, make several passes to make the board stable on the planer tables, prior to achieving a finished surface.

Planing the face edge

1 With the machine switched off, check that the fence is at a right angle—90 degrees—to the tables. Or, for a beveled edge, set the fence to the required angle. Lower the guard and slide it across, so that the wood can pass between it and the fence.

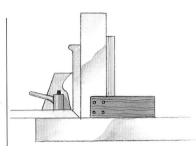

Set the fence at a 90-degree angle for the face edge.

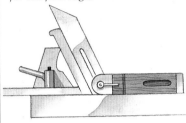

Set the fence at the appropriate angle for a bevel.

2 Switch the machine on and position the timber on the infeed table. Hold the face side firmly against the fence and feed it over the cutter block, passing it from one hand to the other.

Pass the wood from hand to hand as you feed it over the cutter.

Thicknessing with a combination plane

With a perfectly flat face side and face edge, it is now possible to plane the board to the required width and thickness.

1 Remove most of the excess material with a table saw in order to help make the board manageable.

2 Ensure that the surfacing tables are correctly adjusted and that the cutter-block guard and shavings deflector are in position.

3 Stand slightly to one side of the machine. Position the board on the infeed table and use push sticks to feed it through the thicknesser—keep your hands away from the rollers.

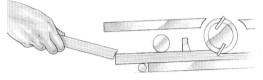

Use push sticks when the wood nears the base and the feed rollers.

4 As the board moves across the rollers, move to the other end of the machine to receive it. Do not force the board by pulling or put your hands anywhere near the rollers— make sure that you wait for the board to feed through naturally, keeping your hands well away.

Planing thin pieces to width

Very thin pieces of wood can be difficult to plane to width because they may not stay upright. Either make a special jig to ensure their stability or carry out this operation using the same method described in "Surfacing with a combination plane," having first sawed almost to width.

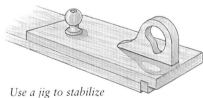

Use a jig to stabilize very thin material during planing.

Planing the face edge of thin timber pieces

To plane the edge of thin wood, use a special jig to hold the board safely. Set the machine fence at the correct angle (as above) and take extra care.

Turn to pages 150–2 and use the small shelf exercise in order to practice and develop your planing skills.

Dust/chip extraction

Even small machine planers produce a lot of waste chips. Most machines have attachments by which an extraction unit can be fitted to remove waste, thus keeping both the job and surrounding air clean. Although the unit is normally a separate investment, most woodworkers find that it is well worth the additional expense.

FINE SAWING

In addition to rough sawing lumber to size, you will also need to be able to perform much finer saw work. This section looks at the tools and skills needed for fine work, such as cutting precise joints and difficult shapes.

Hand tools

There are many saws available to the woodworker for fine cutting.

Backsaws

Backsaws are used for precise work. They have a strip of brass or steel attached to the top of the blade—this both keeps the blade straight and adds weight to the tool, to help make cutting easier.

A **tenon saw** is the largest of the backsaws. Its blade ranges between 10 and 14 in. in length, with a 12 to 14 tpi. As its name suggests, this saw is used mainly for cutting fairly large joints, particularly tenons.

A **dovetail saw** is similar to a tenon saw, though it is slightly smaller. The blade is 8 in. long, with 15 to 21 tpi. The teeth on this saw are generally set very fine. Again, its use is quite specific—for cutting dovetails and other fine sawing work.

A **bead saw,** or gents saw as it is sometimes known, is designed for very delicate work. It normally has a straight handle and is a much finer backsaw than the dovetail. The blade is about 6–8 in. long, with 15 to 25 tpi.

Tenon saw

Dovetail saw

Bead saw

Curve-cutting saws

There are several saws used for cutting curves.

The **bow saw**, although not used very much these days, is a traditional curve-cutting saw that has a lightweight wood frame. The removable blades are between 8 and 12 in. long with 8 to 16 tpi. The blade is tensioned with a tourniquet and can be turned through 360 degrees.

A **coping saw** has a sprung metal frame, which holds the blade in position by tension. The handle turns to add or release tension. The blade is 6 in. long, with approximately 15 tpi. The blade is very narrow, and can be disposed of when blunt since it is inexpensive to replace. The blade can be revolved in the frame by turning the end fittings. Unusually, this saw cuts on the pulling stroke.

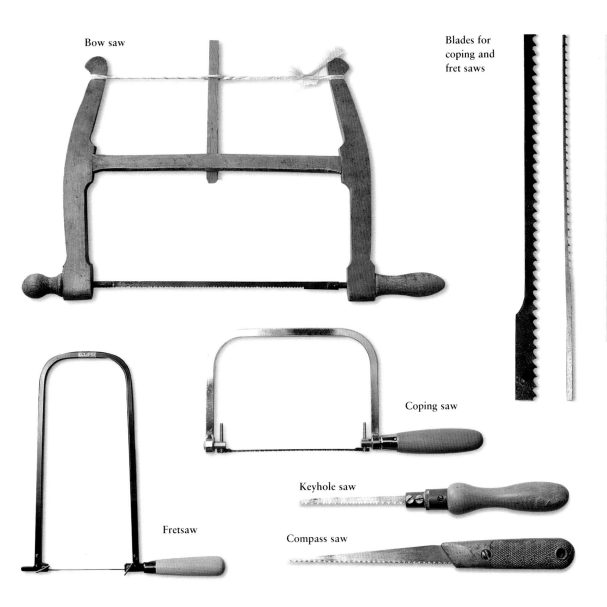

Bow saw

Blades for coping and fret saws

Fretsaw

Coping saw

Keyhole saw

Compass saw

The best hand power tool for fine sawing is the jigsaw (see page 70). This is able to saw relatively tight curves, both on the inside and the outside of the curve, and with care can handle very intricate work. The main problem is that the saw cuts on the upstroke, and when cutting across the grain, this can cause grain breakout or pickup. The tool must be held flat against the surface of the work. Always cut on the waste side of the line.

A **fretsaw** is similar to the coping saw but it has a deep throat in the steel frame and is designed for cutting very tight curves. The blade is 6 in. long, with approximately 15 tpi. The fretsaw uses very thin blades—as thin as $\frac{1}{8}$ in.—that are held in with thumbscrews at both ends and are very fragile.

A **keyhole saw,** or pad saw, is used for internal cuts when a bow saw is unable to reach the area to be cut. It has a straight handle, which can be more comfortable for some tasks. You may come across a compass saw with a shaped

or straight handle, which performs the same operation as the pad saw.

Using a backsaw

Backsaws are generally used for fine, accurate saw work.

1 Measure and mark the lines with a marking knife.

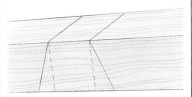

Use a marking knife to mark the saw lines on your board.

2 Secure the work in a vice. Use the tip of your index finger to position the saw blade on the waste side of the cut line. Begin with a few backward strokes, guiding the saw with your finger.

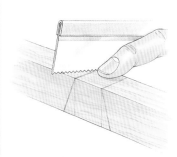

Start the cut on the waste side and guide the saw with your finger.

Japanese saws

Japanese tools have become increasingly popular with Western woodworkers in recent years. Japanese saws have superb cutting performance and cut on the pull stroke rather than needing pressure to cut the way European saws do. The range of Japanese saws shown here includes the most commonly known example to Westerners, the ryoba noko (double-edged saw), shown in the center. It is used for work where both crosscutting and ripping are necessary. A small ryoba noko is often employed in the making of cabinets or when framing doors. The unusual-looking saw on the left is known as azebiki nokogiri; it has a short blade with curved edges. The curves allow the woodworker to begin in the center of a piece of wood, which can be extremely useful. It is also used to cut sliding dovetails.

3 Extend the strokes along the cut line, keeping to the knife mark. The saw cuts on the forward stroke, so release pressure on the return stroke. Guide the saw on the forward stroke; the weight of the back strip aids the actual cut.

Using a bow saw

1 Begin by fitting the blade into the bow saw. Do this by loosening the tourniquet and positioning the blade in the slots in the handle rods. Carefully insert the pins through the holes in the blade and rods and take up the slack on the tourniquet.

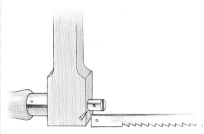

Fit a blade in a bow saw.

2 Turn the handles to adjust the blade to the required position in relation to the frame for the intended cuts. The blade may be revolved as for a coping saw.

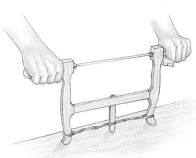

Turn the handles to adjust the blade position.

3 Tension the blade by twisting the tourniquet with the center piece of wood, or the toggle. Ensure that the toggle is sitting against the center rail.

4 Hold one end of the saw with both hands. It is vital to have a proper grip on the tool, with the index finger of the first hand extending in line with the blade. Even though the saw has a handle at both ends, it is normally used holding one end only with both hands; make careful strokes making sure that you keep to the line.

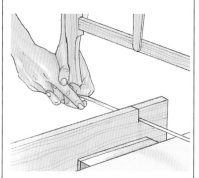

Hold the bow saw correctly.

Using a coping saw

1 To replace a blade, unscrew the handle to bring the pins closer together and release tension. Insert the blade in one end and slightly flex the frame against the bench; insert the blade in the other end and tighten by turning the handle.

Flex the coping-saw frame and fit the blade.

2 Secure the piece of wood in a vice, grip the handle of the saw firmly, and position the blade on the waste side of the cut line. Pull the saw toward your body in order to make the cut.

Pull the coping saw toward you as you make the cut.

3 To change the direction of the blade or to prevent the frame from falling foul of the edge, loosen the handle slightly, rotate the blade in the frame, and retighten before continuing with the sawing. This allows the frame to be turned over the nearest edge without changing the cutting direction.

Using a fretsaw

1 To fit a blade, loosen the thumbscrews at each end and insert the blade. As you retighten the thumbscrews, spring the frame closed; this will give the blade tension.

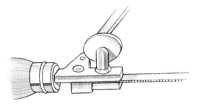

The fretsaw blade.

2 Clamp the wood to the bench with the work area overhanging, and sit so that you are near the cutting area.

3 Position the blade on the waste side of the line, so that it cuts on the downstroke and you can cut to the marks on the top surface. These saws cut with a pulling action, not pushing as other saws do.

Use a pulling action with a fretsaw.

Using a compass saw or keyhole saw

1 To make an internal cut, drill a hole in the marked area of the piece, on the waste side.

2 Insert the saw blade and use the forward, thin edge of the blade to start the cut. Gradually increase the length of the strokes.

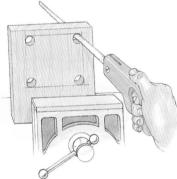

Use a compass saw to cut a hole.

Bandsaw

The best machine tool that you can use for intricate, fine sawing is a bandsaw. Unlike most other types of machine saws, this has a continuous band of metal with teeth on the leading edge. The band runs around two or three wheels and the blade passes through a slot in a machine table.

The blade is tensioned by the top wheel, and it is powered by a motor working on the bottom wheel. Various

thicknesses of blade and different sets of teeth mean that very small curves can be sawed, and the large blade makes it an extremely good general-purpose machine. The machine is supplied with various fences, but once mastered, it is often easier to use by sight than with guides or fences.

Using a bandsaw

1 Before starting the machine, select the correct blade that you need for the job. It is important to check this for faults before you start work. The blade needs to be tensioned and the top wheel needs to be tracked in order to keep the blade running in the center of the wheel. A hand wheel or knob tilts the top wheel to align the blade. Set the guide blocks so that they just miss the sides of the blade; usually there is a set above and below the table.

2 Next, the friction wheel needs to be set approximately $1/16$–$1/8$ in. from the back of the blade—too far back and the blade may come off, while if it is put too far forward, it could break the blade.

3 Once the saw is set-up test run it for 5 to 10 seconds on full speed; stop the saw and check that the blade is still set in the correct position; adjust as required.

4 Before sawing, adjust the blade guides so that there is only about $1/8$ in. between them and the work.

5 Switch on the machine and align the saw blade with your marked line, ensuring that it is on the waste side.

6 Carefully feed the work into the blade, constantly checking that it is following the line.

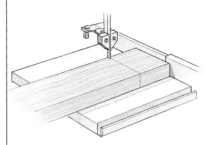

Carefully feed the timber into the blade of the bandsaw.

7 At the end of the cut, use a push stick to feed the remaining edge of the work through the blade. Always be sure that your fingers are out of the way when the saw breaks through.

Safety first

• Wear the appropriate safety equipment.

• Always ensure that the blade is properly tensioned, and that the blade guides and rear thrust wheel are properly positioned.

• Never force the work. The blade should be sharp enough to do the cutting; you are only directing its path.

Turn to pages 153–5 and use the mail rack exercise to practice fine sawing.

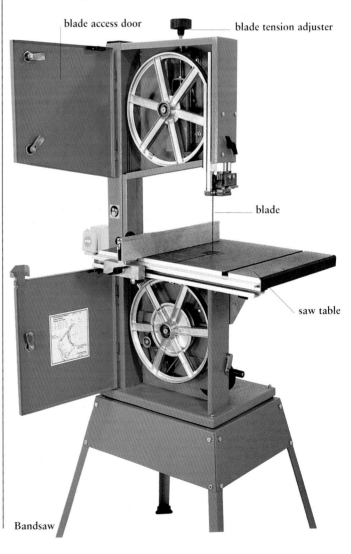

blade access door

blade tension adjuster

blade

saw table

Bandsaw

CHISELING

Together with saws and planes, the chisel is one of the most important tools in a woodworker's workshop. It is used for creating neat, accurate joints and also for removing waste material.

Chisels

Chisels come in a wide range of sizes, and it is important to have a good selection in your tool kit to cover the full range of tasks. Like all edge tools, chisels function best when they are very sharp. This ensures that less effort is needed to cut, and the tool is also much easier to guide, which means you will get greater accuracy. Paring, which is the removal of very fine shavings with the chisel, can be carried out either horizontally or vertically.

A **firmer chisel** is the strongest type of chisel and has a rectangular shaped blade. It comes in sizes ranging from 1/8–2 in. and is used for general-purpose chiseling tasks.

Bevel-edged chisels also come in various sizes and have two shallow bevels ground along the edges of the upper face. This makes the chisel more suitable for joint making.

A **paring chisel** is the same as a bevel-edged chisel, although it has a much longer blade, which is particularly useful when paring housings. One type of paring chisel is cranked (has the blade at an angle) so that the blade can be kept flat, even when paring very wide boards.

Firmer chisels

Bevel-edged chisels

Paring chisels

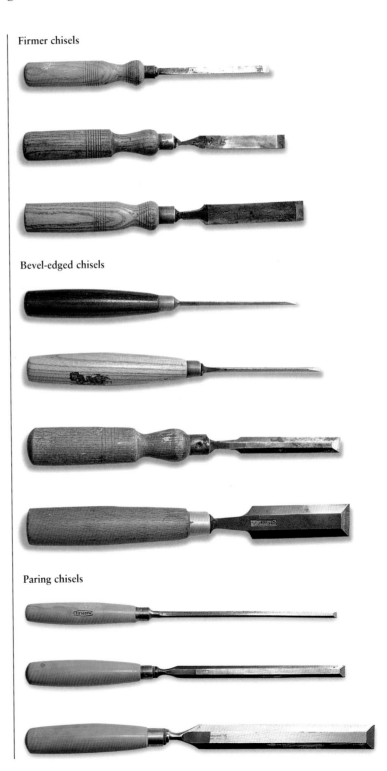

Gouges

A gouge is, essentially, a type of chisel, which has a curved cross-section to the blade. There are two types of gouges available for different purposes: an out-cannel gouge and an in-cannel gouge.

The **out-cannel gouge** has a cutting edge ground on the outside and is used for paring convex shapes.

The **in-cannel gouge** is ground on the inside and is used for paring concave shapes.

Mortise chisels

Mortise chisels are stronger than the chisels described on the left, and are designed for tougher work, such as cutting deep mortises. Whereas most chisels are normally used only with body pressure, mortise chisels may require a mallet to drive the tool firmly into the work. For this reason, these chisels normally have some form of cap, such as a metal ferrule, to protect the top of the handle from splitting. However, keep the mortise chisel sharp, so that only a slight tap with the mallet works.

The **sash-mortise chisel** has a thick, substantial blade for very heavy-duty work. It has wide sides that help to keep the blade straight. This enables it to lever out waste from deep mortises.

The **registered mortise chisel** is a heavier pattern, having a thicker blade, and is used for cutting larger joints.

A **drawer-lock chisel** may be used to cut mortises or housings in tight spaces.

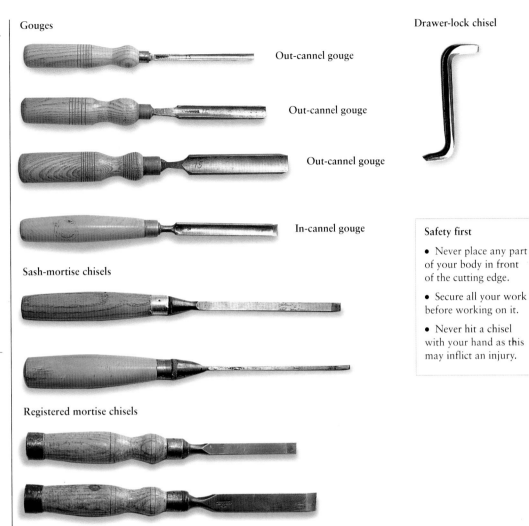

Gouges

Out-cannel gouge

Out-cannel gouge

Out-cannel gouge

In-cannel gouge

Sash-mortise chisels

Registered mortise chisels

Drawer-lock chisel

> **Safety first**
> - Never place any part of your body in front of the cutting edge.
> - Secure all your work before working on it.
> - Never hit a chisel with your hand as this may inflict an injury.

Japanese chisels

As an alternative, you may want to invest in some Japanese chisels for your tool kit. They are made up of a lamination of a thin bottom layer of very hard steel and a thicker layer of softer steel. The Oire nomi (butt chisel) shown here on the near right is a general, all-purpose chisel. It has a thin blade and the top face has a wide chamfer on both edges to make it lighter and easier to reach corners with. The Kama nomi (sickle chisel) on the far right gets its name because of the way it looks. It has beveled sides and is used to clean up the insides of dovetails and the side grooves of plane blocks.

A selection of Japanese chisels.

Using chisels

Paring horizontally

1 Lay the work flat on the bench and secure it with C-clamps or, if it is a suitable size, in the vice.

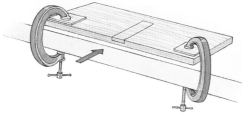

Secure the work on the bench, ready to be pared horizontally.

2 Stand with your chest and shoulders at right angles to the board, with your legs apart and the elbow of your dominant hand tucked into your body.

The correct stance to adopt when paring horizontally.

3 Hold the chisel handle in your dominant hand. Hold the blade between the thumb and forefinger of your other hand, behind the cutting edge. Apply pressure with the forearm of

your dominant hand in order to make the chisel cut. Use the other hand to steer and guide the direction of the chisel.

Hold the blade between your thumb and forefinger for horizontal paring.

Guide the chisel carefully and pare away the waste.

Paring vertically

1 Place the work on the benchtop and secure in position with a C-clamp. It is preferable to fix a piece of spare wood underneath the work.

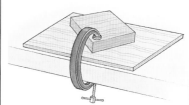

Secure the work on the bench, ready to be pared vertically.

2 Bend over your work so that your shoulder is directly over the chisel, and apply a controlled, downward pressure on your hand. This action will help you to keep the chisel straight while cutting.

The correct stance to adopt when paring vertically.

3 Grip the handle of the chisel firmly by placing your thumb over the end of it. Use the thumb and forefinger of the other hand to control the blade carefully, as before, when paring horizontally. Apply firm downward pressure in order to chisel out the waste.

Control the blade with your thumb and forefinger.

Apply a downward pressure as you chisel away the waste.

Cutting mortises with a chisel

1 To remove the bulk of the waste, hold the chisel in one hand with the blade positioned between the gauge lines—approximately $\frac{1}{8}$ in. in from the end of the mortise—and apply pressure. Repeat several times along the mortise to chop out the initial layer.

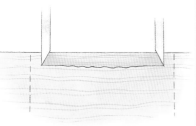

Remove the first layer of waste from the mortise.

2 To remove deeper levels, strike the handle of the chisel squarely with a mallet. Do this first at each end of the mortise, with the bevel facing the center of the recess. The chisel will cut straight down. Then hold the chisel at a slight angle a little farther in from the end and strike the chisel with the mallet. This will raise the waste from the bottom of the mortise. Pry out the waste and continue these steps until the required depth has been reached. If cutting a through mortise, work from both sides.

Use a mallet to raise the waste from the bottom of the mortise.

3 Finally, finish the mortise by cutting it back to the required shoulder lines. Do this by paring away the waste to the end of the mortise, using the technique shown in "Paring vertically," opposite. It is important that you keep the chisel square during this process.

Using gouges

Use gouges in the same way as chisels, ensuring that the cutting edge is sharp. Use the in-cannel gouge when you are trimming curved shoulders, and the out-cannel gouge for hollowing out shapes.

Use an out-cannel gouge for hollowing out shapes.

Turn to pages 156–7 to practice chiseling to make animal shapes.

Examples of chiseled shapes – see pages 156–7 for instructions.

MAKING GROOVES

Grooves are long narrow channels cut either along or across the grain. They can be used for joints that fit pieces of wood together or for decorative effect. Grooves are often used to hold drawer bottoms and cabinet backs.

Hand tools

Before power tools were introduced into the workshop, grooves were cut with a hand plow plane, or one of the more complex tools that derived from it, such as the combination plane (see page 75).

The plow plane has bits ranging from ⅛–½ in., which are held with a screw at the correct cutting angle. The tool is fitted with a depth gauge and a fence, which means that it will only cut straight grooves parallel to a given edge. The combination plane has features that make it suitable for tongue-and-groove work, while the multi-plane has extra bits for moldings.

Power tools

Good quality hand power routers can be used for carrying out grooving and operations such as rabbeting and molding. For people starting out in woodwork, a small power router is ideal because it is more versatile than a plow plane.

Power routers

Power routers consist of a motor held in a mounting, beneath which is fixed a socket to hold varying sizes of bits. The baseplate guides the

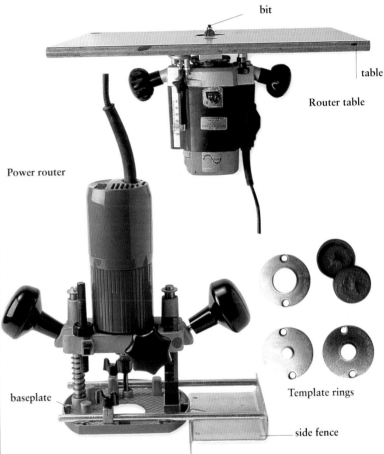

bit

table

Router table

Power router

baseplate

Template rings

side fence

tool over the work surface and is fitted with clamps for securing rods and accessories. The depth stop is used to adjust the projection of the bit from the baseplate, while the handles are used to steer the tool.

Most large routers work by a plunging action. The motor body rises and falls on a pair of columns and the bit is plunged into the wood, before being retracted at the end of the job. The motor size varies but all routers give a speed without load of between

22,000 and 27,000 rpm. However, because the speed drops as soon as the bit touches the work, high-powered motors are preferable for high-quality finishes.

The socket accepts the shank of the router bit and can be found in several sizes. The lightest routers have sockets of either ¼ or ⅜ in. in diameter, while larger machines have a capacity of ½ in. The larger the socket capacity, the larger the size of bits that can be fitted.

Safety reminder

- Always follow the manufacturer's instructions.
- Hold the router firmly when starting up and operating.
- Use both handles.
- Use safety glasses, ear protectors and a dust mask.
- Never start the router when the bit is in contact with the work.
- Always disconnect the power supply when you are making any adjustments, especially when changing bits.
- Use sharp bits.
- When cutting, the router should move from left to right.
- Secure the work well.

Groove-forming bits

V-grooving bits

Plug bit   *Dovetail bit*   *Combined bit*

Edge-forming bits

Router bits

While high-speed steel bits are adequate for most jobs, tungsten-tip bits maintain their sharpness for longer. However, when these bits do need sharpening, they must be sent to a specialist. There is a wide range of bits available,

and these can be categorized as either groove-forming (straight) or edge-forming (molding).

Groove-forming bits come in a range of styles. Straight bits cut square grooves, while V-grooving bits create a V-shaped indent, largely for decorative work. Veining and core-box bits produce round-bottomed grooves, while a dovetail bit is used for dovetail housings and joints.

Edge-forming bits can have pin- or ball-bearing race guides. The latter is preferable as it reduces the risk of damage along the edge of the wood. The most common types are rabbet, chamfer, rounding and trimming varieties. For shaping edges, cove, ogee, and beading bits create decorative edges along the wood.

Router table

One main advantage of the router is that it can be mounted upside down in a frame so that the bit projects from the surface, with safety fences in place. This is a very useful and safe way of working. Instead of taking the router to the work, the wood is fed over the router, in the direction of the bit.

Proprietary **router tables** can be bought, but you can also make one using material such as plywood. Cut and construct

Construct a homemade router table.

a box with one open side so that the router is readily accessible. Cut a hole in the top of the box for the bit to protrude through and fix the router baseplate in the box, directly below the hole in the top.

Biscuit jointers

Even though the furniture maker can use the jointing methods described previously, if you need to make a lot of cabinets or boxes, the biscuit jointer is a very useful tool.

The **biscuit jointer** is a small circular saw that cuts slots into both faces of a joint. A wood oval—the biscuit—available ready-made of compressed beech, is inserted into the slots. The biscuit joint is often used in place of tongues and grooves or dowel joints and can even replace some traditional cabinet- and drawer-making joints.

The biscuit jointer can make butt joints, both from edge to face and from edge to edge, as well as miter joints. It can also be used to cut small grooves and to trim panel edges.

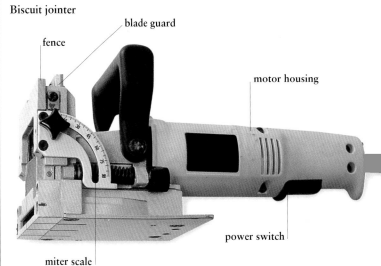

Biscuit jointer

fence
blade guard
motor housing
power switch
miter scale

Using a power router

Compared with some tools, power routers are relatively safe to use, provided you maintain them properly and follow the manufacturer's instructions.

Fitting a bit

When fitting a bit into a socket, first unplug the router from the electrical supply.

1 Lock the spindle, using either the button provided, or the metal rod that passes through a hole in the spindle. Some routers have two wrenches—one for the spindle and one for the socket nut.

2 Use a wrench to loosen the nut and unscrew the socket.

Unscrew the socket with a wrench.

3 Insert the bit into the socket, carefully pushing it into position. Be careful not to cut your fingers.

Insert the bit with the retaining nut into the socket.

4 Then, tighten the socket nut using the wrench and unlock the spindle.

5 Use your fingers to check that the bit is tight. Test-run the router, so that it gains full speed for 5 to 10 seconds. Turn off the router and recheck the bit.

Cutting grooves with a side fence

To produce a straight, grooved line, parallel with the edge of the wood, use a side fence. This should be positioned to the right side of a clockwise-rotating bit, so that the force of the blade does not pull the fence too much towards the work. It is a good idea to test-run a scrap piece of wood first before routing your work.

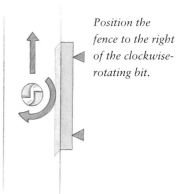

Position the fence to the right of the clockwise-rotating bit.

1 Choose the required bit for the job and insert it into the tool as explained above.

2 Adjust and lock the fence in the correct position.

3 Set the depth of cut so that the bit will plunge only as far as you require. In many instances, it is better to make deep cuts in small stages. This will help to prolong the life of the bit and prevent the machine from overheating.

4 Hold the router firmly, using both handles. Switch on the machine, with the router motor in position above the base. Twist the locking handle to unlock the router body and plunge the bit into the work to the preset depth. Lock the router into position.

Cut a groove, using a router and side fence.

5 Continue the cut to the end of the piece of wood. To make a stopped groove, plunge the router at the start mark, guide the tool until the bit reaches the end mark, and release the plunge mechanism.

Cutting a groove using guide battens

Guide battens can be used for making grooves that are some distance from the edge of the wood. You can use any straight pieces of wood that are long enough to project beyond the start and finish marks of the groove.

1 Using C-clamps, fix the guide battens to the work. The bit has to line up with the center of the router base, so that the groove will end up being midway between the battens.

2 Select the required bit and fit it carefully into the power router.

3 Plunge the router and cut as before. Remove the battens when finished.

Cut a groove, using a router and side battens.

Cutting edge moldings

Edges are molded for decorative effect or to soften sharp corners.

1 Select the required bit and insert it in the socket. Use molding bits with a bearing at the tip, rather than a simple steel tip, because this reduces the risk of burning the wood.

2 Fit the fence securely, bearing in mind that the bit will tend to draw the fence to the edge.

3 Clamp the work to the bench as shown below, ensuring that nothing is obstructing the fence.

The edge to be molded needs to overhang the bench sufficiently.

4 Plunge the router to the correct depth, lock, and start the motor. Bring the bit up to the edge of the wood, and holding the fence or bearing against the work, cut the molding, moving from left to right.

Routing with a template

In addition to using fences and battens, shaped edges and internal shaping can be carried out using a template. Most routers have a collar or ring that can be fixed to the tool's faceplate, which will act as a guide when using a template. The diagram shows a section of the collar and the bit, and how the aperture along the edge and inside the template has to account for the differences in diameter. For example, a $\frac{3}{8}$-in. bit with a $\frac{5}{8}$-in. outside diameter collar will need the template cut $\frac{1}{8}$ in. bigger than the finished cutout.

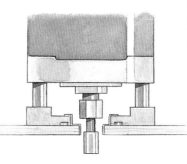

The collar and template.

1 Mark a template on a piece of $\frac{1}{4}$-in. medium density fiberboard. Draw out the whole pattern that you want to reproduce, with the outer line representing the edges of the final job. Remember you can cut shaped outside or inside edges. Now measure the bit and the collar to determine the differences in diameter, as described above.

2 Make the template, cutting as closely as you can to your second line with a bandsaw or jigsaw. Finish off with a rasp, file, or sandpaper.

3 Fix the template in position. If the surface has not been finished, you can use nails to secure it. If any finish or veneer

has been applied, use double-sided tape. In some instances, depending upon the desired shaping, it may be possible to use C-clamps.

4 Switch the router on and plunge the bit to the required depth; guide the collar against the template as you rout around the edges.

Cutting joints

The router is a versatile tool that can be used to cut many types of joints—even some of the complex ones such as mortise-and-tenons and dovetails. Unless you need to cut a number of joints, these can be done by hand. However, any joints based on rabbets and grooves, such as tongue-and-groove, lap, and housing joints (both barefaced and dovetail) are suitable for the router.

Using a biscuit jointer

The instructions below show you how to make a simple butt joint.

1 Set the cutting depth to suit the biscuits you are using, and adjust the fence so that the blade aligns with the center line on the first component. Press the fence against the work.

2 Start the machine and plunge the blade to make a cut. Use the same procedure to cut the rest of the slots. Then cut those on the edge of the second component.

3 To assemble the joint, spread adhesive into the slots and insert the biscuits. The adhesive will make the biscuits swell, producing a very strong joint. You will need to work rapidly to apply the adhesive, insert the biscuit, and clamp the joint.

Expert tip

When molding the edges of solid wood panels, particularly across the grain, there may well be some breakout at the end of the pass. For this reason, use the tool on the two sides of the end grain first. Then, as you mold the long sides, this breakout should be removed.

Turn to pages 158–9 where the hot plate stand will give you practice in grooving.

Machine tools

A machine tool equivalent of the power router is a large industrial machine with a fixed head containing the motor with larger capacities and speeds. Nowadays the hand power tools are so efficient that you may never need to investigate the machine alternative. Another industrial machine is the spindle molder, and again the power router is so efficient for most purposes that this industrial equivalent will not be necessary.

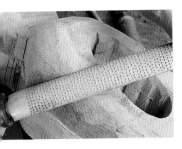

SHAPING

The ability to shape curved surfaces and edges moves furniture away from the solely functional. When you want to introduce a freer approach to your work, you will need to use the tools and techniques described in this section.

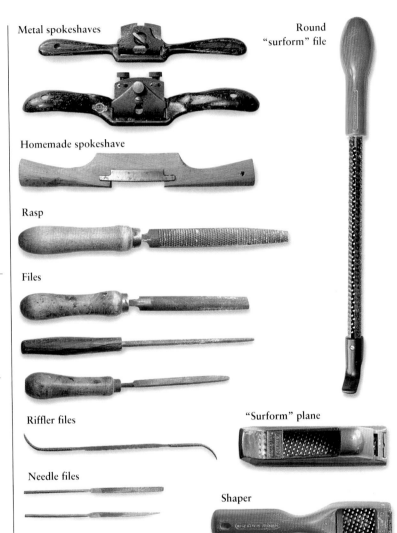

Metal spokeshaves

Homemade spokeshave

Rasp

Files

Riffler files

Needle files

Round "surform" file

"Surform" plane

Shaper

Using a second-cut file

The distribution and size of teeth on rasps and files determine the degree of coarseness— or cut—of the tool. A bastard cut is the coarsest, a smooth cut is the finest, and a second cut is in between the two.

Drawknives

A traditional tool used by chairmakers, wheelwrights, or coopers, drawknives have similarities to axes, and remove wood very quickly. They do not produce a very refined finish, and are most suitable for initial shaping before using a plane or spokeshave. The tools are now not really in general use, and tend to be found only in specialized trades. The one pictured here is a curved drawknife.

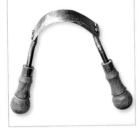

Shaping tools

Even though some work on convex and other curved surfaces can be carried out with planes and chisels, narrow edges require a smaller tool to prevent slipping. Spokeshaves are ideal for such work. Rasps and files are also used for shaping work, particularly when curves are tight.

Spokeshaves

Although spokeshaves are ideal for shaping, they can be quite difficult to control and will require some practice. There are two main types—one for convex shapes and the other for concave. Spokeshaves are usually made of metal but, traditionally, furniture makers would have made their own tools from wood—normally beech—into which a metal blade was then fitted.

Round-face spokeshaves have convex blades that are ideal for use on wood with a concave face. The blade is held in position by a cap iron, and the depth of the blade can be adjusted by loosening this cap and jiggling the blade into the required position. Alternately, some spokeshaves have screws at the top two corners of the blade, which can be loosened and tightened for making precise adjustments.

Flat-face spokeshaves are the same as round-face versions, except that they have flat, narrow faces. This feature of the tool makes it suitable for skimming a convex curve.

A **half-round spokeshave** has a deep, concave blade and face, and is suitable for rounded tabletops and chair legs.

A **chamfer spokeshave** can be used to cut bevels up to 1½ in. wide.

A **combination spokeshave** is dual-purpose, and has both a straight and half-rounded blade. Because it is useful on work with a range of surfaces, it saves changing blades as you move from one area to another.

Rasps and files

Most commonly used by carvers for initial shaping, rasps and files also remove a lot of material. Rasps produce a fairly rough surface, which then needs to be smoothed with a file. The teeth on rasps range from coarse to quite smooth, and the tool is available in flat, round (rat-tail) and, most usefully, half-round shapes.

Files are much finer than rasps and help to remove roughened wood left by the other tool. For a finer finish, they can be used with abrasive paper wrapped around them. **Riffler files** are designed for use in tight curves, while **needle files** are used for metalwork and are useful when adapting hardware such as hinges.

"Surform" tools are available in a range of plain or file types. The main difference lies in their carefully punched teeth, which enable wood shavings to pass through the metal. This means that the tool can move over the wood's surface more quickly, because it is less likely to get clogged. The most commonly used surform tools are the flat surform file and the round surform file.

Adjusting the blade on a spokeshave

1 Remove the blade by undoing the locking screw on the cap iron. Sharpen the blade by grinding and honing, as required (see pages 72–3).

2 Carefully reposition the blade ground-side down and tighten the lead screw. If this screw is the sole means of adjustment, tighten the blade gradually and position the blade with your fingers until it protrudes at the correct depth. If the tool has adjustment screws, use these to achieve a more precise setting.

Adjust the blade in the spokeshave to the desired projection.

Using a spokeshave

Effective shaping with a spokeshave can take time to master. It pays to practice on scrap wood, before attempting a job on a piece of furniture. Keep the cutting edge of the blade sharp to ensure the best results, and remember to adjust the position of the blade to vary the depth of cut as required.

1 Secure the work in a vice. Hold the tool with both hands, so that your fingers curl over the front of the handles, and your thumbs rest at the back.

Secure the work in a vice and hold the spokeshave with both hands.

2 Rest the tool on the work and move it forward and backward, so that the blade cuts a shaving. Work in the direction of the grain, changing the position of the wood in the vice as you go, if necessary.

Using rasps and files

There are frequently occasions when curves are so tight that edge tools are not suitable for the job. In these instances, it is best to use a file or rasp.

1 Fit a handle to the rasp or file. If possible, secure the work in a vice before you start. Use your spare hand to hold the wood securely, preferably with your fingertips near the area to be filed, to maximize the pressure.

2 Hold the rasp firmly with your dominant hand and apply forward pressure in order to cut away the wood.

Cut away the wood with a rasp.

3 After making a series of rough cuts with the rasp, use a wood file in order to remove some of the rough surface.

4 Then finish the job with sandpaper wrapped around a file or a piece of hardwood in order to achieve a more refined finish.

Cleaning rasps and files

When rasps and files become clogged, use the wire bristles on a file cleaner—or file card— to loosen the shavings. Then remove the shavings with the coarse fiber brush on the other side of the file cleaner.

DRILLING

In woodwork and furniture making, you often need to make holes, either to use with special saws or to insert a range of screws, dowels, and other hardware. It is important to be able to drill accurately to a specific depth and angle.

Hand tools

With the advent of the power drill, hand drills and braces are less commonly used today. However, they still have an important role to play in the woodworker's workshop.

A **bradawl** is a simple tool for marking pilot holes for small screws, or for creating the center-mark for drilling.

A **gimlet** is similar to the bradawl, but it creates deeper holes by actually cutting into the wood.

Hand drills

A **hand drill** is the simplest type of drilling tool. By operating the handle, a series of gear wheels rotates the chuck shaft. The drill bits, which are held in the chuck, are subsequently rotated. There are several types of drill bits that can be used in this tool and powered varieties to perform different functions.

Drill bits

The following bits can be used in hand or powered drills. **Twist drills** come in a range of sizes. It can be difficult to drill precisely with these bits—they can easily move off course with the vibration of the tool. You could mark the drilling location with a bradawl, making a slight recess in the surface for the bit.

Dowel bits, or centerpoint drills, also come in a range of sizes

and have a point at the center of the tip and two spurs. The center tip can be placed exactly on the drill mark, and the two spurs help to prevent the bit from moving off course.

A **countersink bit** cuts a tapered recess around the main hole. This provides a useful home for the head of a screw, so that the top of the screw sits flush with the surface of the wood. This makes for a very clean and smooth finished look.

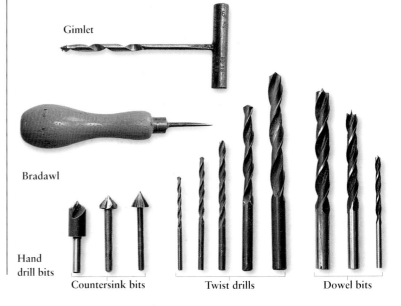

Gimlet

Bradawl

Hand drill bits

Countersink bits

Twist drills

Dowel bits

Hand drill

chuck

handle

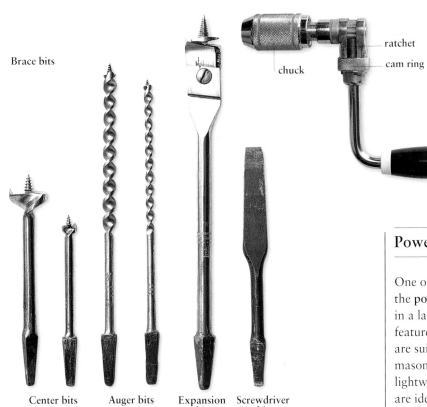

Brace bits

Center bits   Auger bits   Expansion   Screwdriver
                               bit   bit

Ratchet brace

ratchet

cam ring

chuck

Braces

A **brace** is also used to drill
holes, but the whole frame
of the tool is rotated in a
clockwise direction while
pressure is at the same time
applied to the rear, domed
handle. Most types of braces
have a ratchet mechanism, so
that the tool can be used in
restricted spaces. The chuck of a
brace has jaws that are designed
to house bits with square
shanks. However, some braces
can accept the same round-
shanked drill bits that are
used in power and hand drills.

Brace bits

Center bits come in a range
of sizes from $1/4$–2 in. A single
spur on one side of the bit scores
the edge of the hole. Then the
cutting edge on the other side
of the bit cuts into the wood.
A lead screw protruding from
the center pulls the spur

and then the cutting edge into
the wood. This ensures that
a neat, crisp hole is made.

Auger bits are similar to center
bits, but they cut deeper holes.
The long, spiral body behind the
cutting edge keeps the drill in
line and removes waste wood.

Expansion bits are similar to
center bits, but have a cutter that
can be set to different diameters.
Available in two sizes, the total
cutting capacity ranges from
$1/2$ in. to 3 in.

Countersink bits work in the
same way as those for drills,
but they have square shanks to
fit in the brace chuck.

Screwdriver bits enable braces
to be used as a heavy-duty
screwdriver for long screws.
However, many people use
electric screwdrivers or light
power drills with screwdriver
bits instead.

Power drills

One of the first electric tools,
the **power drill** is now available
in a large range of sizes and
features. Heavy-duty versions
are suitable for such work as
masonry and concrete, while
lightweight, rechargeable types
are ideal for fine drilling, such
as for small screws.

Like hand drills, power drills
have a chuck that holds the
required bit. It is worth
remembering that the shank of
the bit corresponds with the
diameter of the hole that the bit
cuts. So large drills, which tend
to have a large chuck capacity—

Safety first

- Wear safety glasses.
- Secure the work.
- Do not wear any loose clothing.
- Keep hands well away from drill bits.
- Tie back long hair securely.
- Always select the correct speed.
- Never use a tool to do a job for which it was not designed.
- Make sure that you use sharp drill bits.
- Never force the tool—let the bit do the work.

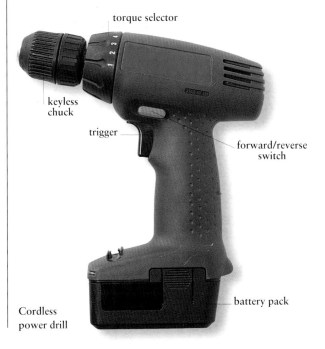

torque selector

keyless
chuck

trigger

forward/reverse
switch

battery pack

Cordless
power drill

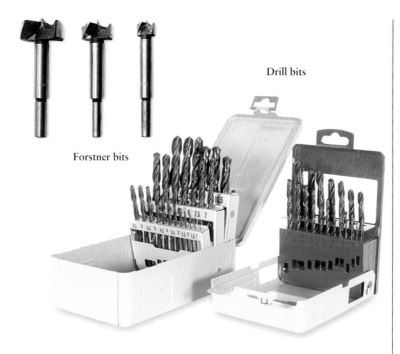

Forstner bits

Drill bits

Pillar drill

Usually known as a drill press, the **pillar drill** is a heavy-duty machine tool and is very useful in the workshop. In fact, unless you are planning to carry out a lot of site work, a pillar drill is probably the next step after a small power drill, rather than investing in a large tool and separate stand. Pillar drills can be either bench or floor mounted, and are ideal for precise, repetitive drilling.

The tool has an adjustable table to accommodate a range of sizes of wood, and a feed lever that works in much the same way as the lever on a vertical drill stand (see box, left). A depth gauge can be set to determine the depth of the hole, while a guard helps to prevent any obstructions or clothing from getting in the way of the rotating chuck. Remember never to wear loose clothing while you are using a piece of machinery.

A vertical drill stand

This is another useful attachment, as it transforms a hand-held power drill into a temporary drill press. The feed lever is used to lower the drill, with its rotating bit, into the work. When this lever is released, a return spring brings the drill back to the starting position. A depth gauge on the stand can be used to limit the movement of the tool, so that stopped holes can be drilled. To drill through holes, position a piece of plywood under the work. This helps to prevent the underside surface from splintering as the drill passes through.

up to ½ in.—can take larger bits, which means that they are capable of drilling larger holes. Smaller, lighter drills have less chuck capacity and are used for smaller holes.

Most drills come with a speed selector. Some larger drills have a hammer action, which is useful when attaching battens to masonry walls.

Power drill bits

There is a wide range of drill bits available.

Twist and **centerpoint drill bits** are the same as those used for the hand drill, although if they are to be used on metal at any stage, it is worth investing in high-speed steel types. Large twist drills are made with reduced shanks, so they can fit in standard power drill chucks.

Spade bits have long points for positioning on the exact center of the hole mark. This is especially helpful when you are

drilling at an angle to the face surface, since the point prevents the drill from wandering.

Forstner bits are high-quality drill bits that have a special serrated ring around the main point. These teeth help the bit to stay on course, boring through difficult areas and preventing knots from deflecting the drill.

Countersink bits with reduced shanks (again designed to fit ordinary power drills) are also available, as are drill-and-countersink bits, which produce both a hole and countersink in one action.

Drill-and-counterbore bits perform similar actions to the drill-and-countersink bit, except that they also produce a neat counterbored hole, which can be plugged with a piece of wood, to conceal the screw beneath. To cut the plug, use a plug cutter, which will cut a cylindrical piece of wood exactly the right size for the hole made by the drill-and-counterbore bit.

Pillar drill

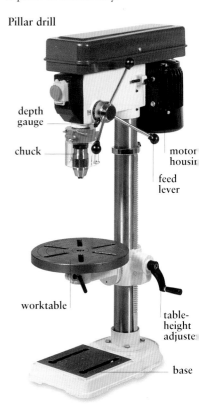

depth gauge

chuck

motor housin

feed lever

worktable

table-height adjuste

base

Using a hand drill

It is possible to use a hand drill from most positions. However, it is most common, and generally easier, to drill from a vertical position, so that you can apply a steady pressure to the rear handle.

1 Select the drill or bit you require. Open the jaws of the hand drill by holding the chuck with one hand and rotating the drive wheel counterclockwise with the other. Or, some hand drill chucks are opened with a chuck key, just like power drills.

2 Insert the bit into the chuck and tighten the jaws, either by turning the drive handle clockwise or, if appropriate, tightening with the chuck key. Check that the bit is centered in the chuck jaws.

3 Mark the center of the hole on the wood's surface, preferably with crossed hairlines. Twist a bradawl on the exact center of the mark, which will produce a starter hole.

Mark the center of the desired hole before you indent it with the bradawl.

4 Put the tip of the drill on the starter hole. Bring the body of the drill to the correct angle— normally square with the face. Stand two try squares near the mark so that you can sight the drill bit to ensure accuracy.

Rotate the hand drill's drive wheel.

5 Hold the drill steady by applying a moderate amount of pressure to the rear handle. Begin to rotate the drive handle, so that the drill cuts into the surface. Continue rotating the handle while holding the drill steady and at the correct angle. You should not require a great deal of pressure or speed— experience will teach you how all the different woods respond and how much pressure is required for each.

Using a brace

1 Select the required bit for the job. Center the cam ring so that the brace ratchet is locked in position. Then hold the chuck and rotate the frame clockwise, to open the jaws.

2 Insert the bit and tighten the jaws of the chuck by rotating the frame counterclockwise. Ensure that the tapered shank of the bit is firmly in the chuck.

3 When you are drilling horizontally, place the work in a vice so that you are drilling at lower chest level.

4 To drill vertically, secure the work on the bench or in a vice. Hold the brace upright with one hand while you turn the brace with the other hand.

Turn the frame of the brace steadily.

5 Hold the brace steady. Most drills have a screw that pulls the bit into the work, so only the minimum amount of pressure is required. Turn the frame with your other hand, taking care to keep the tool level. Remember that the bits used in a brace are designed for slow and methodical cutting.

6 At the required depth, reverse the handle a couple of times to release the screw. Then gently pull the tool away from the hole, rotating the brace at the same time in order to clear the waste from the hole. If you are boring through holes, stop drilling as soon as the lead screw shows on the opposite side. Remove the brace and drill bit, as described, and then reverse the work to repeat the drilling from the other side.

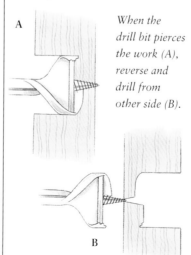

A

B

When the drill bit pierces the work (A), reverse and drill from other side (B).

7 If there is not enough room to make a full sweep with the frame, set the cam ring on the ratchet. When the ratchet is set, it will turn the bit about one-quarter of a turn. Then reverse the handle direction and make another cut. This technique is useful when you are forced to work in confined spaces.

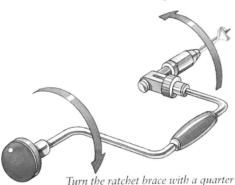

Turn the ratchet brace with a quarter sweep to cut and then return.

Making a depth stop for a twist drill

Even though it is possible to buy metal depth stops for twist drills, it is very easy to make your own version. Take some square scraps of hardwood and drill a hole of the required size down the center. Slip the wood over the drill bit, and mark the length of the hole required. Cut the wood on the mark. Slip the depth stop back on the drill and drill the hole until the stop touches the surface. You can keep several lengths of wood drilled to fit the drill sizes that you most commonly use so that you can cut suitable lengths when needed.

Now turn to pages 162–4 – the wine rack will be a good exercise to practice precise drilling.

Homemade depth stops.

Using a power drill

Power drills are relatively easy to use—on wood there is less vibration than on materials such as concrete or masonry.

1 Select the required bit and fit it into the chuck. This is usually done with a chuck key, in the same way as a hand drill, but some power drills have keyless chucks. Pull back the casing of the chuck, insert a bit with an appropriately grooved shank, to fit the type of drill, and release the chuck casing. The chuck will automatically grip the bit.

2 Select the required speed on the drill. With some tools, the speed of the rotating chuck will depend on the amount of pressure applied to the trigger. Although knowledge of the desired speed comes with experience, it is generally best to have a fast setting for drilling holes in wood, and a slower speed for masonry.

3 Hold the rear handle with your dominant hand and the secondary handle, if there is one, with the weaker hand. Stand comfortably with your body squarely facing to the work. Position the tip of the bit on the drill mark and pull the trigger.

Position the drill bit and start to apply pressure to the trigger.

4 As the drill bit moves into the wood, keep the tool steady and at the required angle to the work.

5 When you have achieved the depth of hole required, gently pull the tool away, with the bit still rotating, and release the trigger when the bit is clear of the work.

The power drill is used in a similar way when fitted with a screwdriver bit, although a slower speed is usually required to ensure accurate results. All power drills also have a reverse-action switch, so that the tool can be used both to tighten and loosen screws.

Using the pillar drill

When using a pillar drill (see page 98), take extra care to hold the work securely. If possible, use C-clamps to hold it in position, and use a fence and end stop to drill identical holes in separate pieces of work.

1 Select an appropriate bit and unlock the chuck of the drill with the chuck key. Insert the bit, tighten the chuck, and be sure to remove the chuck key. It is extremely dangerous to leave the key in position when the machine is switched on.

2 Lower the safety guard and switch the machine on. Holding the work securely, use the feed lever to lower the bit onto, and through, the wood. Keep your hands well away.

3 After you have achieved the required depth, use the lever to raise the bit. Once the bit is completely clear of the workpiece, you can turn off the machine.

MAKING HALF-LAP JOINTS

Learning to make joints is a fundamental skill in woodwork, and marks the first step of proper construction. Half-lap joints are among the simplest of all the joints to make, although they still require accurate skills in measuring, marking, sawing, and planing. They are used when two pieces of wood cross each other; the joint is made by removing half the thickness of the wood from each piece.

Types of half-lap joints

There are several types of half-lap joints. The most common that you might come across in your woodworking are described below.

Cross half-lap joints are used when two rails meet square to each other. It is usual for the vertical piece to look as though it continues through, but both halves are actually the same.

Corner half-lap joints are similar to cross half-lap joints, but the pieces meet at the corner, rather than in the main body of the rail, and may need additional reinforcement.

Oblique half-lap joints are made in a way similar to cross half-lap joints, but the cutouts are set at an angle.

"T" half-lap joints are used when the end of a rail meets flush with the outside edge of another.

Dovetail half-lap joints are virtually the same as "T" half-lap joints, but the pieces are cut to a specific dovetail shape—giving the joint additional strength.

Note that half-lap joints are not integral structural units and

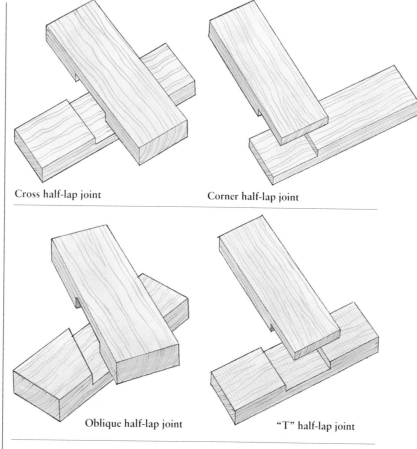

Cross half-lap joint

Corner half-lap joint

Oblique half-lap joint

"T" half-lap joint

so they will need to be secured with either adhesive or screws.

The illustrations show examples of half-lap joints where each joint is cut on the wood's thickness. However, you will find the joint is often cut the other way around for certain types of underframes—for example, on the small table project (see pages 178–81).

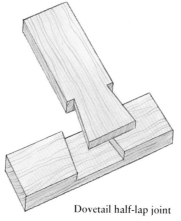

Dovetail half-lap joint

Making a cross half-lap joint

1 Take two pieces of wood of the same width and thickness and lay one across the other in the position of the finished joint.

2 Use a try square and marking knife to mark the width of one piece on the face side of the other where the material will be removed, and square those lines halfway down the edges. Repeat on the other piece. Note that the top half is removed from the first piece, while the bottom half is removed from the second.

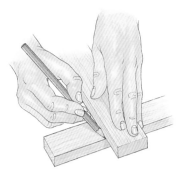

Mark the face sides.

3 Use a marking gauge, set to half the thickness of the wood, in order to scribe a line in between the knife marks. Work from the face side of both pieces of wood.

Gauge the edges.

4 Use a tenon saw to saw across the two shoulder lines down to the gauge line, working on the waste side of the lines.

5 Make some extra saw cuts across the joint to make it easier to chisel out the waste.

Make cuts across the grain to facilitate chiseling out waste.

6 Secure the piece in a vice or clamp. Pare away the waste across the grain until you have a flat surface. Chisel from both side edges to stop breakout and pare the shoulders of the joint to ensure a good fit.

Pare away the waste.

7 Repeat on the other piece. To ensure that the joint is square and flush, dry-test it before gluing the pieces and clamping them together.

Dry-test the half-lap joint.

Making corner or oblique half-lap joints

A corner half-lap joint is made in the same way as a cross half-lap joint. However, all cuts can be made with a saw, so little chiseling should be required.

The photograph above right shows oblique corner half-lap joints. Exactly the same principles apply but the cross is angled rather than square.

Dining table cross rails made with a cross half-lap joint (see pages 218–22).

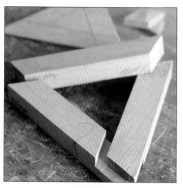

Oblique corner half-lap joints.

Making a "T" half-lap joint

This joint is made in a way similar to the cross half-lap and corner half-lap joints.

1 Put one wood piece in place on the other and mark its width. Mark the area to be cut out, including the depth.

2 Measure and mark the end of the other butting piece, and use a marking gauge to mark the depth of cut on all three sides.

Gauge and mark the depth of cut.

3 Saw away any excess from the lower cross piece, then use a chisel to cut the wood to depth.

4 Secure the butting piece in a vice and saw down the gauged line, before you cut across the shoulder.

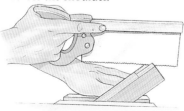

Saw down the gauged line.

Making a dovetail half-lap joint

Although the principle behind this half-lap joint is similar to that of a "T" half-lap joint, this joint requires very precise measuring and setting out. If possible, use a template for accurate results.

1 Measure and mark the butting piece, preferably using a template for the dovetail shape.

Use a template to mark out the dovetail shape.

2 Cut out the dovetail with a saw.

3 Trace the cut dovetail on the face side of the cross piece and square the lines down the edges. Gauge the depth of the joint. Use the dovetail as a template for drawing the area to be removed on the cross member.

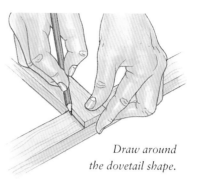

Draw around the dovetail shape.

4 Cut the half-lap across the angled lines with a tenon saw down to the gauge lines.

5 Chisel away the material until the two pieces fit snugly.

Trivet made with oblique half-lap joints (see pages 168–9).

Turn to pages 168–9—the triangular trivet is a good exercise to practice half-lap joints.

MAKING MORTISE-AND-TENON JOINTS

The mortise and tenon is generally a joint between a vertical piece, a stile or a leg, and a horizontal piece, a rail. When glued, it makes a very strong structural unit. The two components are usually the same thickness and both mortise and tenon are one-third of that thickness. The tenon can travel right through the vertical piece, a through joint, or be stopped within its width, a stopped joint.

Through mortise-and-tenon joints

Through joints are mainly used for decorative effect. The tenon on the end of the rail projects right through the stile or leg and shows on the outside. It can be wedged from the outside for extra strength.

Wedged through mortise-and-tenon joints

Through joints can be strengthened by inserting wedges in the end of the tenon. This forces the tenon to splay and lock tight in the mortise.

Loose-wedged through mortise-and-tenon joints

This is an old joint that is used on benches and tables. It can be assembled dry and therefore can be pulled apart and put back together—a knock-down capability.

Stopped mortise-and-tenon joints

If a through mortise-and-tenon joint is not required, and this will be true in many frames, a stopped mortise-and-tenon joint can be used instead. In this type of joint, the tenon and mortise stop short of the outside face. This is the most common type of mortise-and-tenon joint. It is usually strong, but for extra strength it can be fox wedged. Wedges can be inserted into the mortise-and-tenon joint before it is closed.

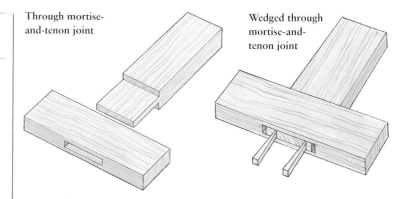

Through mortise-and-tenon joint

Wedged through mortise-and-tenon joint

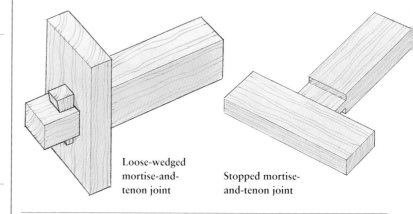

Loose-wedged mortise-and-tenon joint

Stopped mortise-and-tenon joint

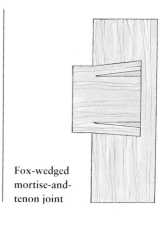

Fox-wedged mortise-and-tenon joint

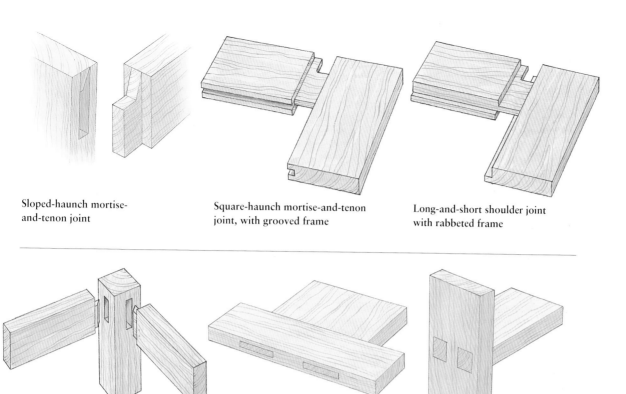

Sloped-haunch mortise-
and-tenon joint

Square-haunch mortise-and-tenon
joint, with grooved frame

Long-and-short shoulder joint
with rabbeted frame

Corner mortise-and-tenon joint

Wide mortise-
and-tenon joint

Twin mortise-
and-tenon joints

Sloped-haunch mortise-and-tenon joints

When the top of a stile has to be level with the outside face of a rail, the tenon will only usually be two-thirds the width of the rail. With a simple tenon, the rail could break away from the stile at the top. Therefore, to give the mortise and tenon as much contact as possible, an angled haunch is made to help keep the rail in line but this does not show on the top surface.

Square-haunch mortise-and-tenon joints

This kind of joint is used where the components are either grooved or rabbeted. When making a frame with a groove on the inside edges, the groove is normally worked the whole way a long each edge.

Therefore, the haunch of the tenon must be square, thus filling the outside end of the joint and the groove.

Long-and-short shoulder mortise-and-tenon joints

This joint is also used for grooved or rabbeted components. In traditional cabinet making the rabbet is made before the tenon is cut. When making a frame with a rabbet, one shoulder of the tenon needs to be long in order to reach across the rabbet into the mortise and the other needs to be short to sit against the top of the rabbet. In this situation it is possible to make a square top on the haunch.

Corner mortise-and-tenon joints

When two rails join together at the top of a leg the mortises

will intersect at the center point. Therefore the end of the tenons are cut at an angle so that they do not foul each other when the piece is assembled.

Wide mortise-and-tenon joints

Sometimes in a frame a rail has to be quite wide and it will weaken the joint too much to have one wide tenon going into a wide mortise. Therefore, two tenons and two mortises are made so as to retain the strength in the stile or leg. This joint can be through as well as stopped.

Twin mortise-and-tenon joints

On wide, thick components, the two mortises and tenons sit side by side rather than in vertical alignment as they are in the previous joint. This joint can be through as well as stopped.

Making a through mortise-and-tenon joint

When making a mortise-and-tenon joint, it is best to start by making the tenon and then the mortise. Mark all the lines to be cut with a knife and gauge. Other marks can be made with a pencil.

Marking the tenon

1 With the rail length slightly oversized, mark the shoulders all round with a knife. Then mark the length of the tenon plus ⅛ in. waste.

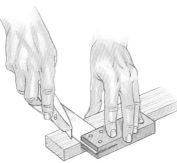

Mark the shoulders and length of the tenon.

2 Set a mortise gauge to the exact width of a mortise chisel, which is close to one-third the thickness of the wood.

3 Gauging from the face sides, mark the thickness of the tenon from the shoulder lines toward the end of the rail, using a mortise gauge. Ensure that the mortise marks are in the center of the rail.

Mark the thickness of the tenon with a mortise gauge.

4 Cut the tenon to length and mark across the end with the mortise gauge.

Cut the tenon to length and mark out the end.

5 If the tenon is to have a haunch or side shoulders, mark these on the face of the rail.

Mark the waste area of the tenon with a pencil.

Cutting the tenon

Place the work in the vice and make the following cuts with the tenon saw, ensuring that your saw is just on the waste side of the line.

1 With the tenon upright make some careful cuts across the end grain to a depth of about ⅛ in.

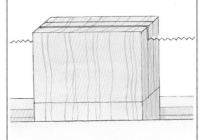

Make a series of careful cuts across the end grain.

2 Now reposition the rail and saw at a 45-degree angle from the first cut down the tenon, stopping short of the shoulder line.

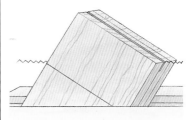

Make the first cut and stop just short of the shoulder line.

3 Turn the tenon around and saw down the other side. This will give you sawn lines across the top and down both sides. Secure the rail vertically in the vice and saw directly down to the shoulder line.

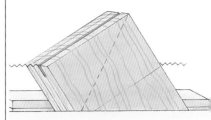

Turn the tenon around and cut from the other side.

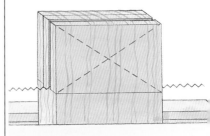

Make the final cut and remove the waste from each side.

4 When both sides of the tenon have been cut, lay it flat against a bench hook. Saw across the shoulder line with a tenon saw in order to remove the waste from each side of the tenon.

The finished tenon.

Marking the mortise

1 Mark the position and width of the mortise all round. Use a pencil initially to mark all around the stile.

2 If the stile is the same thickness as the rail, use the mortise gauge as already set to scribe the mortise on the face side.

3 If the stile is thicker than the rail, reset the mortise gauge so that it marks the mortise in the center and mark on the joint face.

4 In this situation most tenons will have shoulders all the way around. The shape of the mortise will therefore need to account for this. With this in mind, mark the actual width of the mortise with a cut line on both the mating and outside surfaces of the piece of wood.

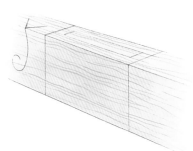

Mark out the mortise, ready to be cut.

Cutting the mortise

1 To cut the mortise, start approximately ⅛ in. from the cut lines at each end, which indicate the mortise's true width, and make a series of cuts in the wood using a mortise chisel to about ⅛ in. deep.

Make a series of cuts in the mortise using a chisel.

2 Remove the waste from your first series of cuts.

3 Make several more cuts and remove the waste until you get approximately one-half to two-thirds of the way through the piece.

4 Turn the piece of wood over and start to cut from the other side.

5 Make another series of cuts until the two parts meet in the middle.

6 Pare the faces within the mortise, if required.

7 Pare the ends of the mortises back to the cut line from both sides.

If you are making a stopped mortise rather than a through mortise, you will need to stop chiseling when you reach the required depth (see page 108).

Bench constructed with mortise-and-tenon joints (see pages 257–65).

Choosing the best method

There is little to distinguish between different methods of cutting a mortise—it is a matter of preference. However, the methods using the mortise chisel are suitable if you have only a few mortises to cut. The drilling method has great advantages where you have a pillar drill or drill in a drill stand and have a lot of mortises to cut. Square mortise drill attachments are also available for pillar drills.

Alternatives for cutting the mortise

There are alternate ways of cutting a mortise.

Using only a mortise chisel, start from the center of the mortise and take a series of cuts so that you make a "V" in the center of the mortise; then turn the chisel around and cut out the edges. Always leave the final cut to the end of the mortise until the rest has been cleared of waste.

Cut a central "V" in the mortise with a chisel.

Alternately, the bulk of the material can be removed from the mortise using a drill. It is best to use a pillar drill or drill in a stand. Set a guide on the drill table and drill a series of holes along the mortise; then use a mortise chisel at the ends, and a wider paring chisel to true up the inside faces of the mortise.

Chisel away the waste from the mortise after drilling a series of holes.

Making a wedged through mortise-and-tenon joint

A wedged through mortise-and-tenon joint is made in a way similar to a through mortise-and-tenon joint. Note that the tenons are marked and cut over length so that the projection can be planed flush with the outside face after assembly. Adapt the basic method as follows.

1 Make saw cuts in the end of the tenon that are two-thirds the length of the tenon.

2 Slightly enlarge the mortise aperture from the outside face, by ⅛–³⁄₁₆ in. at each end, to about two-thirds the width.

3 Make the wedges. Fit the joint and glue and clamp it before driving the wedges into position. The clamps can be removed after the joint has been wedged if you prefer.

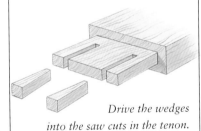

Drive the wedges into the saw cuts in the tenon.

Making a loose-wedged through mortise-and-tenon joint

A loose-wedged mortise-and-tenon joint is made in the same way as a through mortise-and-tenon joint, but the proportion of the tenon has to allow for the removable wedge. Therefore, it needs to project out of the mortise some distance.

1 Make a hole in the tenon, ensuring that its position will enable the wedge to tighten the joint. The outside edge of this hole or mortise must be at the same bevel as the wedge.

2 Make the wedge, and when the joint is clamped, tap it into the joint. As the wedge is driven in, the tenon is pulled forward and secured in place.

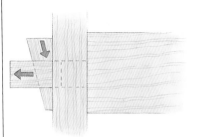

Tap the loose wedge into the mortise-and-tenon joint.

Making a stopped mortise-and-tenon joint

All the steps are similar to the description for a through joint as detailed above except:

1 The tenon will be shorter than the width of the piece into which the mortise is cut.

2 The mortise will be cut only to a specific depth—that is, approximately two-thirds of the rail's width.

Making a sloped-haunch mortise-and-tenon joint

A sloped-haunch mortise-and-tenon joint is commonly used in constructions such as frames, where the outside rail is level with the top of the stile and you do not want the haunch to show.

1 Cut the mortise to match the full length part of the tenon, two-thirds the width of the rail. Make the space for the haunch by making two saw cuts at an angle from the top edge of the stile into the mortise.

Make two saw cuts either side of the space for the haunched tenon.

2 Pare away the waste wood from the mortise with a chisel.

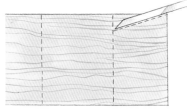

Use a chisel to pare away the waste wood.

3 Cut a full tenon. Then saw the sloping haunch across from the outside edge to two-thirds the width. Finally cut along the tenon to remove the waste.

Making a square-haunch mortise-and-tenon joint

When making a frame that has a groove on the internal face it is easiest to cut that groove right through from end to end; the square haunch is made so that it exactly fits the groove.

1 Carefully mark out the square-haunch joint to allow for the groove. Remember that the mortise will be shorter than the width of the rail.

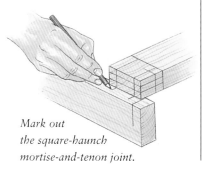

Mark out the square-haunch mortise-and-tenon joint.

2 Cut the mortise as before.

3 Mark and cut the square haunch on the tenon.

Making a long-and-short shoulder mortise-and-tenon joint

Making a frame with a rabbet on one face will require a tenon that has one shoulder shorter to fit on the top of the rabbet. The longer shoulder fits into the mortise. The face of the tenon should line up with the face of the rabbet because this makes for easier construction.

1 Carefully mark out both the mortise and tenon of the long and short shoulder joint.

Marked out long-and-short shoulder joint.

2 Cut the mortise as before.

3 Cut the tenon with one long and one short shoulder to match the depth of the rabbet.

Making a corner mortise-and-tenon joint

A corner mortise-and-tenon joint is used when two rails meet a leg at the same level.

1 When the mortises are cut, ensure that they meet in the center of the leg.

2 When the tenons have been cut, make a 45-degree bevel on the end of each tenon, ensuring that they are cut the right way so that the mortise will be filled.

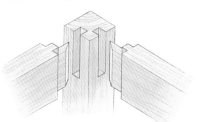

Detail of the corner mortise-and-tenon joint.

Chair with stopped and through mortise-and-tenon joints (see pages 250–6).

The small table on pages 178–81 was designed especially as an exercise in mortise-and-tenon joints. It is good practice and a lovely piece of furniture in its own right.

MAKING DADO JOINTS

Dado joints are grooves that are cut across the grain of the wood and are generally used when installing intermediate shelves or dividers in cabinets. The through dado joint is the most common and easiest to make. The dovetail dado joint is more complex and requires more practice, but it is much stronger and more stable than the through joint.

Through dado joints

A **through dado joint** is simply a groove—or dado—that accepts the full thickness of the shelf or divider and shows on the front and the back edges.

Stopped dado joints

The **stopped dado joint** is the same as the through dado joint, except that one end of it stops short and cannot be seen on the front edge of the side panel.

Dovetail dado joints

In a **dovetail dado joint**, the end of the shelf is cut to a dovetail to run in the dado in the side panel.

Dovetail joints can show on the front but they are usually created as **stopped dovetail joints**—that is, cut short of the front edge so that the joint cannot be seen.

The dovetail can be on one side only—a **barefaced dovetail dado**—or on both sides.

When long dadoes are needed, a tapered dovetail dado joint is frequently used so that the

Through dado joint

Stopped dado joint

Through dovetail dado joint

Stopped dovetail dado joint

Barefaced dovetail dado joint

dovetail "bites" in the last few fractions of an inch.

Cutting a stopped dado joint

1 Start by marking your guides on the inside face of the side to be cut. Use a marking knife to cut lines in order to indicate the desired position of the shelf—that is, the shoulders. Square these lines down the edge.

2 Then, use a marking gauge to mark the depth of the dado—one-third the thickness is normal—and also the stopped part of the dado.

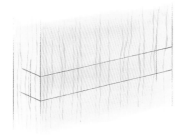

Mark the position of the shoulders.

3 To cut the dado joint, chisel a cutout at the end of the stopped groove to the required depth. This will enable you to saw the groove from the rear.

Chisel out the end to the required depth.

Saw the sides of the dado.

4 Chisel out the waste a little at a time across the grain down to the gauge line. Check the bottom for flatness.

5 Now mark the end of the shelf using a marking gauge along the two faces and the front. Then you can gauge the waste at the stopped end.

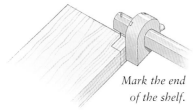

Mark the end of the shelf.

6 Cut away the waste with a tenon saw and fit the joint. Adjust as required.

Cutting a stopped, tapered dovetail dado joint

1 Mark the dado as for the previous joint.

Mark the shelf position in pencil.

2 Mark the dovetail on the edge with a sliding bevel. Mark the stopped end of the dado with a marking gauge. Mark the tapered and straight shoulders of the dovetail groove with a knife—a taper of about $\frac{1}{8}$ in. on the bottom; the top is usually square to the edge.

Mark with a knife.

3 In order to be able to saw the joint, cut out a pocket at the end of the stopped groove to the required depth.

Chop the front recess.

4 Saw the dovetail angle from the rear on the waste side of the shoulder lines. Place an extra saw cut in the center to help remove the waste.

Saw to the dovetail shape.

5 Now chisel out the waste by paring across the grain, taking care because the waste will be hard to remove since it is wider than the top of the dado.

6 Now mark shoulders for the dovetail on the shelf using a cutting gauge along the two faces. Use a pencil and square for the back edge.

7 Gauge the stopped end. Then, mark the taper of the dado, and using the sliding bevel as set for the dado, mark the dovetail angles on the back edge of the shelf.

8 Cut away the stopped part with a tenon saw. Then saw the shoulders and pare the dovetail angles across the grain.

9 The shelf should now slide in smoothly from the back, making for a very sturdy and securely fitted joint.

Slide the shelf into the dado.

The small mirror and shelf on pages 174–7 is an ideal project to practice both dado joints and fretwork.

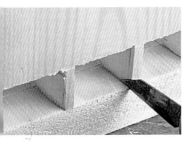

MAKING DOVETAIL JOINTS

The dovetail is considered to be the most beautiful of decorative joints. Fine craftworkers proudly use dovetail joints when making a piece of furniture to demonstrate the highest levels of their craftwork. So, in this case the joints should definitely be seen and the most common type is a through dovetail, possibly positioned on the corner of a cabinet or box.

Through dovetail joints

The **through dovetail joint** is the simplest of the dovetail joints, but still requires careful marking and cutting. It is a traditional joint used for joining the ends of solid-wood pieces, often on cabinets and other box constructions. The pins and the tails show on the outside faces.

Single-lap dovetail joints

The **single-lap dovetail joint** is a common joint in cabinet making. It is mostly used for connecting drawer sides to a thicker drawer front—cases in which the dovetail joint is required for strength but must not interfere with the finish of the piece. With the single-lap, the dovetails are visible on the sides, but the front piece is unbroken and clean-looking.

Double-lap and secret-miter dovetail joints

Although great satisfaction can be derived from making double-lap and secret-miter dovetails, the craftwork will never be seen unless it is a demonstration joint that will be taken apart.

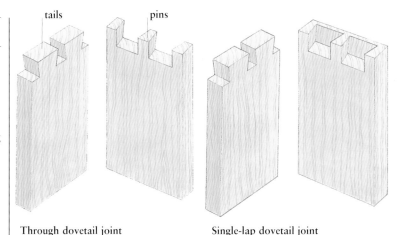

tails   pins

Through dovetail joint   Single-lap dovetail joint

Double-lap dovetail joint   Secret-miter dovetail joint

The growing use of routers—for making tongue-and-groove joints—and biscuit jointers makes these joints an interesting, but not very practical option.

The **double-lap dovetail joint** is used on cabinets or boxes where you do not want the joint to be seen. You will only see a thin strip of end grain on one lap—either the tail or pin member.

The **secret-miter dovetail joint** is often used in very fine woodworking and requires extremely careful marking and cutting. In this instance, the dovetail joint is completely enclosed and will never be visible from the outside.

Pins or tails first?

Some craftworkers prefer to cut tails first, but it is easier when making a double-lap dovetail or a secret-miter dovetail to cut the pins and mark from them to the tail side. This description is for the latter method, but the step-by-step instructions for the small casket project (see pages 182–5) describe making the tail first and then marking the pin.

Dovetail angles

The angle of the dovetail should not have too much slope; otherwise it will be weakened by short grain. Not enough slope will reduce the potential strength of the joint. Experience has shown that in hardwood the angle should be 1:8 and in softwood 1:6.

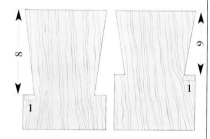

Too much slope.   Too little slope.

Hardwood angle.   Softwood angle.

Making a through dovetail joint

There are different approaches to dovetailing. The main options are to mark and cut to the exact length of the dovetail as described here or to mark the length, but add an extra ¹⁄₁₆ in. waste to be cleaned off.

1 Mark the lengths of the wood pieces, including the dovetail. Cut to length and carefully plane the ends straight and square on both halves of the joint.

2 Set the gauge to the thickness of the wood and mark the shoulder lines on both of the pieces.

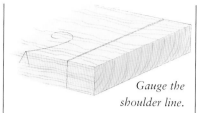

Gauge the shoulder line.

3 With a pencil, set out the pins on one piece to the required spacing and number. To do this, mark the full width of the first pin parallel to the edge (b). Divide the remaining width of wood into equal parts (c).

4 Transfer these marks to the top edge and set out the wider ends of the pins (d). Set a sliding bevel to the required pitch (1:6 or 1:8) or use a dovetail template and mark the beveled sides of the pins, back to the narrower ends, where the tails will fit (e). Make sure you mark the bevel on the end pin marked in step 3 and that all the bevels slope the correct way.

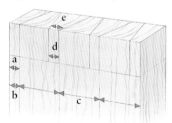

Set out a dovetail joint—the pins must have beveled lines either side of original squared back line.

5 When you are satisfied, mark the pins on the end of the wood with a knife.

6 Using a knife and square, mark the pin sides down to the shoulder line. With a pencil, mark the areas to be removed.

Mark the waste areas carefully, ready to saw.

7 With a fine dovetail saw, saw down the waste side of the cut lines. Be sure to stop before you reach the shoulder line.

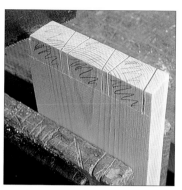

Saw carefully down the marked pin lines.

8 Using a coping saw, remove most of the waste between the pins.

9 Pare right down to the shoulder line using a sharp chisel. After some practice, you will be able to pare from one side only. But when you are starting out, you may find it easier to pare from the shoulder lines on both faces.

10 Mark the tails from the pins. Lay the wood that will have the tails on the bench. Hold the pins upright in the correct position between the shoulder line and edge of the wood. Mark the tails using a knife or a scriber.

Mark the positions of the tails by drawing around the pins with a knife or scriber.

Nejiri arigata— Japanese dovetail joint

This traditional Japanese joint is fascinating because it looks so mysterious and intricate. It is extremely strong and, unlike a conventional dovetail, cannot be taken apart in a straight pull in either direction once it is assembled. Although it may look incredibly difficult to make, it is not that hard to cut because all the angles are based on 75 degrees. It is just important to make sure that each piece is accurately marked before cutting. This joint was introduced into British furniture making by Alan Peters in his own Devonshire workshop. He was taught the secret of how to do it by Japanese furniture maker Kintaro Yazawa.

11 Square the lines across the ends of each joint and use a pencil to mark off the waste (the pin areas).

Square the lines across the ends of the joints.

12 Cut the tails carefully on the waste side of the cut mark.

13 Remove the waste and pare between the tails as before.

Making a single-lap dovetail joint

Since the dovetail in this joint is stopped short of the front face of the wood, you must chisel as well as saw to remove the waste.

1 First, gauge the thickness of the side—the tail piece—on the inside face and edge. Then, you can mark the dovetail pins using a sliding bevel or a dovetail template and a steel square.

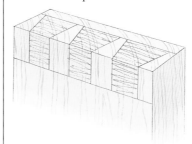

Mark the pins with care and accuracy.

2 Next, place the wood in the vice and secure in place. Saw down the dovetail angle and the square line. Remember to make sure that you are sawing on the waste side of the cut line.

3 Make some saw cuts in the waste area to relieve the wood and to make the process of chiseling easier.

Saw out some narrow cuts, ready for paring.

4 Pare the waste at an angle from shoulder to shoulder, and then pare away the remaining waste in order to produce the dovetail socket.

5 Mark the position of the tails from the pins, holding the pins upright between the shoulder line and edge of the wood. Then, cut the tails carefully on the waste side of your mark.

The simple through dovetail joint can be an attractive feature on wooden boxes, and when cut to a beveled edge as on this box (see pages 182–5), it is also an impressive illustration of quality craftsmanship.

The small box on pages 182–5 is a good way for you to practice your dovetail joints.

USING ABRASIVES

You may produce a satisfactory surface with a plane or scraper, but in most cases,

before you apply a finish, you will need to smooth with abrasive paper, also called

sandpaper—sheets of paper with a variety of abrasive materials glued to the face.

Abrasive papers

There are different "sandpapers" available, usually named for the type of abrasive grit that is used.

Glasspaper is used on softwoods but not usually in fine cabinet making.

Garnet paper is generally a reddish-brown color with hard particles that form sharp cutting edges. It is a good general-quality abrasive.

Aluminum-oxide paper is harder than garnet paper, and is widely used as the abrasive sheet for power sanders.

Silicon-carbide paper is generally used for finishing metals or for smoothing paint surfaces between coats. It is usually lubricated with water and therefore called wet-and-dry paper. For woodwork, a silicon-carbide paper dusted with zinc-oxide powder is used, with the powder acting as a lubricant. This gives a very good finish between coats when using lacquers and polishes.

Grades of abrasive papers

You should always work from the coarse to the fine grades, the idea being that the next finer grade will remove the scratches caused by its rougher

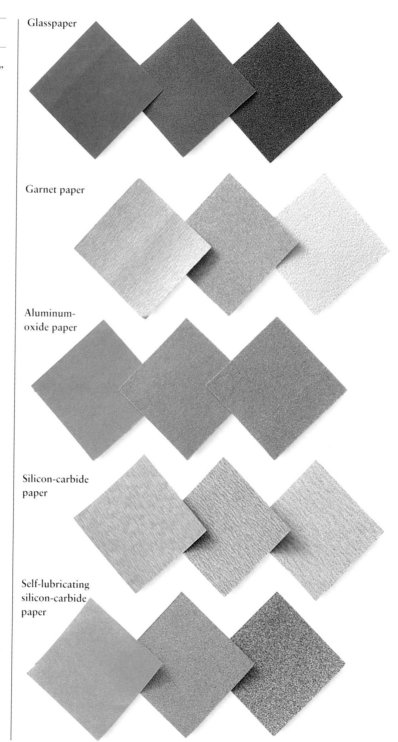

Glasspaper

Garnet paper

Aluminum-oxide paper

Silicon-carbide paper

Self-lubricating silicon-carbide paper

De-nibbing

The coarser abrasive papers are used for smoothing the surface. The finer grades are used after a finish has been applied to remove any slight runs or blemishes in the finished surface. This is known in the trade as de-nibbing.

Using steel wool

A small pad of very fine steel wool can be used after applying a finish, to obtain a final smooth surface or to apply a coat of wax polish for a surface that is attractive to touch. Dip the steel wool in the wax and apply with the grain. Finish with a soft cloth.

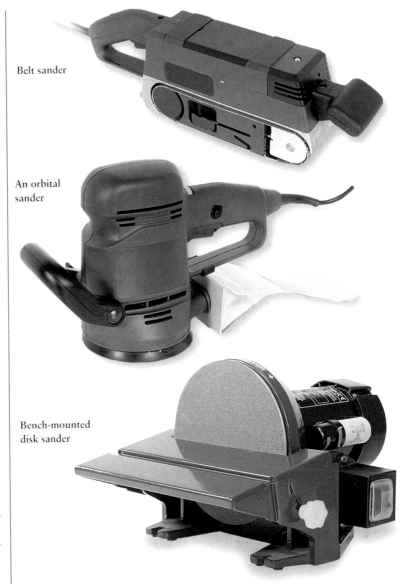

Belt sander

An orbital sander

Bench-mounted disk sander

predecessor. Generally, with good planing and scraping, you should not need to use the very coarse grades. As well as being graded from very coarse to very fine, sandpaper is also graded by number—the higher the number, the finer the grit.

Sandpaper grades

Very coarse	50–60
Coarse	80–100
Medium	120–180
Fine	220–280
Very fine	320–600

Medium grades, and some fine grades, are used for general cabinet making, while some fine and very fine grades are used when finishing. Abrasive papers can also be termed closed-coat, where the particles are closely grouped for fast sanding, whereas open-coat papers have larger gaps between the particles and thus clog less readily.

Power tools

Generally it is best to sand by hand since you can see and feel how the surface is changing. However, when confronted with large areas, a power tool will save much effort. Some hand-sanding is generally still required to remove any minute scratches left by a power sander.

Orbital sanders

The orbital sander is a useful tool and has the advantage of being unlikely to remove too much material by accident and spoil the surface. Care must be taken, however, when using it on veneered surfaces. Most machines are similar in that the rubber-covered baseplate

has the sandpaper stretched over it, and the motor causes this plate to move in an orbital, elliptical or a reciprocating pattern. Although special abrasive sheets are available, standard sheets can generally be cut to fit.

Belt sanders

The belt sander needs very careful handling because it is very easy to remove more material than you intend, unless you have extremely careful control over the tool when working on flat surfaces.

However, it is a useful tool when bench mounted and used to undertake specific small sanding jobs, either along the grain or when shaping parts.

Bench-mounted disk sanders

As with the belt sander, disk sanders can be very fierce on flat surfaces. A disk sander is best used as a bench-mounted tool for sanding and shaping small pieces. Orbital disk sanders are also available and are ideal for finishing because they produce virtually no surface scratches.

Sanding by hand

It is advisable to use a sanding block for most work. Very occasionally you may want to use the abrasive paper without a sanding block, either for curved work or very light sanding. If you need to sand moldings, make a block to the appropriate shape to match the face of the mold.

1 Choose your starting grade of sandpaper depending on the work that you are planning to sand.

2 Fold the paper backward and carefully tear it to fit the block. When using standard sized sheets, you can generally tear each into four pieces.

3 Before you begin, wrap the abrasive paper tightly around the sanding block.

Wrap abrasive paper securely around a sanding block.

4 Always sand with the grain of the wood and work down through the various different grades of abrasive paper until you achieve the desired finish.

5 Turn the sanding block at 90 degrees to the surface grain in order to avoid catching the grain with the edge of the sandpaper.

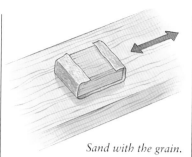

Sand with the grain.

Using power tools

Using an orbital sander

Cut or tear the paper in half lengthwise and fit on the sander. When using an orbital sander, grip the tool with both hands and maintain an even balance.

1 Switch the sander on before placing it on the work surface. Carefully lower the sander flat onto the surface and guide it over the work before applying a light pressure only. Too much pressure will tear or wear out the abrasive paper prematurely.

2 Use long and slow backward and forward strokes, keeping the sander moving evenly over the whole surface of the piece. Do not dwell on one spot or lift the sander up on one edge; you will create an indentation in the surface.

3 Lift the sander clear of work before turning it off. You may want to finish sanding by hand.

Using a belt sander

1 Before you begin, hold the sander upside down on a firm surface and inspect the belt carefully. If it is damaged or worn, be sure to replace it before starting work.

2 Start the sander and note any sideways movement. Operate in short bursts, and

correct any sideways movement by turning the tracking adjustment knob until the belt runs evenly, flush with the outer edge of the baseplate.

3 Secure the work. Hold the sander above the surface with both hands, maintaining a well-balanced stance. Lower the sander onto the surface. Move the sander backward and forward along the work, maintaining an even contact with the baseplate.

4 There are times when you will find it easier to secure the belt sander to your workbench and lower the work onto the belt. This is particularly useful for sanding long edges or end grain, or for shaping wood pieces.

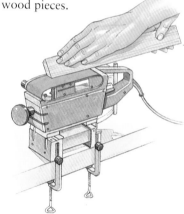

Sand long edges by mounting the belt sander on a worktop and securing with C-clamps.

Using a disk sander

1 Make sure the supporting table is square with the face or set it at the required angle. Start the sander, allowing it to reach full speed.

2 Press the wood carefully against the sanding disk. Make sure that you apply only short bursts of moderate pressure, otherwise the wood may burn.

SCRAPING

On some wood the grain will make it difficult to achieve a good finish

with a plane and the final surface finishing will have to be carried out with

a scraper. A scraper will take very fine shavings from difficult surfaces.

Scraping tools

The basic **cabinet scraper** is a thin rectangular sheet of tempered steel. It is very useful for finishing surfaces of irregular or interlocked grain where the cut of a plane is not fine enough.

Continued use of the scraper may cause your thumbs to become sore. If you have a lot of scraping to do, use a **scraper plane**. This is a cast-metal tool with a double handle that holds a scraper blade in the right position and at the correct angle. While a cabinet scraper is sharpened on four edges, the blade for the scraper plane is generally sharpened on only one edge of the two long faces.

A **hook scraper** is a versatile tool that can be used instead of a scraper plane and will also remove paint or varnish.

Another useful tool is the **burnisher**. This is made from hardened steel with a round, oval, or triangular section. It is used to form a burr on a scraper.

Sharpening a scraper

The long edges of the scraper have to be sharpened to produce a burr that will remove small amounts of wood when pushed across the surface.

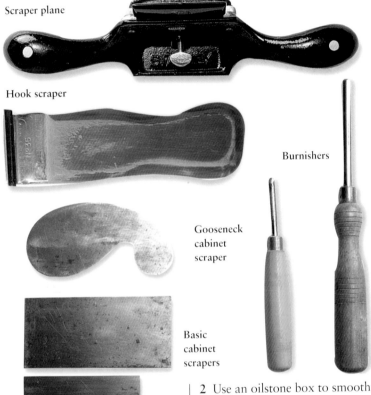

Scraper plane

Hook scraper

Burnishers

Gooseneck cabinet scraper

Basic cabinet scrapers

1 Ensure that the edges of the scraper are square by drawing a file along the edge.

2 Use an oilstone box to smooth the edge and remove the file mark. Simply place the edge of the scraper between the top and bottom parts of the oilstone box and move the scraper backward and forward a number of times.

Square the edge of the scraper using a file.

Smooth the edge of the scraper in an oilstone box.

3 True the sides of the scraper on the stone to produce a perfectly square edge.

True the sides of the scraper on the side of the oilstone box.

4 You now need to create a burr on the edge of the scraper. To do this, run a burnisher or a small gougel along the flat edge at an angle in order to create the burr.

Create a burr on the edge of the scraper with a burnisher.

5 You will probably have to practice this technique a number of times in order to produce a satisfactory edge on the scraper.

6 When using the tool, you will frequently have to reraise this cutting burr, so use the burnisher in order to flatten the edge of the scraper. Re-turn the edge over the face before starting the sharpening process over again.

Burnish the edge of the scraper.

Re-turn the edge of the scraper.

Using a scraper

1 Hold the scraper in two hands with the fingers positioned as shown. Bend the scraper slightly, and keeping it at an angle, carefully take thin shavings from the wood's surface. The angle will depend on the burr and wood's surface.

Hold the scraper with both hands.

2 Cabinet scrapers usually have four edges on which burrs have been created, but if you are scraping a very hard wood with difficult grain you will have to resharpen your cabinet scraper quite often.

Using a scraper plane

1 First, take the blade out of the scraper plane so that you can sharpen it. Now, carefully work a burr on the edges of the blade, as described above.

Work a burr onto the blade of the scraper plane.

2 When you are happy with the burr that you have produced, set the blade back into the scraper plane. Make sure that you allow the scraper to protrude just a little above the surface.

3 Holding the two handles of the scraper plane, carefully scrape the tool over the wood's surface until you achieve the desired finish.

Carefully scrape the plane across the surface.

4 You will probably find that you have to sharpen the blade of your scraper plane frequently.

ASSEMBLING PROJECTS

Whatever the piece of furniture being made, a crucial stage is that of assembly. It can be a complex operation. You need to plan the process carefully, often putting a piece together in separate stages to make handling easier. Most joints and assemblies will use some form of adhesive that will need to cure with the joint closed under pressure.

When assembling furniture, it is recommended that you always try out the process first with dry joints—that is, without any adhesive. This is a good method of finding and solving any fitting problems that may arise before you are committed to final assembly with adhesive.

Clamps

There is a wide range of clamps, and even though they will mainly be used for dry or final assembly, they are often useful to hold components on a bench during the making process.

Sash or bar clamps

For assembly the most common type of clamp is the **sash** or **bar clamp**. Sash clamps have a bar with a screw pressure shoe at one end and a moveable shoe, which will accommodate different lengths, at the other. A rectangular bar is adequate for light use, but a T-bar is better where larger or heavier pressures are needed.

It is possible to make your own sash clamp using clamp heads that can be used on a wooden bar (some woodworkers use a round pipe for the bar). Clamps that have a rapid action enabling them to slide along the bar until pressure is applied are also available, but their very construction means that it is not possible to obtain the same pressure that is achieved with traditional sash clamps.

Sash clamps can be used for assembling frames or cabinets. Always remember to use wooden clamping blocks between the work and the shoe to prevent bruising the work surface. When used for frames, ensure that the clamps close the joints and remember to check that the assembly is square. To do this, use a try square or, preferably, measure across each diagonal. If both are the same, the frame is square. If a frame is out of square, a slight adjustment of the position of the clamp in order to shorten the longest angle should bring it square.

Measure across the diagonal to see if the clamped frame is square.

It is worth investing in a number of clamps rather than just one. When assembling cabinets more than one clamp may be needed at a time, and

It is useful to have a number of clamps for assembling large projects.

Sash clamp

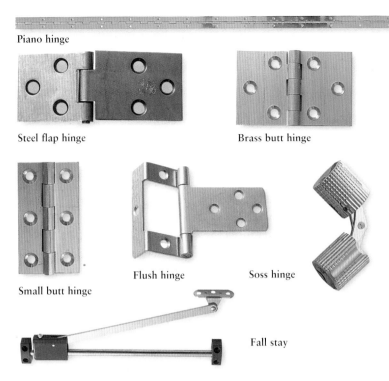

Piano hinge

Steel flap hinge

Brass butt hinge

Small butt hinge

Flush hinge

Soss hinge

Fall stay

The fitted butt hinge.

very heavy doors. It is invisible when the door is closed.

The **cranked hinge** is normally used for finer work with lay-on doors. The door can swing through an arc of 180 degrees, allowing clear access to the cupboard.

The **flap hinge** is an adjustable hinge where the flap lies flush when open.

The **backflap hinge** has wide leaves recessed into the wood, and is used for attaching writing desk door flaps. The hinged door "falls" down to provide a desk work surface.

Fitting a butt hinge

When fitting hinges, precise marking, cutting, and screw positioning is essential.

1 Set two marking gauges from the center of the hinge pin—the first to the outer edge of the leaf to gauge its width and the second to the face of the hinge to gauge its thickness.

Chisel out the recess for a butt hinge.

2 Mark the length of the hinge with a square and knife in position on the door or flap, and then gauge the width and thickness of the recess.

3 Chisel out the recess, keeping inside the set-out lines, by first tapping the chisel $\frac{1}{8}$ in. within the squared lines. Hold the chisel at a 45-degree angle and lightly tap it to raise the grain. Pare across the recess from the depth-gauge line, guiding the chisel by hand and leveling the bottom of the recess. Test the hinge to make sure that it fits and adjust as required.

4 Using the hinge as a guide, mark the center of the screw holes with an awl. Remove the hinge and drill pilot holes for the screws. If using brass screws, insert steel screws first as guides to prevent damage to the softer brass. Then remove the guide screws, and place the hinge in position using the brass screws.

5 Fit the other leaf of the hinge using the same technique.

Hinges can be used to make falls (see pages 268–73).

Escutcheon is a heraldic term to denote either a whole coat of arms or the field on which the arms are painted. The term is used in cabinet making to describe the carved armorial shields that are sometimes used as a central feature on the pediments of large pieces of case furniture. It also refers to the ornamental metal plate and pivoted metal cover that surrounds a keyhole. When a key is inserted in a lock it very rarely locates on its pin at once without striking the drawer front first—the escutcheon protects the drawer from damage. This type of escutcheon was used on cupboard doors as well as on desk and drawer fronts. They are often found in brass, which was first used from about 1650. By 1770 escutcheons began to vary in size and often formed part of larger designs found on the overall piece. For example, late 18th-century backplates had Neoclassical motifs embossed on them and the escutcheons were often made to match. The one shown here is made of brass.

Fall lock

Cabinet lock

Sliding-door locks

Locks and catches

A variety of locks can be fitted to furniture and boxes.

The traditional **cabinet lock** is normally used to secure cupboards and drawers.The **fall**, or **fall-flap lock**, is a cylinder lock that is designed to fit flush with the inside surface of a fold-down desk. The key can be removed only when the flap is shut.

The **sliding-door lock** is another type of cylinder lock that can be used to lock overlapping sliding doors.

Small metalwork shops may also produce individual hardware.

A variety of catches are also available, including the magnetic catch, the ball catch, and the magnetic latch.

Stays

Stays are designed to support a fall-flap in a horizontal position, and take the strain off the hinge. The simplest fall-flap stay is the **joint stay**. The sliding stay is a better-quality version, which slides on a bar fixed to the inside of the cabinet. The friction stay controls the movement of the flap so that it moves smoothly under its own weight.

Joint stay

Knock-down hardware

It is often convenient to be able to disassemble large pieces of furniture for transportation. The industry has developed a range of hardware so that furniture can be sent flat-pack. You will probably not have

access to a wide range of these but the following might be available in your local hardware store.

It is better to use **machine screws** than wood screws since with frequent assembly and disassembly wood screw threads and holes can become slack. The machine screw has a metal thread—like a bolt— and different lengths, gauges, and thread size can be found. However, some type of insert such as a screw socket needs to be placed in the wood component to act as a nut. It has a thread in the center that accepts the machine screw, but on the outside has a screw that can be driven. The insert cannot be seen.

A machine screw and socket.

The **tee-nut** is used in material where there is not enough depth for a screw socket to be used. It is often used when attaching upholstered seats to chair frames. The nut is a disk with a central threaded socket. The socket accepts a machine screw and four prongs that bite into the surface. This keeps it in position when it is inserted into a clearance hole on the side that will not be seen.

A **barrel nut** is used when connecting a rail to an upright—for example, when fitting rails between a bed's headboard and foot. It is a cylinder that has a thread drilled and tapped perpendicular to the barrel direction. To fit, drill a longitudinal hole for the bolt, and a cross-hole in the rail for the barrel nut. Insert the barrel nut, align the thread and tighten the bolt. You can also use bolts with nuts and washers if you cut a square mortise or recess to accept them. Another extremely useful approach is to use metal studding—lengths of threaded rod—that can be cut to the necessary lengths to suit the size of the job in hand.

A barrel nut and screw.

Saw sets can be used for connecting cabinets together and are a development of the saw sets that are used to hold saw blades in saw handles.

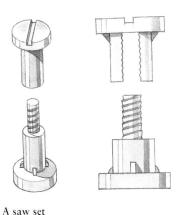

A saw set

Handles

Even though many woodworkers prefer to make their own handles as part of the overall design, there are very many proprietary handles available in all shapes, styles, materials, and colors.

Proprietary handles include **traditional door** or **drawer knobs**, which are available in wood, metal, or ceramic. These are usually fixed from behind, where a screw passes through the cabinet front into the knob. **D-shaped handles** are a modern-style handle, which are fitted in the same way and available in metal, plastic, or wood.

Cabinet handles are available in a variety of forms, including the swan neck. This type of handle is suspended from two pivots— one at each end of the handle.

Period handles are still available.

Drawer-pull handles are very strong handles, and are often used for large or heavy drawers.

For smaller drawers, the **drop handle** is common. Both the drop handle and the drawer-pull handle are fitted from the front.

The **flush handle**, as its name suggests, fits flush with the surface. Used for drawers, it is fixed with flat head screws.

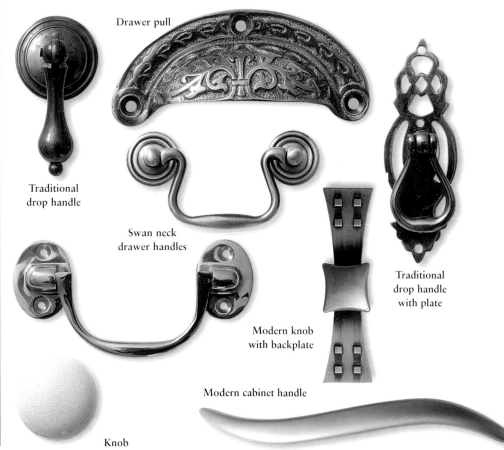

Drawer pull

Traditional drop handle

Swan neck drawer handles

Modern knob with backplate

Traditional drop handle with plate

Modern cabinet handle

Knob

USING ADHESIVES

Adhesives were traditionally derived from natural substances and could suffer degradation if exposed to moisture or heat. During the last century, however, a vast range of adhesives was developed for industrial applications and these became available to the woodworker. Adhesives that are totally moisture- and heat-resistant are now available.

Early adhesives

Early adhesives or glues were often made from animal skins and bone. A **double-container glue pot** was used. The inside container held the glue and the outside held the water, which, when boiled, softened the adhesive. It would usually come in slab or cake form, which first needed to be softened in water, and then brought to the right temperature and viscosity in the double container. Later, adhesive was available in the form of fine granules or **pearls**. These glues are seldom used today and generally only in the restoration trade or when laying veneers by hand. They have little resistance to heat and solvents.

Types of adhesives

The first popular synthetic adhesive developed was based on urea-formaldehyde (UF). Another very popular adhesive is polyvinyl-acetate (PVA). UF and PVA have become the mainstay for cabinet makers, although special adhesives are available for specific purposes.

Urea-formaldehyde

Urea-formaldehyde (UF) usually comes as a powder that has to be mixed with water before use. It is essential to ensure that the correct balance of water and powder is used and that it is well mixed in order to remove all lumps. The curing takes place by moisture evaporation and chemical reaction. This adhesive can be supplied as two liquids—one being a separate catalyst or hardener. The two liquids are applied to the two different mating faces of a joint, with curing taking place by chemical reaction.

Polyvinyl-acetate

Polyvinyl-acetate (PVA) is available as a white liquid and, when applied to a joint, sets by water evaporation. Initially, it had poor water and mechanical

Double-container glue pot

Pearl glue

Urea-formaldehyde

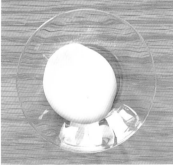

Polyvinyl-acetate

Epoxy-resin adhesive

Contact adhesive

Cynoacrylate

resistance, being limited to interior applications. It was not deemed suitable for laminating purposes. Now, however, there

have been many developments and PVA can achieve high standards of moisture and mechanical resistance.

Glue brushes

Adhesive spreader

Glue roller

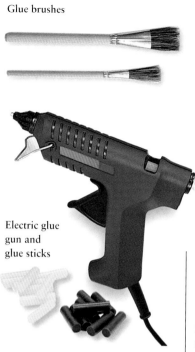

Electric glue
gun and
glue sticks

Plastic glue
syringe

Epoxy-resin adhesives

Epoxy-resin adhesives are useful
for joining different materials
together, but are less satisfactory
for general woodwork. They are
ideal for exterior work, although
they are very expensive.

Contact adhesives

Contact adhesives are generally
solvent based and are applied
to both surfaces, left until
tacky and then brought
together under pressure. They
are often used for applying
decorative plastic laminates to
manufactured board or when
gluing fabric. It is not advisable,
however, to use such adhesives
for laying veneer because the
latex rubber base allows too
much movement to occur.

Cynoacrylates

Cynoacrylates are instant glues
and are available in different
consistencies. The thinnest
variety is like water and is used
for parts that fit together snugly.

It cures in 5 to 10 seconds.
Then there is a somewhat
thicker liquid—the consistency
of syrup—that can fill small
gaps between ill-fitting parts. Its
setting time is slightly longer, at
10 to 25 seconds. The thickest
of the glues is molasses-like and
has the best gap-filling ability.
Its slow cure rate (30 to 50
seconds) means that you can
realign components after you
have assembled them. But you
can use an accelerator spray with
the glue so that it cures instantly.

Hot glue

Hot glue is available in
cylindrical sticks, which can
then be applied using a
convenient hot glue gun. The
gun is electrically heated, and
the adhesive sets within
seconds, making it ideal for
constructing mock-ups.

Applying adhesives

Adhesives can be applied with
a **brush, flat stick,** or **roller.**
A **plastic glue syringe** is useful
when trying to reach inaccessible
joints. When applying UF or
PVA, a **hand-held adhesive
spreader** can save time and help
to ensure a thin, even spread of
adhesive. An **electric glue gun** is

an extremely useful applicator
to use for large jobs. Used
with solid glue sticks, it melts
the adhesive and forces it
out through the nozzle in a
liquid form.

Using adhesives

Choose the adhesive that
will best suit the assembly
process, considering factors
such as drying time, moisture
resistance, and strength.

Apply adhesive to flat surfaces
using a brush, spreader, or
roller. Apply the adhesive to
joints using a brush or a stick.

Almost all assemblies will
need clamping to fix the pieces
together securely. Pressure
will need to be maintained
until the adhesive has cured
completely. The curing time
of the different adhesives varies
from product to product so
be sure to check the packaging.
It is worth remembering that
heat will accelerate the curing
of most adhesives.

Expert tip

When assembling work
adhesive will invariably
squeeze out of the joint
when finally clamped.
If adhesive is left in
place until it has cured,
the surface of the work
is bound to be damaged
by its removal. You
could remove the excess
when the adhesive is
still wet, using a cloth
and water to remove
all traces. Or, wait until
the adhesive has cured
to a "rubbery" state,
when it can be removed
easily by scraping across
the surface with a chisel.
It will still need to be
wiped down with a
damp cloth to remove
all traces of the
adhesive. Do not drown
the work with too much
adhesive or water as
this can stain wood,
especially hardwoods.

WOOD FINISHING

Wood finishing is sometimes viewed as the final but brief operation of a woodwork project. However, it actually needs to be carefully considered at the outset in order to decide on the most appropriate finishing method and when it is best to apply it. Make sure that you leave enough time for finishing and prepare and plan thoroughly before you start any project.

Even though finishing is generally the final process that you will undertake in any woodworking project it can often be useful—and sometimes essential—to prefinish your wood components before assembly. This is so that the finish can be applied to all the nooks and crannies that cannot be reached after assembly.

Finishing technology has developed to satisfy two criteria for when the object is in use— practicality and appearance.

Tack cloth

Putty/filler knives   Paintbrush   Solvent-based putty   Water-based putty

Shellac sticks

Wax sticks   Plastic wood filler   Fine surface filler

Use may often dictate the finishing strategy—for example, the amount of physical or environmental wear that the piece will have to resist. Will it be used indoors or outdoors, or will it be subjected to continuous wear?

There is a wide range of finishes available today: natural clear, synthetic-colored, as well as some unusual surface finishes. Before you apply finish though, it is important to prepare the wood surface as necessary.

Fillers

You will often have to fill small cracks and holes in order to prepare the wood for finishing. There is a range of filling materials available.

A **putty**, or **filler**, **knife** is used to apply a filler. A putty knife is a thin, flexible piece of stainless steel fixed to a handle. It is used to work the putty or filler into the defect within the surface of the work before sanding and applying a finish.

Small cracks and holes can be filled with a **putty** as near as possible to the wood's color. You can also use preparations based on shellac. **Shellac sticks** come in wood colors and are ideal for repairing small cracks or knotholes.

Wax sticks are made from carnauba wax and mixed with resin and coloring pigments. Wax sticks are normally used for repairing small hairline cracks in the wood surface. Remember that you should use wax sticks only when you intend to use a wax finish on the work (see pages 132–3).

Wood filler is made from natural and/or synthetic materials, and is normally used to fill wood defects, such as splits and knotholes. It can be readily sanded down to provide a smooth surface for a polish. It is available in a variety of colors to match almost any wood, and can also be mixed with lighter or darker filler or paint pigments for a perfect color match. Most filler for cabinet work is water-based although alcohol-based types, which dry more quickly, are also available.

Grain fillers are much the same as wood fillers, except that they are more watery. Grain fillers are rubbed into the surface with a cloth, left to dry, and then fine sanded. Even though powdered grain fillers are available, it is preferable to use successive coats of lacquer cut down between each application.

The resin in softwoods can bleed, especially from knotholes. **Shellac**—a resin dissolved in denatured alcohol—prevents bleed.

Shellac

Preparing the surface

Decisions made as to the practicality and appearance of wood finishes are closely linked, and the brief history of finishes (see box, right) will help explain the reasons for some of our choices over the centuries.

1 Before applying any finish, be sure that the surface is well prepared by planing, scraping, and using abrasive papers.

Plane before applying finish.

2 Ensure that the surface is free of dust or other particles by wiping it with a tack cloth.

3 In some situations you may need to fill the grain, or any defects, with a filler. Place the filler between the putty knife and the defect. Apply pressure with the knife while dragging it across the surface. This forces the filler into the defect. As with any putty or filler, slightly overfill the defect. When dry, sand back to a flush finish.

If you are using a softwood that has knots you may need to use shellac at this stage.

Wood partially filled with filler.

Ebonizing

This is the European process of staining and polishing wood to give a surface finish that resembles ebony. It was particularly popular in the 18th and 19th centuries and was influenced by the craze for all things Asian. Edward Godwin, for example, had an intense interest in Japanese art and used ebonized wood to create a lot of his designs. In fact, he pioneered what came to be known as Anglo-Japanese furniture. In the late 19th century Japanese mania was at its height within furniture design— European shapes were retained but Japanese details added, and ebonized wood was used a lot to create the furniture.

An example of 19th-century designer Philip Speakman Webb's work with ebonized wood appears below. Ebonized furniture very quickly became an accepted part of the Victorian interior. English furniture makers had also been heavily influenced by France, which had ébénistes—specialized carvers who worked mainly in ebony. The English makers, however, relied heavily on ebonized oak and mahogany in their designs but borrowed techniques and ideas from the French.

Natural clear finishes

When quality wood is used nowadays, there is generally no need to change the color, but only to bring out the natural qualities of the wood species. It is worth remembering that on exposure to light the color of most will usually tend to darken anyway. For this reason, the clearest finish possible is often the most desirable.

French polish

French polish is made out of shellac, a natural substance made from beetles dissolved in denatured alcohol. It has been used for many years and used to be the furniture maker's standard finish during the 19th and early 20th centuries. It can be finished to a very high gloss but unfortunately is vulnerable to both water and alcohol. There are various types of French polish available today.

Button polish is the highest grade of French polish and is a golden-brown color.

Garnet polish is a dark red/brown and is used on wood to make it look like mahogany.

White polish is made from bleached shellac and is used for pale-colored woods.

Transparent polish is used where minimum color change is required on light woods such as ash and sycamore.

Colored polish contains an alcohol-based stain and is used in order to modify the color of the wood.

Penetrating oils

Oils soak into the wood, giving a beautiful rich finish that enhances the grain rather than simply coating the surface. When applying oil finishes, it is best to thin the first coat to encourage penetration into the wood, and then follow this with several coats to build up a good finish. This is better than simply flooding on a thick coat. Oil is the most easily repaired of all wood finishes. Simply sand down and re-oil. A range of oils is available today.

Linseed oil can be raw or boiled. Raw oil takes a long time to dry, boiled less so. Since drying has to be done naturally, the resulting finish is not as hard as with other oils. Its performance can be improved by adding dryers, such as gold size or terrabin.

French polish on maple.

Button polish on beech.

Tung oil on teak.

Tung oil on maple.

Limed wax on oak.

Brown Boot Tan wax on teak.

Danish and teak oils have dryers already added. Different formulations will give very good results in terms of penetration and hardness.

Tung oil is from the tung tree, and is also known as Chinese oil. It is very durable and is also heat and alcohol resistant.

Waxes

Wax polish is made from beeswax or carnauba wax in turpentine. Each of these waxes can be used alone but it is generally better to seal the grain with a thin lacquer or with white shellac before building up wax coats. Wax is often used as a final finish on top of other materials. A very fine steel wool is used to apply a soft wax, giving a semi-matte surface. The surface is then buffed with a soft cloth. With so many ready-made preparations available, waxes are no longer so popular.

Applying French polish, oils, and waxes

Some of these finishes are combustible and prone to self-ignite, so after you have applied the finish, be sure to unfold the cloth or pad and leave it outside to dry completely.

Application by cloth pad
French polish is applied with a thick, soft pad.

Other finishes such as oils can also be applied in the same way.

1   Make the pad from a square of white linen cloth with a ball of batting cotton placed over the cloth. Fold the cloth over the batting, and then turn in the edges. The pad is then held in the palm of the hand.

2   The batting can be charged with shellac, oils, or some of the other finishes.

3   Dip the pad in the finish, letting it soak up a reasonable amount of the finish; it should not be dripping wet.

Application by cloth

Apply polish with a rubber.

A cloth is usually used for applying waxes and oil. Cotton is best for this process.

1   When applying oil, soak the cloth thoroughly in a finish of your choice.

2   Rub the cloth over the wood surface with even strokes.

Apply oil with a cloth.

It is very important when you have finished with the cloth to unfold it and leave it outside to dry to avoid spontaneous combustion.

Application with steel wool
This method is used for applying wax.

Steel wool

1   Wax can initially be applied with a pad of very fine steel wool, rubbing in the general direction of the grain.

Apply wax with steel wool.

2   Subsequent burnishing is made with a lint-free cotton cloth formed into a pad. This is then used to rub the wax to a dull shine.

Fold the cloth over the batting to make a pad.

Spraying wood finishes

Setting up spray equipment in a proper working environment is expensive. It is essential that the area is clean, that there is adequate extraction/ventilation for the noxious chemicals and that lighting is suitably flameproof. Unless you already have experience in spraying or want to turn your hobby into something more, it is preferable to use the other techniques described here.

Synthetic clear and colored finishes

With the rapid developments that have taken place in the manufacturing processes in recent years, there is now a wide range of different types of synthetic finish available: stains, resins, lacquers, and paints. Each is suitable for a particular purpose and so be sure to choose carefully.

Stains

Staining was traditionally done to modify the color of wood when the original did not suit the maker's requirements. More recently, makers have chosen woods for their specific virtues, and a small range of other colors has been developed. They add an overall finish that will color the wood but still show the grain. These stains are available in water-, alcohol-, and oil-based forms. Water-based stains have been formulated to give results as close as possible to traditional products, without using dangerous substances. The table below shows the variety of effects that you can achieve by applying the same stains to three different base woods.

Lacquers (varnishes)

Lacquers, or varnishes as they are sometimes called, also have a long history, but are not as popular today. They create a fairly hard, resistant surface and can be used in clear form over another surface or as a flat, opaque color that disguises the grain. They are available in gloss, semi-gloss and matte finishes and can be water- or solvent-based. Water-based lacquers have the same benefits as water-based stains.

Paints

Interesting effects can also be produced with paint, either completely disguising the grain allowing some hint of the wood to show through, or with a broken finish. Traditional paints have been oil-based but water-based and more recently plastic-based paints have become very familiar, and all come in a wide range of colors. When completely dry, finish the effect with wax for a soft finish or a clear lacquer for a more durable finish.

Applying lacquers, stains, and paints

These finishes are often applied with a brush, although stroking a stain on with a cloth is also effective. Taking the care to achieve an even finish is always a priority.

Pine alcohol stain on beech.

Canadian Cedar alcohol stain on beech.

Burmese Teak alcohol stain on beech.

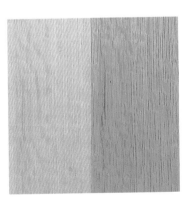

Pine alcohol stain on oak.

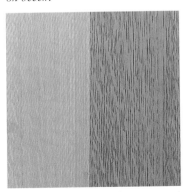

Canadian Cedar alcohol stain on oak.

Burmese Teak alcohol stain on oak.

Application by brush

1 Take a scrap piece of the same wood as that used in the project you are working on and apply your chosen stain to check if it gives a suitable result. You can create a deeper color by applying more coats.

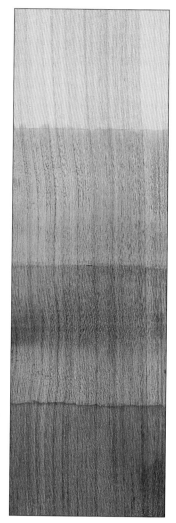

Test a strip of wood with varying degrees of stain.

2 When you are happy with your test piece you can then proceed with your project.

3 Apply the finish with straight strokes of the brush along the grain and let the film settle naturally. When using paint you need to brush initially in different directions, finishing off with light strokes in one direction. This should be with the grain if the piece is solid wood. If you are painting up to an edge always brush outward.

Apply the finish with a brush.

4 Wipe off any excess with a cotton cloth. Lightly take the brush across the grain again to avoid leaving any cloth marks.

5 When it is dry, rub down with self-lubricating silicon-carbide paper.

6 Remove any sanding dust and apply additional coats of finish as needed.

7 When you have achieved the color that you want, a clear finish can be applied.

Unusual surface finishes

If you are seeking an interesting finish for your work, a variety of options are available, including fuming, blasting, scrubbing, and scorching.

Fuming oak

Oak and other woods that contain a proportion of tannin can be fumed effectively when exposed to ammonia, which makes the wood darken. Take an airtight container into which the project can be placed after final finishing. Place some saucers of strong ammonia in the compartment with the project and seal it. After a time the oak will change color to an attractive gray. When the desired color is obtained, remove the ammonia and apply a transparent finish. Take the utmost care when using ammonia because the fumes are very toxic. Always wear a face mask and goggles.

Sand blasting

Sand blasting is an industrial method of cleaning components prior to other finishing treatments. When wood is sand blasted the softer grain is removed and the hard grain remains. It is then usual to apply a transparent finish. This process should be carried out by a specialist.

Scrubbing

Until recently, wooden work surfaces in kitchens were scrubbed for cleaning purposes. The resulting finish was a light, bleached wood surface. As with sand blasting, this is because the soft grain was worn away. For the right piece of woodwork this can be a very interesting effect.

Scorching

Scorching is not normally a method that is used on fine furniture because this finishing technique uses a blowtorch in order to burn the surface of the wood. The resulting charred material is then carefully wire brushed away. Subsequent finishing with a lacquer or an oil gives an unusual finished effect, particularly when used on softwood species of wood.

Unusual surface finishes

Fumed finish

Sand-blasted finish

Scrubbed finish

Scorched finish

VENEERING

Although not widely used these days, hand veneering is an important process in furniture restoration. When using modern adhesives a constant pressure needs to be exerted over the area to be veneered. In industry, large presses are used for this task, but it is possible to make your own caul, or press. This section looks first at hand veneering and then at caul, or press, veneering.

Veneering tools

Veneer work uses many of the basic woodworker's tools, including measuring and marking equipment, planes, a fretsaw, chisels, scrapers, and sanding equipment. If veneering is something you would like to do, then a number of more specialized tools are also needed.

Specialized veneering tools include a selection of **craft knives.** For intricate work, use a fine scalpel blade; for cutting a straight edge along the grain, use a curved blade; for cutting across the grain, use a straight,

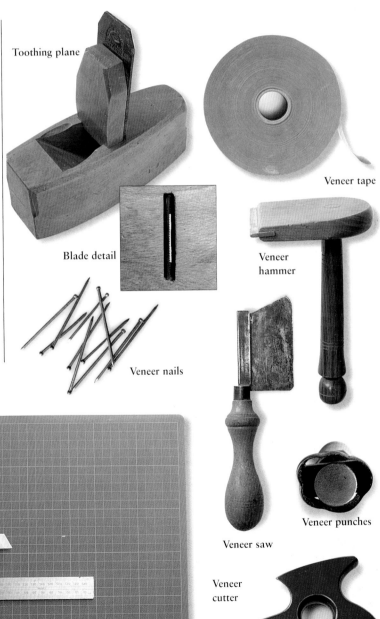

Toothing plane

Veneer tape

Blade detail

Veneer hammer

Veneer nails

Veneer punches

Veneer saw

Veneer cutter

Craft knife, cutting mat, and ruler

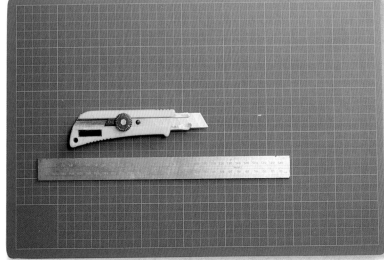

pointed blade, and for preparing veneers ready for jointing, a bevel blade is best.

The **veneer saw** is a fine-toothed tool, which is used to cut through any thickness of veneer. Use it with a straightedge for accuracy. The saw is about 6 in. long and has a curved blade.

A **veneer hammer** is used for hand-laying veneers and for squeezing excess adhesive, air, and moisture out from under the veneer.

Veneer punches come in a variety of sizes and are used to fix any defects in the veneer.

Veneer nails are used to hold the veneer temporarily in place while the joints are taped with veneer tape.

A **toothing plane** provides a key on the groundwork surface ready for gluing. The blade of the plane is set almost vertical.

A double-container glue pot, adhesive granules and other adhesives (see pages 128–9) are also needed for veneering.

Preparing the board

You will need a good-quality board upon which to lay the veneers—a waterproof plywood or blockboard is preferable. Prepare the board by applying lips—edge strips—to all four edges. These are made from solid wood, which is normally of the same species as the veneer. They should be mitered at the corners.

1 Plane all the edgings, but leave the width over size to the thickness of the board.

2 Trim the board to accept the edgings so that the finished size of the project will be correct.

3 Carefully mark and cut the miters on the ends of the edgings so that they fit exactly.

4 You can join the edgings to the board with loose tongues or by gluing them to the board's edges. If using tongues and grooves, work these with a router prior to cutting the miters.

5 Glue the edgings in place, and make sure that the miters match perfectly.

6 When the adhesive has cured, carefully plane the excess edging flush to the surface of the board on both sides, taking care not to round over the edging.

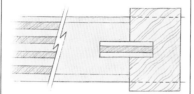

Glue the edgings into place and trim them to shape.

Since veneers can exert a pull on the face of a board, you must put a backing veneer on the secondary face.

Preparing the veneer

Many common veneer woods are available in flat sheets with very little ripple or distortion. These can be used without preparation. When using exotic veneers, and those with difficult grain, the sheets may be distorted with curls and burls. If this is the case, you will need to dampen the veneers and press them between two boards to make them flat.

Laying the veneer by hand

1 Begin by soaking the adhesive granules in a little water, using a double-container—either a double-container glue pot or use a can and an old saucepan as an alternative.

2 Heat the water in the outside container so that the soaking granules are heated until they dissolve and the adhesive has reached the correct consistency. You can tell if the consistency is right when there are no lumps present and the adhesive runs evenly off the brush.

Soak and then heat the adhesive granules gently.

3 Texture the faces to be veneered on the baseboard with a toothing plane to provide a key.

4 Brush some slightly thinned adhesive onto the surface of the board—the ground or groundwork—to act as sizing, or a coat to seal the surface. Let this soak in and leave it to dry.

5 Next, apply the adhesive to the top surface of the groundwork and the back of the veneer. While the adhesive is still tacky to the touch set the veneer in place.

6 Use a veneer hammer to press the veneer down; squeeze any air and excess moisture from under it. Use zigzag strokes and always work from the center to the outer edges.

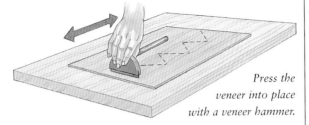

Press the veneer into place with a veneer hammer.

7 If the adhesive begins to cure, place a damp cloth over the veneer and use an old iron set to a low heat to soften the adhesive. Press down with the hammer again.

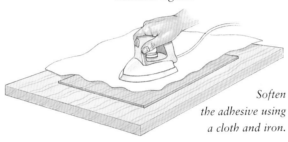

Soften the adhesive using a cloth and iron.

8 Check for blisters under the veneer by tapping the surface with a fingernail. You will hear if there are any areas that have not adhered correctly.

9 If you are applying extra veneer pieces, such as a border, prepare the new veneers for application.

10 Working from the center to the edges, lay the new pieces of veneer overlapping the original.

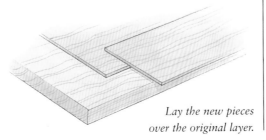

Lay the new pieces over the original layer.

11 Using a sharp craft knife and a metal straightedge, cut along the required line.

Cut the veneer with a craft knife.

12 Soften the adhesive with the cloth and iron, remove the waste pieces and press down with the veneer hammer using zigzag strokes.

13 Continue to lay the veneer to complete the desired pattern.

Caul, or press, veneering

A caul is a press that applies pressure to the groundwork and veneer. It is made from two sheets of manufactured board at least 1 in. thick, which should be slightly larger than the piece of work to be veneered. For small areas it is possible to use C-clamps on the caul as long as their throats are deep enough to give some pressure near the center. For larger areas, however, you need to make clamping strips or bearers that have a slight curve in the center to span the caul. As clamping force is applied, maximum pressure is initially concentrated on the center, while subsequent pressure spreads to the outside.

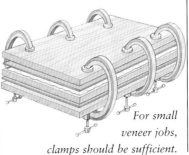

For small veneer jobs, clamps should be sufficient.

Making the caul

The caul is quite easy to make.

1 Having decided upon the size of the component you want to veneer, cut the two thick sheets of manufactured board, which need to be approximately 2 in. larger than the work.

2 Make some bearers that will apply pressure to the two boards. In order to ensure that the initial pressure is at the center of the boards and progresses toward the edges as the clamps are tightened, make a slight curve on one face.

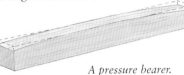

A pressure bearer.

3 Prepare two sheets of polyethylene to place between the work and the boards to keep the veneer from sticking to the caul face.

Pressing veneer in a caul

1 Prepare the package that is to be pressed. There will be the element to be veneered, normally called the groundwork, a face veneer on the show side and a backing veneer on the other face, all sandwiched between two sheets of polyethylene. Also, a paper pad or rubber sheet can act as a softening pad, and sometimes an aluminum sheet that is able to be heated can be inserted to help the adhesive cure.

Prepare the veneer package.

and bends and works easily, brass is harder but can still be worked and bent, while steel can be much more difficult.

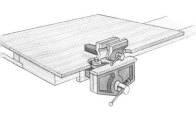

A workbench cover for metalwork.

Sawing a metal bar, rod, or tube

Use a hacksaw for cutting a metal bar, rod, or tube with any substantial thickness.

1 Mark the line to be cut with a scriber. Take care not to mark or damage any finish on the metal.

2 Cut with firm strokes; hacksawing will take much longer than sawing wood.

Cut the metal tube with a hacksaw.

3 When the cut is almost finished, support the waste.

Cutting sheet metal

If you are using sheet metal that is not too thick, it can be cut with metal shears or snips, used in the same way as scissors.

1 Mark the shape to be cut.

2 Cut to the line. The sheet will bend as it is cut and you will probably have to beat the sheet flat with a hammer on a rigid surface if it curls up too much. However, if you use the correct shears this should not be too much of a problem.

Finishing and filing

The cut edge will nearly always need some finishing with metalworking files and/or needle files.

1 Set the work in the vice.

2 Holding the file firmly at both ends, use it to remove material in a forward motion. With a little practice you will be able to file accurately to a line. Always be sure the handle is on the file.

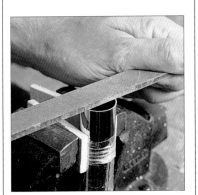

File across the metal tube.

Joining metals

It is quite difficult to join metals with most adhesives, and the two main methods are heat and hardware. Very high levels of heat are needed to melt and fuse most metals together. Unless you happen to have an engineering background or facilities, you will most likely need to have this type of work undertaken by a metal workshop.

Hardware is more easily used, and can range from screws to bolts and nuts for structures to rivets for sheet materials. Screws can be self-tapping and/or self-drilling.

Using plastics

Plastics, other than adhesives and finishes, are less likely to be used even though it may often be better to use transparent clear plastics than glass. Plastics are generally easy to work. Some plastics can be joined with solvent adhesives, and modest heat can be used to soften local areas so that sheet can be bent. After sawing plastics, smooth the sawn edges first with a fine metalworking file and then with wet-and-dry paper.

Filing a plastic edge.

Sanding a plastic edge.

THE PROJECTS

Small shelf Basic

This small shelf has no apparent supports, which helps to give it a compact, attractive appearance. Provided it is hung on a substantial wall, the shelf is perfectly safe and should be able to take the weight of normal household items. However, do not place very heavy articles on it, or extend the shelf width, as this will reduce its strength.

Tools

Jack plane

Drill and ½ in. and countersink bits

Tenon saw

Smoothing plane

Screwdrivers

Measuring tools

For all projects, a ruler or tape measure is needed for setting out. A try square is needed to square any set-outs across an edge or face.

MATERIALS		
Part	**Materials and dimensions**	**No.**
	Hardwood	
Shelf	28 x 5 x 1½ in.	1
Other materials: one 12 x ½ in. diameter dowel; four 2-in. 10 gauge flat head screws; adhesive (PVA recommended); wax; finish.		

1 Plane all of the surfaces of the wood to the correct overall length, width, and thickness with a jack plane. Ignore the bevels for the moment—you will not complete these until steps 8, 9, and 10. Using a try square and ruler,

measure and mark a line ⅝ in. in from one of the long edges of the piece. This is the line where the wood will later be cut into two pieces to make the shelf and its support (rear strip). Following the measurements given on the drawing below,

mark on the back edge of the wood the position of the three support dowels and the four screw holes in the center.

Mark the positions of the rear strip, support dowels, and screw holes.

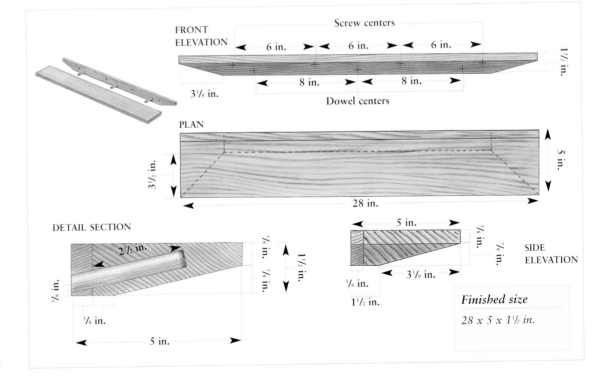

FRONT ELEVATION

Screw centers

6 in. 6 in. 6 in.

1½ in.

3⅛ in.

8 in. 8 in.

Dowel centers

PLAN

3½ in.

5 in.

28 in.

DETAIL SECTION

2½ in.

⅝ in.

1½ in.

⅞ in.

⅝ in.

5 in.

5 in.

⅝ in.

⅞ in.

3⅛ in.

SIDE ELEVATION

⅝ in.

1½ in.

Finished size

28 x 5 x 1½ in.

Skills required for project

Measuring and marking *pages 64–7*

Basic sawing *pages 68–71*

Planing *pages 74–81*

Drilling *pages 96–100*

Using adhesives *pages 128–9*

Wood finishing *pages 130–5*

4 Set up a sliding bevel to measure the angle of the dovetail on the batten. You will then be able to repeat this angle in step 6 to make sure that the slats are cut to exactly the right shape.

Use a sliding bevel to work out the angle of the dovetail battens.

5 On the battens mark where the slats will be positioned at ¹⁄₂-in. intervals (see the drawing on page 153) and, for each slat, drill a ³⁄₁₆-in. clearance hole for the screws. Countersink the screw holes on the bottom of the rack. All the slats will be held in the center of the dovetails.

6 Take the slats and use a marking knife to mark precisely the positions of the dovetails that will accept the supporting battens. From the bottom of each slat, measure up ⁵⁄₈ in. and square a pencil line right around the wood. Use the measurements on the drawing on page 153 to mark off the position and width of the dovetails on the slats. Set a sliding bevel to the angle of the

Mark the dovetails on the slats.

the dovetail on the battens that you measured in step 4. Use this and a marking knife to mark the dovetail angles. Gauge a line between these to represent the top cut-line of the dovetails.

7 Cut down the shoulder lines carefully with a dovetail saw, and remove the waste from the center with a coping saw. Pare to the top cut-line with a 1-in. paring chisel, ensuring a square cut is maintained. Cut one dovetail at a time, checking that each fits the batten well.

Use a paring chisel to pare out the waste from the dovetail joints.

8 Try all the slats dry on the battens to check that they are square with the battens.

9 Next, drill a ¹⁄₈-in. pilot hole from the existing clearance hole into the slats; insert and fix the screws in place.

Join the slats and battens together with screws.

10 Now that the slats are held firmly, mark the angles on the top surfaces.

Measure up 3¹³⁄₁₆ in. on the two diagonally opposite corners of the end slats. Then mark 2¹⁄₂ in. up on the other two diagonally opposite corners. To find the heights of all the middle slats, lay a straightedge along the outside of the rack and join the 2¹⁄₂-in. mark at one end with the 3¹³⁄₁₆-in. mark at the opposite end. Mark with a marking knife. Number the bottom of each slat in sequence.

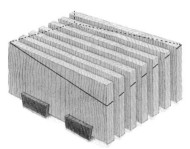

Use a straightedge to mark the heights of the middle slats.

11 Remove the screws and, having marked the positions of all the slats, slide them off the battens.

12 Cut the angles on the top surfaces of the slats. Saw carefully as the surface does not have a right-angled edge but twists from side to side. Hold in a clamp, saw end angles a short way, and then follow the line along the face to the center on both sides. These will act as guides for planing.

13 Plane and sand these top edges. Then sand all the faces and apply a finish to all components before assembly.

14 Now slide the slats, one by one, onto the battens and align with your marks. Reinsert the screws.

15 Apply another coat of finish to the areas that you can still reach if desired.

Animal shapes Basic

A basis of all work is cutting precisely to a line, and then chiseling – or paring – vertically or horizontally. This project gives the opportunity to practice chiseling skills and, since the design is so simple, achieve a very crisp result.

Tools

Smoothing plane

Marking knife

Marking gauge

Tenon saw

Bevel-edge paring chisel

Drill and drill bit

Dovetail saw

MATERIALS		
Part	Materials and dimensions	No.
All pieces	Hardwood length and width to suit the scale of the animals chosen (8¾ x 8 in. used here) x 1 in. thick.	

Other materials: abrasive paper; finish.

1 Use the drawing below in order to choose the scale at which to make the animals.

The size of the grid can be changed to suit your own individual requirements –

if you want to make the animals twice as big, then simply double the size of the grid that you use.

2 When you have chosen your scale, true the timber with a smoothing plane by working systematically all around. Then you are ready to mark the grid on the timber with a pencil.

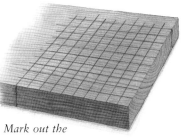

Mark out the grid on the timber.

3 Draw the animal shapes onto the grid with a pencil. Then mark the outside edges and details of the animal shapes across the grain with a knife and along the grain with a gauge. Also mark centers for the eye positions and cut lines for the slot detail.

Maximum size

6¾ in. long and 4 in. high

Each square represents ⅜ in.

Skills required for project

Measuring and marking *pages 64–7*

Planing *pages 74–81*

Fine sawing *pages 82–5*

Chiseling *pages 86–9*

Drilling *pages 96–100*

Using abrasives *pages 115–17*

Wood finishing *pages 130–5*

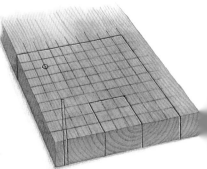

Mark out the animal shapes in the grid, including centers for the eyes.

4 Cut out the rectangle that contains each animal using a tenon saw. Where there are square or rectangular portions to be removed from the main block, cut them out, sawing to the waste side of the line.

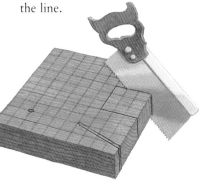

Saw away the bulk of the waste.

5 Carefully pare to the cut lines, vertically paring the end grain and either horizontally or vertically paring the long grain.

Use vertical strokes to pare back to the marked line carefully.

6 Now drill out the holes for the animals' eyes and cut the thin slots with a fine dovetail saw.

7 If your planing, sawing, and paring have been done well, then you may not wish to use abrasive paper on the faces and edges of each piece, but the sharp arrises on all corners will need removing at this stage.

8 If the animals are to be handled by children, then do not apply a finish. As an alternative, you could use a vegetable-based oil.

Hot-dish stand   Basic

This project provides an easy way to develop your skill at creating

grooves. This is quite a simple technique, but a very useful one.

You can use either a hand plow plane or an electric router.

MATERIALS		
Part	**Materials and dimensions**	**No.**
Whole piece	Hardwood 39 x 1¼ x ⅛ in.	2

Other materials: adhesive; sandpaper; finish (oil).

The stand is made out of two pieces of wood ⁵⁄₁₆ in. thick, cut into strips and joined together with adhesive. It is better to use two pieces of wood rather than one, even if it is available in the correct width, and to cut them into strips. This is because heat causes wood movement, which is minimized by alternating the direction of the grain. Also, grooving is carried out along the grain, and turning the two squares through 90 degrees will provide you with a more stable board.

1 Cut the wood with a tenon saw into 18 strips, each ¾ in. wide x ⅜ in. thick and approximately 8 in. long.

2 Join nine strips together to make a square. Arrange the grain so that it is as near as possible to a quarter-sawn board—with growth rings at not less than 45-degree angles to the base. Glue these strips together: apply adhesive to one side of a strip; lay the next one on top and move it from side to side until you feel the suction of the adhesive holding the pieces together. Bring the faces and end flush. Repeat for all the other pieces of the stand. Place in sash clamps, but take care not to overtighten the clamps, as this will cause the work to bow. Repeat with the other nine strips and allow to dry.

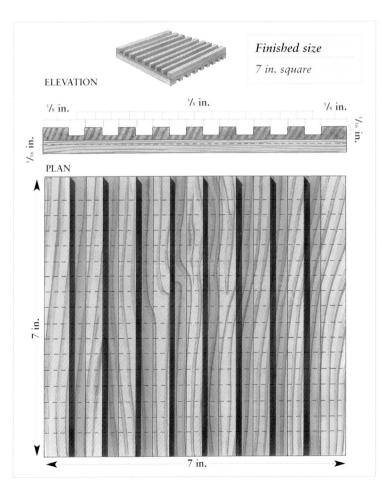

ELEVATION

⅝ in.   ⅜ in.   ⅝ in.

⁵⁄₁₆ in.   ⁵⁄₁₆ in.

Finished size

7 in. square

PLAN

7 in.

7 in.

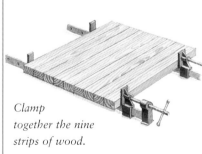

Clamp together the nine strips of wood.

3 With the hand plane, plane each square to give a perfectly flat face side. Test by placing one on top of the other, with the grain at right angles to each other.

4 Once you have fitted the two squares face to face, glue them together with the grain at right angles.

Glue the top and bottom together.

5 With a hand plane, plane the outside edges so that each face is true and perfectly square. Test with a try square.

6 Insert a ³/₈-in. bit or blade into your plow plane or router; set the depth to ¹/₄ in., and the fence to guide the groove ⁵/₈ in. in from the edge. Run the groove along the grain; rotate the work and repeat. Turn the work over and run the groove along the grain on the opposite side; rotate the work and repeat.

Use a router to run the grooves.

7 Move the fence over an additional ³/₄ in.— 1³/₈ in. in total—and run the next groove. Repeat as explained above in step 6. Then, move the fence another ³/₄ in.—2¹/₈ in. in total—and run those grooves. Move the fence by another ³/₄ in. and complete the central grooves.

The finished corner.

8 When you have completed the grooves on both sides of the stand, finish by smoothing the rough ends of wood carefully with sandpaper, removing the arris.

9 Any synthetic finish that you apply to the hot plate stand will probably suffer from the heat of pots and pans, so it is best simply to oil the stand lightly to minimize any future spotting.

159

Early development of furniture

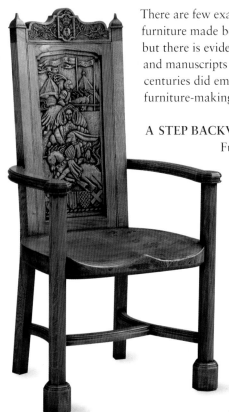

A Catherine of Aragon-style chair, designed by Stewart Linford furniture.

There are few examples left today of furniture made before the 16th century but there is evidence in carvings, pottery and manuscripts that much earlier centuries did employ well-developed furniture-making techniques.

A STEP BACKWARD

Furniture making is an ancient tradition, with its roots going back to early civilizations. In Ancient Egypt there was a tradition of burying furniture in tombs. Throughout the first and second dynasties skills were being developed, including the use of mortise-and-tenon, dovetail, and miter joints. The furniture was mostly crude three-legged stools or armless chairs, and tables were almost unknown. Although through stone carvings and frescoes it can be seen that beds, stools, throne chairs, and boxes were common. Everything was made to be portable and decoration was derived from religious symbols.

Our knowledge of early Greek furniture is mainly taken from painted pottery, but we know they adapted techniques from both Egypt and the Orient. In turn, Greek civilization heavily influenced the Romans and in both cultures the principal piece of furniture was the couch. It was the Romans who first developed cupboards, and wall paintings from Pompeii show plain, undecorated wooden tables, benches, and cupboards with paneled doors.

When the Roman Empire collapsed during the 4th and 5th centuries, Europe sank into the Dark Ages, during which time very little furniture was used. What was in existence was far inferior to the quality of furniture in Greek and Roman times.

During the 14th and 15th centuries there was a shift in furniture making. Previously, it had mainly been monks who worked on furniture but now lay people began to learn the skills involved. There were many developments in Europe during this time—various cupboards and desks evolved and crude dovetailing and mortise-and-tenon joints, secured by pegs, were employed. Furniture remained portable because if a nobleman owned more than one dwelling he still had only one set of furniture that he needed to carry with him. Throughout this period, and into the 16th and 17th centuries, all furniture was scarce and mainly belonged to nobility and the wealthy. Chairs symbolized authority—even a large household may have owned just three;

OPPOSITE LEFT *Mortise-and-tenon joints were first used in Ancient Egypt, as seen in this stool.* ◆ OPPOSITE CENTER *An oak court cupboard from the mid-17th century.* ◆ OPPOSITE RIGHT *An oak refectory table, made in 1540, with carved angel figures on both sides of each upright.*
◆ ABOVE LEFT *A late 17th-century oak settle with turned baluster back.* ◆ ABOVE CENTER *A Jacobean oak bench with turned legs and carved detail.*
◆ ABOVE RIGHT *A Jacobean oak settle with an arcaded design on the back panels.*

one for the lord, one for his wife, and the other for visitors. The peasant households of Europe, even as late as the 18th century, had only rather crude, roughly constructed basic pieces of furniture.

A NEW VISION

In Italy in the 15th century there was a huge growth of the powerful bourgeoisie and this created a new demand for strong, fine furniture. Furniture makers looked to Greece and Rome to draw inspiration from the ancient civilizations. Other countries in Europe were influenced by this new mood. French furniture had been made of oak, which was difficult to carve, but the influence of Italy turned the French toward walnut, which allowed carvers to create elaborate carved heads and strapwork. When Francis I returned for France after captivity in Italy in 1525, he employed several Italian craftsmen and the furniture of 16th-century France became remarkably graceful. For example, chairs became lighter, with heavy paneled sides and bases replaced by carved and turned arms and supports, and legs joined by stretchers.

With a caned seat and back, this chair was made in c1670 out of beech and walnut.

Italy also influenced Germany and the Low Countries. Germany blended classical architectural motifs with animal masks and grotesques. The north of Germany, however, had no direct experience with Italy and heavy oak furniture was still preferred in the north, while in the south softwood was being used.

England was not affected by the Italian Renaissance until about 1525. It was much more conservative, remaining Gothic and heavy in style. But Henry VIII made efforts to bring Britain up-to-date and employed Italian and German furniture makers. Classical motifs began to appear and craftsmen developed framed-panel joiner—furniture that is made up of tenon-jointed rails and stiles. There was also a technical breakthrough in the 1540s, when the true miter was developed. Most furniture in Britain continued to be heavy and made of oak, but richer homes began to prefer walnut and other native hardwoods. Turned decoration, such as balusters, was introduced and Britain started to catch up with the rest of Europe. However, it was not until the reign of Charles I—which marked a new era of artistic patronage—that things began to take off, with the range of furniture expanding and armchairs with scrolled wooden arms beginning to appear.

161

Wine rack Basic

This simple, stylish wine rack requires accurate drilling work. You can achieve good results slowly with hand tools, but if you are making a large rack, it will be easier to use a drill press or power drill. The steps below describe a method where each hole is individually marked. For a larger rack, it would be easier to use a jig to drill the holes in the correct position without needing to mark each piece.

Tools

Tenon saw

Marking gauge

Drill and ⅛-in. dowel bit

Smoothing plane

MATERIALS

Part	Materials and dimensions	No.
	Hardwood	
Slats	1³⁄₁₆ in. square—the total length needed depends on how many bottles you wish to store; for a four-bottle rack you need nine slats, 7½ in. long	1

Other materials: ⅛-in. diameter dowel—for a four-bottle rack you will need 24 lengths each 3¾ in. long; sandpaper; adhesive; finish.

1 First, decide how many bottles you want to store in your wine rack. Then use a tenon saw to cut the required number of wood pieces, each measuring 1³⁄₁₆ in. square and 7½ in. long. To make the four-bottle rack shown here, you will need nine slats.

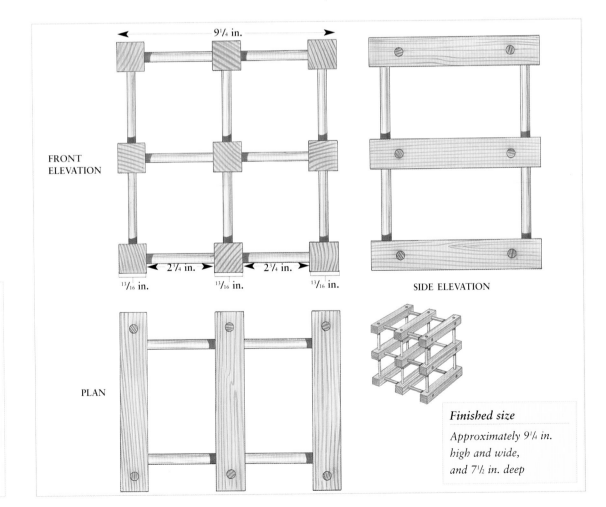

FRONT ELEVATION

9¼ in.

2³⁄₄ in.   2³⁄₄ in.

¹³⁄₁₆ in.   ¹³⁄₁₆ in.   ¹³⁄₁₆ in.

SIDE ELEVATION

PLAN

Finished size

Approximately 9¼ in. high and wide, and 7½ in. deep

Skills required for project

Measuring and marking *pages 64–7*

Planing *pages 74–81*

Fine sawing *pages 82–5*

Drilling *pages 96–100*

Using abrasives *pages 115–17*

Assembling projects *pages 120–7*

Using adhesives *pages 128–9*

Wood finishing *pages 130–5*

2 Next, mark the positions of the holes at each end of the slats. Select a face side and face edge on each piece, marking one set of holes on the face side and its opposite face 1 in. from each end. Then mark holes on the face edge and its opposite face 1⅛ in. from the ends. Square a pencil line across each edge and face at these locations.

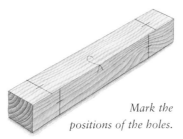

Mark the positions of the holes.

3 Set a marking gauge to ⅝ in., half the width of the wood pieces. Then mark the hole center on each pencil line.

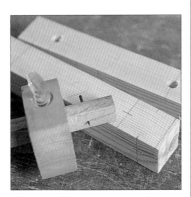

Use a marking gauge to mark the hole centers.

4 It will be easier to locate the drill if you mark the hole centers first with a center punch or an awl.

Mark the hole centers with an awl first so that it will be easier to locate the drill.

5 Drill all the holes with a ⅜-in. dowel bit. You will need to use a proprietary tool or make your own depth stop to be sure all the holes are at the correct depth. The simplest way to make your own drill stop is to drill a hole through a piece of wood and then cut it to size so that the drill bit protrudes ½ in. out the end.

Drill through a piece of wood to make a drill stop.

This will enable you to drill the correct depth in each piece of wood. Drill all the holes as marked— two in each face.

Drill holes in each piece of timber.

6 Next, prepare the dowels that will hold the slats together. Each should be 3¾ in. in length with a shoulder ½ in. in from each end. If your holes have been drilled correctly, you will not need to mark the shoulders.

7 Before assembly, sand the surfaces of all components and remove the arris on the square components. Plane and sand the end grain. Create a small chamfer on each end of the dowel. This will help to locate the dowel in the hole when assembling the rack.

8 Lay out the pieces and start assembling in units of two slats and two dowels. Insert

adhesive into the holes and tap the dowels in place. To ensure that the dowels sit in the holes, use a clamp to squeeze the joints tight.

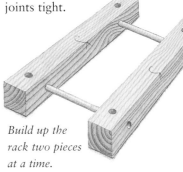

Build up the rack two pieces at a time.

Place adhesive into the holes and press the dowels into place.

9 Assemble to the size of rack you require and remove any adhesive that has exuded from the holes. Check the frame for wind and square. Apply a finish if you wish.

10 To stabilize a large rack and to tip bottles forward to keep the corks moist, insert a thin batten, about ¼ in. under the front edge, and tack into place so that the rack leans backward against a wall. Or, you could use furniture glides.

Stabilize the rack by inserting a batten under the front edge.

Veneered chessboard Basic

The simple chessboard pattern consists of a checkered pattern of dark and light face veneers. This method of veneering uses a caul (or press) and modern adhesives to attach the veneer to the base wood.

MATERIALS

Part	Materials and dimensions	No.
	Manufactured board	
Base	16 x 16 x ¾ in.	1
	Hardwood	
Lips	17¼ x ⅞ x ½ in.	4
	Veneer	
Checkered pattern	Dark and light face veneers both approximately 12 in. square	
Border	17¼ x 2½ in.	4
Underside	Backing veneers	

Other materials: sandpaper; veneer tape; polyethylene; finish.

1 The first stage of the process is to apply lips to all four edges of the board. The final size will need to be 16 in. square—see measurements on the drawing below as a guide. Use a smoothing plane to plane all the lips, but make sure that you leave the width over size to the board's thickness. Trim the board to 15¼ in. in order to accept them. Using a miter square , carefully

Tools

Smoothing plane

Miter square

Straightedge

Router

Sash clamps

Toothing plane

Veneer knife

Caul, tools, and materials

Finished size

16 in. square

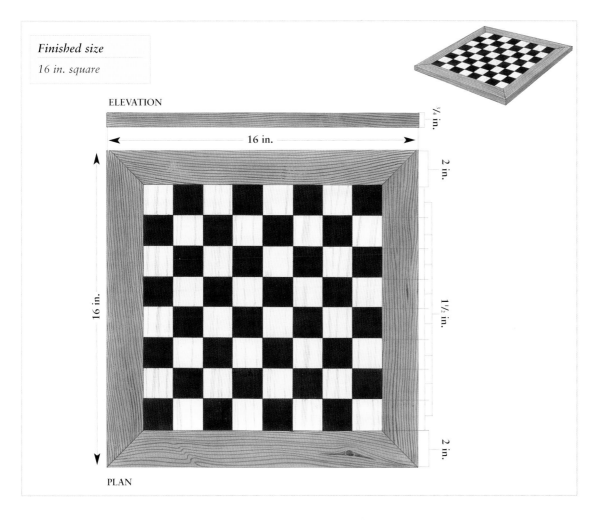

ELEVATION

16 in.

¾ in.

2 in.

16 in.

1½ in.

2 in.

PLAN

Skills required for project

Measuring and marking
pages 64–7

Planing *pages 74–81*

Using abrasives
pages 115–17

Using adhesives
pages 128–9

Wood finishing
pages 130–5

Veneering *pages 136–9*

mark miters on the ends of the lips so that they fit exactly in the corners.

2 You can either join these lips to the board with loose tongues or simply glue them to the edges. If using tongues and grooves, work ¼ x ¼-in. grooves with a router prior to cutting the miters.

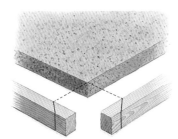

Apply lips to the board, mitering the edges to allow for the corners.

3 If using adhesives, glue the lips in place. Hold with sash clamps as required.

4 When the adhesive has cured, with a smoothing plane very carefully plane the excess lip flush to the surface of the board on both sides.

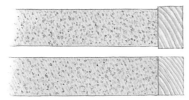

Plane the lips so that they are flush with the board.

5 Key the top and bottom of the board with a toothing plane. Veneers can exert a pull on the face of a board, so put a backing veneer on the underside.

6 Select the veneers for the underside. Carefully cut the light and dark veneers for the top face into precise 1½-in. wide strips. Join nine of these strips in alternating colors with veneer tape.

7 Now carefully cut another nine 1½-in. wide strips at right angles to the first set so that you are left with strips of alternating light and dark squares.

Cut nine more strips at right angles to the first set.

8 Next, shift every other strip up by one square so that you end up with a checkered effect. Fix in position with veneer tape.

Move every other strip up by one square to create a chessboard effect.

9 Lay this matrix in the center of the board and trim the excess squares off the end so that you end up with a chessboard of eight squares by eight squares. Lay the four border strips in position with veneer tape, overlapping and trimming the mitered corners as necessary with a veneer knife.

10 Ensure that, as well as face and backing veneers, you have two polyethylene sheets about the same size. Spread adhesive onto the undersurface of the board and place the backing veneer in position.

11 Apply more adhesive to the top surface of the backing board and place the top veneer assembly in position.

The top veneer assembly kit consists of polyethylene sheet, caul, backing veneer, core board, and top veneer.

12 Lay a sheet of polyethylene on the bottom of the caul and lay the package of backing veneer, core board, and top veneer on it. Lay another polyethylene sheet on top of this and place the top caul in place.

Clamp the assembly together.

13 Apply even pressure to the clamping bearers all the way around.

14 When the adhesive has cured, remove the veneered board from the caul and trim all the edges.

15 Carefully remove the veneer tape, sand all the surfaces, and apply the required finish to the board.

Parquetry

Parquetry consists of mosaics of different colored wood veneers, which are glued onto a groundwork to form geometric patterns. Checkered or diamond shapes are the most common parquetry designs. By skilful manipulation of the color and grain of the wood, an optical illusion of a 3-D image can be created with this technique. Parquetry was most fashionable in walnut furniture from 1670 to about 1715.

Triangular trivet $\boxed{\textit{Basic}}$

A trivet is a small frame that can be put beneath a hot platter or dish to protect the table or kitchen surface. This is a relatively straightforward project, which is put together with oblique halving joints.

MATERIALS

Part	Materials and dimensions	No.
	Hardwood	
Side	24 x 1¼ x ¾ in.	3

Other materials: adhesive; sandpaper; finish.

1 Prepare the wood by planing it until it is rectangular in shape. Measure and cut the three side pieces of the trivet to length, using the drawing below as a guide. Apply face-side and edge marks.

2 Set a sliding bevel to 60 degrees, with a protractor or set square.

Set the bevel to a 60-degree angle and mark with a pencil.

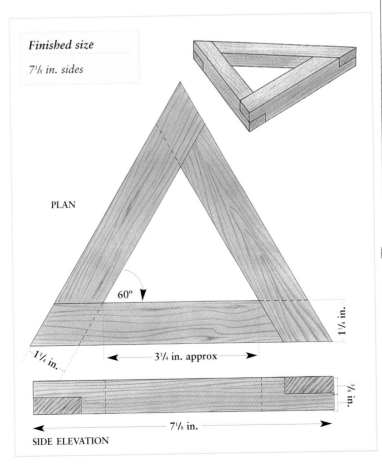

Finished size

7⅛ in. sides

PLAN

60°

1¼ in.

1¼ in.

3¾ in. approx

7⅛ in.

⅜ in.

SIDE ELEVATION

3 First, mark the piece of wood that will be sawed off the end of each piece of wood (A)—measure from one corner up to the opposite edge at a 60-degree angle. Carefully saw off these sections.

4 Next, mark the shoulder—the piece of wood that will be sawed partway through each end to make the half-lap joint (B). Mark a line 1¼ in. in from one end at a 60-degree angle across the face side, parallel with the end that you cut in step 3. Turn the piece over and mark the shoulder at the opposite end in the same way. Check that the distance between the shoulders is 3¾ in. Use a try square to square these lines across the edges. Gauge a center line from the shoulder lines out and around the end of each piece and back to the first shoulder line. Repeat until all the pieces of wood are marked up.

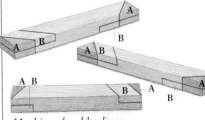

Marking shoulder lines.

5 Go over the shoulder marks with a marking knife, then carefully saw partway down the shoulder lines until you reach the center line. Be sure to saw across the grain.

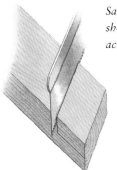

Saw the shoulder lines across the grain.

6 Hold one of the pieces of wood in a vice so that the shoulder line is vertical. Saw down the gauged center line on the waste side of the shoulder. It should be possible to saw accurately to the line but, if you are new to woodworking, you may have to trim the faces of the joints with a chisel. Repeat to achieve shaped ends on all the pieces of wood.

Saw down the center lines on the shoulders.

7 Lay the three components of the trivet together and check that the joints are tight. Adjust as required.

Check the fit and adjust if necessary.

8 Apply adhesive to the joint faces and clamp together with C-clamps.

9 When the adhesive has cured, smooth the outside edges with a plane.

10 Use abrasive paper to sand the trivet and apply the finish of your choice.

Carved mirror frame   Basic

The construction of this piece is very simple and the carving on the face is particularly effective. Here the frame has been used to hold a mirror but you could adapt it to fit a picture or a photograph.

Tools

Smoothing plane

Router with ½-in. straight bit

Mortise gauge

Tenon saw

Mortise chisel

Carving tools

Carver's mallet

Clamps

Drill and ⅛-in. and ¹/₁₆-in. bits

Skills required for project

Measuring and marking *pages 64–7*

Basic sawing *pages 68–71*

Planing *pages 74–81*

Chiseling *pages 86–9*

Making grooves *pages 90–3*

Drilling *pages 96–100*

Making mortise-and-tenon joints *pages 104–9*

Using abrasives *pages 115–17*

Using adhesives *pages 128–9*

Wood finishing *pages 130–5*

Carving *pages 140–1*

MATERIALS

Part	Materials and dimensions	No.
	Hardwood	
Uprights	23 x 2 x 1 in.	2
Horizontals	12¾ x 2 x 1 in.	2

Other materials: one 18½ x 12⅝-in. mirror; one 18½ x 12⅝-in. sheet of ¼-in. plywood and hardwood strips removed when making internal rabbets for use as retaining strips (if you rout rabbets you will need more material for strips); adhesive; sandpaper; finish; ¾-in. 6 gauge flat head screws.

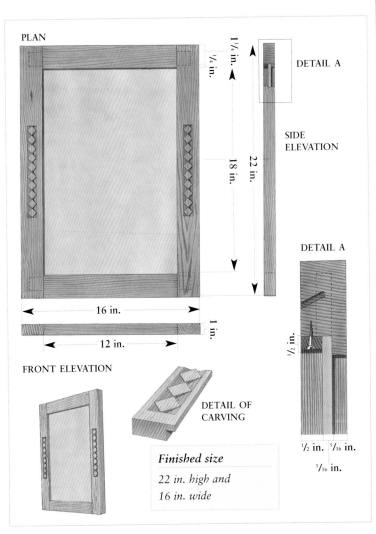

PLAN

1¼ in.

¼ in.

DETAIL A

SIDE ELEVATION

22 in.

18 in.

DETAIL A

16 in.

12 in.

1 in.

FRONT ELEVATION

½ in.

½ in.   ⁵/₁₆ in.

³/₁₆ in.

DETAIL OF CARVING

Finished size

22 in. high and 16 in. wide

1 First, prepare the wood for the basic frame. Plane the two uprights and two horizontals face side and face edge. Apply marks and plane the width and thickness to 2 x 1 in. The finished horizontals will be 14¾ in. long (the internal size of the frame plus the two tenons) and the finished uprights will be 22 in. long. Cut these pieces to length.

2 Use a router to cut the rabbets on the back edge of the internal faces ½ in. wide and ⅝ in. deep.

3 Mark the long-and-short-shouldered mortise and tenons to suit the rabbet size in their respective positions. Mark the tenon with the mortise gauge ⁵/₁₆ in. wide. Grip the horizontals vertically in a vice and cut down to the set-out shoulder lines with a tenon saw. Lay them on a bench against a bench hook and cut the shoulder. Place each horizontal vertically in the vice again and cut ⅜ in. off the outside edge of each tenon. Remove waste by cutting across the long shoulder line.

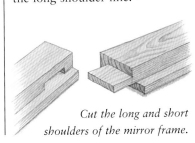

Cut the long and short shoulders of the mirror frame.

4 The mortise lines up with the rabbet on one face. Hold each upright on the edge and chisel out the mortise for each—1 in. deep to suit the stopped tenons. First, pare away the waste within the mortise to the required depth, and then pare back to each shoulder. Check each joint for fit and adjust as required.

5 Mark the shapes of your pattern. Using the relevant carving tool, make cuts to the required pattern. You can practice on some scrap lumber.

Use a chisel and mallet to practice carving on a piece of scrap lumber.

6 When the carving is complete, assemble the frame with adhesive and clamp the joints. Ensure that the frame is square and free of wind.

7 When the adhesive has cured, prepare the frame for finishing and apply the required finish.

8 Make the four retaining strips to fit in the rabbet. Place the mirror or picture in the frame. Lay a couple of sheets of paper over the back to protect it, then a sheet of plywood. Drill holes for the screws through into the rabbet and screw the four strips in place. An angled hole can be drilled at the top of the frame for wall mounting.

From the Baroque style to Rococo

A French armchair made during the reign of Louis XV.

The Baroque style, which originated in Italy, had a tremendous effect on furniture throughout Europe and one of the main features was that furniture began to display theatrical elements. Each country, however, interpreted the style in its own way.

ORIGINS AND DEVELOPMENTS IN STYLE

The Baroque style originally evolved from Italian architecture, painting, and sculpture. Owing much to the Oriental influence that was sweeping across Europe in the 17th century, the characteristics of the Baroque style were grand architectural and sculptural gestures and elaborately detailed ornamentation.

It was in the France of Louis XIV where the quintessential Baroque style took shape, as workshops were founded to create opulent, sumptuous, and monumental furniture that reflected the king's glorious status. New types of furniture were created, most notably the cabinet, which gave rise to the all-important role of the cabinetmaker. New techniques were developed, such as "boulle"—the marquetry of brass and tortoiseshell on an oak backing—named for its originator, André-Charles Boulle.

By the mid-17th century the Low Countries had become important furniture producers in their own right, having gained independence from Spain at the end of the 16th century. Adopting the Baroque style in the 1620s, they continued with it

OPPOSITE LEFT *A William and Mary walnut chair.* ◆ OPPOSITE CENTER *A mahogany chair made in England c1720.* ◆ OPPOSITE RIGHT *Ball and claw foot on a George II carved walnut chair c1740.* ◆ ABOVE LEFT *A French gilded armchair made c1760.* ◆ ABOVE CENTER *A carved mahogany Chippendale period tripod table made c1760.* ◆ ABOVE RIGHT *Chippendale period carved chair made c1760.*

until late into the 17th century, at which time Germany and England began to develop their own distinctive versions of Baroque. Progress in the style and range of furniture in England was interrupted by the Civil War and subsequent Republic, when Puritans introduced strict reforms on the amount of decoration allowed on furniture. When Charles II was restored to the monarchy in 1660, however, he brought back with him the Baroque revolution in taste that he had witnessed while traveling in exile across France and the Low Countries. An influx of European craftsmen followed; they employed new techniques, such as veneering and spiral turning, and introduced new forms such as bun feet. Gateleg dining tables and single-purpose dressing tables made their first appearance and woods such as walnut, cherry, cedar, and yew began to be used.

WILLIAM AND MARY

The Dutch influence on English furniture-making continued with the arrival in 1688 of William and Mary from Holland, accompanied by their designer, Daniel Marot. A simple, elegant style using carved cabriole-legged chairs with ball and claw or pad feet took precedence. There was also a growing preference for intimate surroundings, for which smaller pieces of furniture, such as little tables, began to be developed.

THE RÉGENCE PERIOD

Again, it was the influence of French furniture that was to be dominant in the 18th century. The transitional phase from Baroque to Rococo is termed the Régence period, when a lighter, more fluent and curvilinear style appeared. The Baroque era had been about architectural statements but the emphasis began to shift. The practical consideration of providing comfort to users was at the forefront, hence curved backs that were easier on the sitter were introduced to chairs. Also important was the notion that every piece of furniture should be beautiful and compact. The stocky supports and stretchers of monumental Baroque furniture gave way to graceful, S-shaped cabriole legs just strong enough to hold the dainty new furniture.

ROCOCO

The Rococo style combined this new preference for flowing lines and curves in the structure of furniture, with imaginative designs of graceful foliage, scallop shells, and scrollwork that derived from the ornamentation in garden grottoes. This somewhat frivolous, sugary style led to an anti-Rococo movement that was particularly important in England, where William Kent led the way, designing hefty furniture of Palladian classicism with just a few ornamental concessions to Rococo. In 1720 there was a walnut shortage and mahogany began to be imported to England, which the Palladians used to create striking pieces of furniture.

Despite Palladian resistance, by the 1740s the Rococo style was having a definite impact in England. In 1754, Thomas Chippendale published his "Gentleman and Cabinet Maker's Director," which comprised patterns for English furniture in the Rococo style, as well as its Chinese and Gothic offshoots. Chippendale was a businessman and cabinetmaker, and his name has become synonymous with most mid-18th-century mahogany furniture.

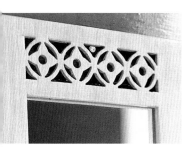

Small mirror and shelf | Basic |

This simple mirror and shelf, ideal for a bathroom wall, will enable you to put several key skills into practice. You will need to make a dovetail dado joint to attach the shelf to the frame, use an electric router to remove the wood to fit the mirror in place and use a fretsaw to produce the fine fretwork detailing along the top and bottom of the frame.

Tools

Marking gauge

Smoothing plane

Marking knife

Tenon saw

Sliding bevel

Paring chisel

Straightedge

Cutting gauge

Electric router or Forstner drill bit and hand router

Fretsaw

Drill

Skills required for project

Measuring and marking
pages 64–7

Planing *pages 74–81*

Fine sawing *pages 82–5*

Making dado joints
pages 110–11

Using abrasives
pages 115–17

Using adhesives
pages 128–9

Wood finishing
pages 130–5

MATERIALS		
Part	Materials and dimensions	No.
Frame and shelf	Hardwood to make both the backboard and the shelf: 22 x 8 x ¾ in.	1

Other materials: one 8⅛ x 5½-in. mirror; adhesive (PVA); silicon; double-sided tape or mastic to fit glass; sandpaper; finish.

1 Prepare the wood face side and face edge. Use a marking gauge and then a smoothing plane to plane to a width of 8 in. and a thickness of ¾ in.

2 First, mark the finished lengths of the two components—16 in. for the backboard and 4½ in. for the shelf. Square all round with a marking knife. Set out the position for the dovetail dado 2 in. from the bottom of the backboard. Use a pencil to square the top and bottom of the shelf across the backboard. Square the other lines on the board with a pencil: Gauge a line 1¼ in. in from each edge to represent the ends of the fretwork and the recess for the mirror, as shown in the drawing on the right.

3 Cut the backboard and shelf with a tenon saw and carefully plane the end grain true to the finished length.

4 Square the two set-out lines for the shelf across each edge of the backboard. Use a marking gauge to gauge a depth of ⅜ in. between these squared lines. Set a sliding bevel to a pitch of 1:4 and mark the dovetail on the edge from the gauge line (see detail Bb on drawing opposite).

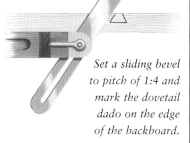

Set a sliding bevel to pitch of 1:4 and mark the dovetail dado on the edge of the backboard.

5 Use a marking knife to square the shoulder lines where the bevel line meets the face. Clamp the piece flat on the bench and cut on the waste side of the line with a tenon saw to the gauge line. Place another saw cut in the center, stopping short of the gauge line.

Use a tenon saw to cut away the dovetail dado.

6 Use a paring chisel in order to remove the waste from both sides; work carefully to the gauge lines. Place a straightedge along the bottom to be sure it is perfectly flat.

7 Next, set out the dovetail on the shelf across each face with a cutting gauge set to ⅜ in., the depth of the dado. Using a pencil, square these lines down each edge of the shelf. Then reset the sliding bevel to the correct pitch and mark the angle of the dovetail from the corner back to the squared line.

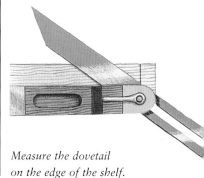

Measure the dovetail on the edge of the shelf.

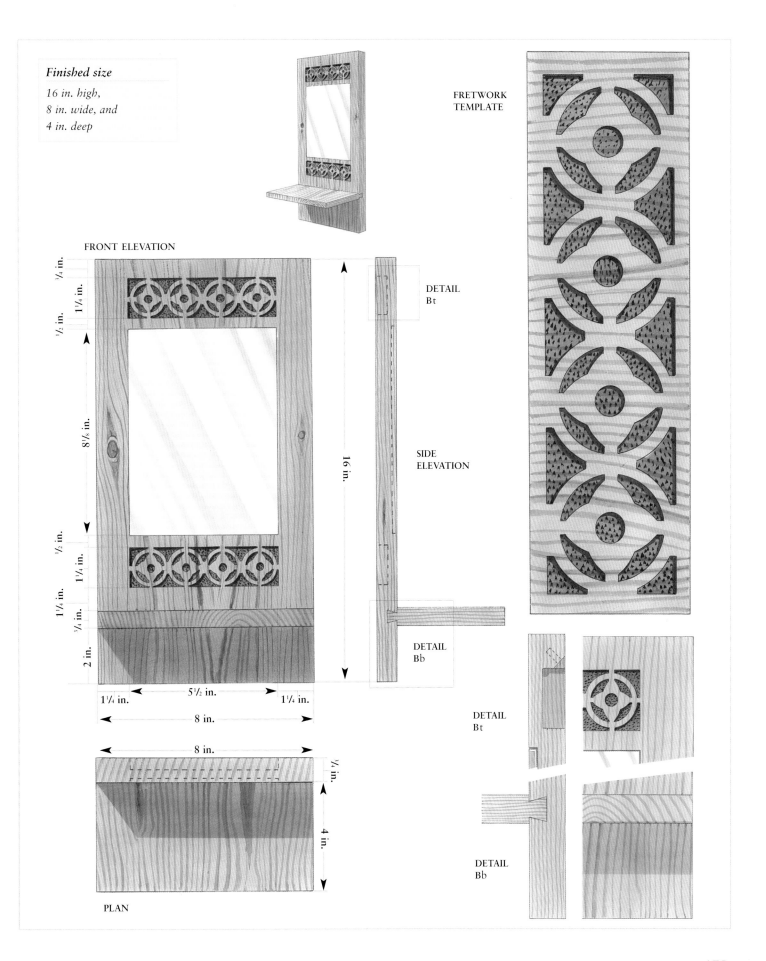

Finished size

16 in. high,
8 in. wide, and
4 in. deep

FRONT ELEVATION

³⁄₄ in.

1¹⁄₄ in.

¹⁄₂ in.

8¹⁄₈ in.

¹⁄₂ in.

1¹⁄₄ in.

1¹⁄₄ in.

³⁄₄ in.

2 in.

16 in.

1¹⁄₄ in. 5¹⁄₂ in. 1¹⁄₄ in.

8 in.

FRETWORK
TEMPLATE

DETAIL
Bt

SIDE
ELEVATION

DETAIL
Bb

DETAIL
Bt

DETAIL
Bb

8 in.

³⁄₄ in.

4 in.

PLAN

175

Fretwork

Fretwork is made from thin wood that has been cut with a very fine saw, called a fretsaw, to form patterns—usually interlocking geometric designs. These are used decoratively on furniture: They are sometimes left open, or applied to a background or can be backed with a different material, such as silk, which shows through the holes. Fretwork was used widely on bookcases, cabinets, commodes, tabletops and chair backs and the term often refers specifically to the mid-18th century Chinese-style of furniture. At this time there was a craze for Oriental designs and chinoiserie (a general term for Chinese decorative work such as motifs or carvings) was applied to a range of furniture. Fretted galleries were added to tables, pagoda-like fretted tops put on cabinets, and fretwork chair backs were designed.

8 Square the lines all around the shelf edge. Hold the shelf flat on the bench and cut each shoulder on the waste side of the cut line to the required depth. Pare away the waste with a sharp paring chisel, working from each side across the grain.

Square the dovetail lines all around the shelf edge and cut to size.

9 On the backboard make gauge marks along the grain and knife cuts across the grain to the precise dimensions of the mirror. It is always better to choose the mirror first and make the recess to fit it, because you cannot always rely on obtaining glass that is cut precisely to size.

10 Now cut away the recess, which will house the mirror. The best tool to use for this is an electric router. Set the router to the correct depth and the fence to enable the tool to cut to the gauge lines. Take a cut from each edge, stopping short of the total length. Leaving the depth setting the same, adjust the fence so that a series of cuts from each side will remove the bulk of the material. When this has been completed, pare to the top and bottom cut lines. If you do not have an electric router, you can remove the bulk of material with a flat-bottomed bit such as a Forstner, setting the depth in a drill press and making a series of holes in the waste area. Use a hand router to remove the remaining waste and carefully pare squarely to the four edges.

Use a Forstner drill bit to cut the recess for the mirror.

11 The thickness of the board is designed to give a stable piece and still allow for jointing. Some material will need to be removed from the back where the fretwork details will be cut, thus giving a thickness of about 5/16 in. Remove this as described in step 10.

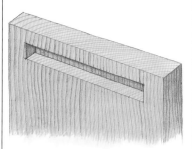

Reduce the thickness of the area where you will do the fretwork.

12 Use the template (see drawing on page 175) to mark out the fretwork detail carefully on the prepared area of the mirror frame. Make knife lines and drill holes to accept the fretsaw blade in each of the areas to be removed. This can be easily achieved by tracing the pattern with carbon paper. Alternately, photocopy the design and glue it down in the required location. The latter is by far the best method to use because the glued-down paper will hold the surface firmly and help prevent chipping.

13 If you have not used a fretsaw before, practice on scrap lumbers, and when confident, cut the patterns. Take your time and follow the lines exactly.

Cut the pattern with a fretsaw.

14 To hang the mirror, make a chamfer and drill a hole at an angle in the center of the top fretwork recess on the back. This can then be located on a screw or nail in the wall.

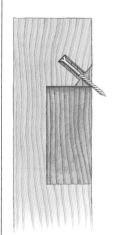

Fix a screw at an angle on the wall and position the mirror over screw.

15 Sand all the wood components, taking care to remove all set-out marks. Glue the shelf in place on the backboard with PVA adhesive. Apply the required finish of your choice.

16 Glue the mirror in position by placing three or four lumps of mastic on it, or use silicon or double-sided tape.

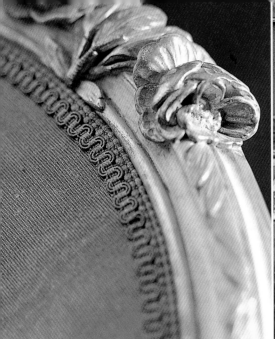

Neoclassicism to eclecticism

This Hepplewhite period dining chair dates from c1780.

THE NEOCLASSICAL REJECTION OF ROCOCO

By the mid-18th century, people were beginning to tire of the Rococo style—critics in Paris spoke against the extravagant, frivolous forms. Designers looked to classical antiquity for inspiration and neoclassicism was born. The sinuous curves of Rococo pieces were replaced with straight, tapered, fluted legs. Decoration included Greek key patterns and rosettes, and chairs had medallion-shaped, oval, or circular molded backs.

ENGLISH EXPONENTS

The Englishman Robert Adam was one of the chief exponents of neoclassicism, along with his brother James. Robert had studied in Italy and drew inspiration from both classical and Renaissance design, using ornamentation such as urns or husks (drop ornaments). He was also thought to have been the inventor of the sideboard. His furniture was copied and modified—

for example, in America the sideboard took on its own unique form, while in England, George Hepplewhite helped to make the Adam style popular. Adam had made great use of soft and pale woods, including American satinwood and Brazilian rosewood, but although Hepplewhite did use these at times, he mainly reverted to mahogany. His rather feminine, delicate designs include heart- and shield-shaped chair backs. This tendency toward greater refinement was widespread in the last 20 years of the 18th century, as represented by Thomas Sheraton's square-backed chairs, which echoed late-18th century French designs.

NATIONAL STYLES

The Empire style began in France at the turn of the 19th century and it marked a triumphant return to a formal, classical vocabulary in furniture. It was during this, the Napoleonic era, that Paris became once again the most important center for cabinetmaking, setting the tone for the rest of Europe. This was aided by the generous patronage of Napoleon, and his military conquests fueled the spread of French ideas. His travels and victories in Egypt gave the style one of its key influences, with sphinxes, lotus leaves, and other Egyptian motifs decorating the new, majestic, masculine furniture, along with the more traditional Roman and Greek motifs. Two of Napoleon's architects, Charles Percier and Pierre Fontaine, did much for the development of this style.

At around the same time, the Regency style took shape in Britain, born out of Sheraton's linear decoration and elongated shapes. Regency was basically Britain's interpretation of the

OPPOSITE LEFT *A carved detail from an armchair in the style of Robert Adam, c1775.* ◆ OPPOSITE CENTER *Triumphant military motifs were often used in Empire pieces.* ◆ OPPOSITE RIGHT *A fine example of painted detail in the arm of this Sheraton period chair.* ◆ ABOVE LEFT *An early 19th century Biedermeier period Swedish birchwood armchair with turned front legs.* ◆ ABOVE CENTER *Influenced by the Biedermeier style, Benedick Holl designed this mahogany writing desk in 1808.* ◆ ABOVE RIGHT *A Victorian neo-Gothic chair designed by Cottingham.*

Empire style and was similarly influenced by classical motifs. However, exoticism was also a major influence, which can be seen in the outlandish architecture and interior decoration of Brighton Pavilion, designed and built during this period. Exotic woods such as zebrawood, amboyna, and satinwood were favored by furniture makers, and veneering was used extensively on chairs.

In Germany, Austria, and parts of Sweden, Biedermeier furniture appeared in prosperous middle-class homes. This style, often seen as a complete contrast to Empire, was actually born out of it and was similarly characterized by classical simplicity. Chairs had curved legs, sofas had rolled arms, and both received generous upholstery. The accent was on light-colored woods such as maple, cherry, and pear. A noted Viennese cabinetmaker, Benedikt Holl, also drew inspiration from Sheraton to develop his own Biedermeier style.

THE BIRTH OF ECLECTICISM
The general Empire style actually sparked a series of mix-and-match styles that harked back to various forms and decorations from the past. The style of furniture design during the reigns of Louis-Philippe in France (1830–48) and

This gilded chair was designed in the style of Sheraton in 1795.

Carlo Alberto in Savoy (1831–48) was a fusion of Baroque, Gothic, and neoclassicism. The vogue was for softer, curvaceous furniture, and carved and relief friezes. This moved into the Second Empire style, which further developed the eclecticism of the Louis-Philippe style. A similar fusing of styles occurred elsewhere. In Italy furniture combined Baroque and Gothic with Greek, Chinese, and Babylonian motifs. Makers employed all manner of imitation, and exotic ornamentation and lavish upholstery were also very much in vogue.

The originality of Italian furniture declined and in the late 19th century the Umbertino style (after King Umberto) confused many styles, but was predominantly neo-Renaissance (although the makers stuck to a somber, heavy look). At the same time, in England and Germany they turned back to the styles of the Middle Ages, evoking their nations' most glorious eras with Romanesque and Gothic designs.

The late 19th century saw a revolution in technology and mechanization that provided simple alternatives to time-consuming crafts like wood carving. This was to have a huge impact on the styles of furniture in the future, although some designers were more favorably disposed to the advances than others.

187

All-purpose workbench

Intermediate

A sound and sturdy workbench is essential in order to achieve the best possible results in your woodworking. As such it is advisable to make this workbench one of your first major projects. The joints are basic mortise-and-tenon joints, held secure with dowels and bolts. A well-constructed workbench will serve as a good investment for the future.

Tools

- Jack plane
- Straightedge
- Marking gauge
- Hand saw
- Mortise gauge
- C-clamps
- Power drill and ⅛-in., 3/16-in., ¼-in., ⅜-in., ¾-in., and countersink bits
- ⅜-in. and ¾-in. mortise chisel
- 1¼-in. firmer or paring chisel
- Tenon saw
- Sash clamps
- Sanding block
- Screwdriver
- Wrench
- Electric router with ½-in. straight bit

Skills required for project

- Measuring and marking *pages 64–7*
- Basic sawing *pages 68–71*
- Planing *pages 74–81*
- Fine sawing *pages 82–5*
- Chiseling *pages 86–9*
- Making grooves *pages 90–3*
- Drilling *pages 96–100*
- Making mortise-and-tenon joints *pages 104–9*
- Making dado joints *pages 110–11*
- Using abrasives *pages 115–17*
- Assembling projects *pages 120–7*
- Using adhesives *pages 128–9*
- Wood finishing *pages 130–5*

MATERIALS

Part	Materials and dimensions	No.
	Solid wood: softwood can be used for the underframe, but hardwood is needed for the backboard and the worktop.	
Underframe		
Legs	35⅝ x 3 x 2½ in.	4
Cross-rails	24 x 3 x 2½ in.	4
Front/back rails	52 x 3 x 1¼ in.	2
Backboard	60 x 8 x 1¼ in.	1
Worktop	60 x 12 in.	1
	Plywood	
Tool well	60 x 12⅝ x ½ in.	1

Other materials: eight 15 x ⅜ in. bolts/nuts/washers; ten 1-in. 8 gauge flat head screws; four 2-in. 8 gauge flat head screws; four 3 x ⅜-in. coach screws with washers; woodworker's vice; adhesive (PVA); sandpaper (120-grit); finish (oil).

1 Prepare the wood by cutting and planing all components to size. Apply face and side marks. Wood that is already planed is available to buy.

Making the underframe

2 The first parts of the bench to be made are the two end frames, which consist of the front and back legs and two cross-rails each. These are held together with wedged mortise-and-tenon joints.

3 Begin by measuring up 4 in. from the bottom of one leg and square a line around the wood in order to represent the top of the cross-rails. Mark a second line on the face edge 3 in. down from this point and square as before. A mortise will be set out between these lines with a ⅜-in. shoulder.

4 To make the shoulder, measure in ⅜ in. from the marked out lines and square around all faces of the leg. Set a mortise gauge to scribe a ¾-in. wide mortise between the shoulder lines.

5 Set out a second mortise of the same dimensions for the top cross-rail on the same face. The top edge of the rails will be level with the top of the legs. Mark the other three legs.

6 Hold each leg in turn face up on a firm flat surface with a C-clamp. Use a power drill with a ¾-in. bit, and drill out the mortise, removing the bulk of the waste. Take care to drill in the center of the mortise and keep the drill straight. Drill approximately halfway from both sides. Clean out the waste with the ¾-in. mortise chisel, by cutting back to the shoulder lines from the center of the mortise. Pare the sides with a 1¼-in. firmer or paring chisel. Work from both sides of the leg, cutting a little at a time back to the set-out lines.

7 To cut the tenons, mark the shoulders by squaring a line around the four cross-rails 3 in. in from both ends. Using the already-set mortise gauge, gauge the tenons toward each end, down and back to the shoulder line.

8 Hold each in turn firmly on edge in a vice or on a saw stool and cut the tenons using a tenon saw. Clean up the face of the tenons with a sharp chisel. Remove ⅜ in. off each edge of the tenons to reduce its width to match the mortises. Check for fit and adjust as required.

9 The mortise-and-tenon joints are secured with wedges. Place a saw cut for the wedge along the tenons ³/₈ in. from each edge, and approximately two-thirds the length of the tenons. You can either make the wedges out of the waste from the tenon (as shown here) or cut them from another waste piece of wood.

Mark the wedges that will be cut from each edge and make a saw cut into which they will be secured.

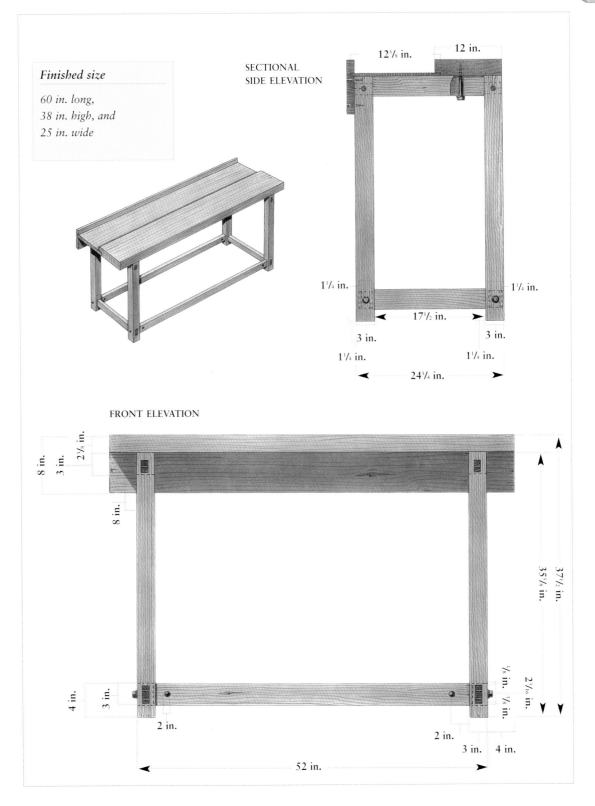

Finished size

60 in. long,
38 in. high, and
25 in. wide

SECTIONAL
SIDE ELEVATION

12⁵/₈ in.   12 in.

1¹/₄ in.   1¹/₄ in.

17¹/₂ in.

3 in.   3 in.

1¹/₄ in.   1¹/₄ in.

24³/₄ in.

FRONT ELEVATION

2⁷/₈ in.

8 in.   3 in.

8 in.

37¹/₂ in.

35⁵/₈ in.

²/₁₆ in.

⅛ in.   ⅛ in.

4 in.   3 in.

2 in.

2 in.

3 in.   4 in.

52 in.

189

10 Dry fit each end frame. If satisfactory, they may now be glued with PVA. Do not use an adhesive that is brittle when set because the joint will be subjected to a lot of vibration. Apply the adhesive to the tenons and place in their respective mortises.

Fit each end frame together.

11 Place one of the frames in a pair of sash clamps and apply a light pressure. Check that the rails are parallel and the whole frame is square and not in wind. Adjust the job as needed so that the frame is true. Tighten the clamps and recheck. Lay a straightedge along the rail across each leg to make sure the joint is flat. The sash clamps may need to be adjusted to correct any faults. Repeat with the other frame.

12 Once the adhesive is dry, clean up the faces with the plane, and 120-grit sandpaper and sanding block. Cut any excess length off at the top to finish flush with the rail.

Making the front and back cross-rails

13 Next, you will need to mark and cut the mortises for the front and back cross-rails, which will join the two end frames together. These have a stopped mortise-and-tenon joint that is secured by a nut and bolt. Set these out as

before on the face side of the legs using the measurements on the drawing on page 189. The mortise only needs to be chiseled out ⅜ in. wide and ⅜ in. deep. Cut the 3 x 1¼-in. rails 52 in. long, and set out the stopped tenons on each end ⅜ in. long. Fit each into the corresponding mortise and adjust as required.

14 Drill a ⅜-in. hole right through the leg from the outside to correspond with the center of the mortise just cut. Hold the rail in its mortise and place the drill back in the hole. Start the drill to make the location on the end of the rail. Remove the rail and drill the hole in the end 2¾ in. deep.

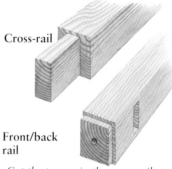

Cross-rail

Front/back rail

Cut the tenons in the cross-rails and the front and back rails.

15 Lay the rail flat and set out a mortise 2 in. in from the shoulder, ⅜ in. wide and approximately ¾ in. high to allow for fitting the nut. Chisel this deep enough so that the bolt will align correctly with the thread of the nut.

16 Fix each rail in place by putting the nut and a washer into the mortise. Position the rail and insert the bolt with the washer through the leg into the end of the rail. Tighten with a wrench and check to make sure it is square.

Fix the lower rails to the end frames with a nut and bolt.

Making the backboard

17 Next, make the backboard, which is 8 x 1¼ in. and set at the same height as the front work surface. Set up a router to cut a ½ in. wide groove ⁵⁄₁₆ in. deep and down 1⅞ in. from the top edge. Secure the board on a flat surface and run the groove.

18 Fit the backboard to the back of the underframe. Cut the backboard to 60 in. long and set out a dado joint 4 in. in from each end to attach to the back legs. Square these lines from the groove down and across the bottom edge. Gauge the dado ⁵⁄₁₆ in. deep between the lines. Cut the dado with a tenon saw, or with the router, which should already be set at the correct depth.

Components of back of bench.

Screw the four uprights into the cross-pieces to make each leg.

14 Next, decide on the length of the horizontal beams. Check with local building codes as to any regulations specifying span or section sizes. Allow for an 8-in. overhang past each leg and cut them to length. Finish off with bevels cut on the top edges.

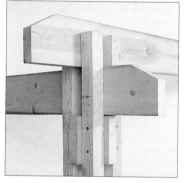

The horizontal beams overhang the uprights and have beveled edges.

15 Lay the beams flat on a sawhorse and sight along the wood to detect any bowing. If bowing is evident, place the bowed edge as the top edge. Mark and cut the bevel on the top edge with a power saw. Apply a finish as required.

16 Finally, install the uprights by drilling additional holes in the baseplate for bolting down or setting them into a concrete footing.

Feature table   Intermediate

This is an interesting and unusual feature table that is constructed from solid wood. It shows the wood to excellent effect and, with its glass top, gives an open visual space, which creates a useful display area. Its simple and effective appearance requires the marking and cutting of extremely fine dovetail dado joints.

Tools

Smoothing plane

Straightedge

Winding sticks

Steel square

Power saw

Marking gauge

C-clamps

Hand saw

$\frac{1}{2}$-in. and $1\frac{3}{16}$-in. chisels

Marking knife

Tenon saw

Router

Miter square

Drill and $\frac{1}{8}$-in., $\frac{3}{16}$-in., and countersink bits

Screwdriver

Skills required for project

Measuring and marking
pages 64–7

Basic sawing *pages 68–71*

Planing *pages 74–81*

Fine sawing *pages 82–5*

Chiseling *pages 86–9*

Making grooves *pages 90–3*

Making dovetail joints
pages 112–14

Using abrasives
pages 115–17

Assembling projects
pages 120–7

Using adhesives
pages 128–9

Wood finishing
pages 130–5

MATERIALS		
Part	**Materials and dimensions**	**No.**
	Any stable hardwood—elm was used here	
Structural shelf	36 x 26 x 1 in.	1
Legs	18 x 13 x 1¼ in.	4

Other materials: one 40 x 20 x ⁵⁄₁₆ or ⅜-in. toughened glass top with polished edges; eight furniture glides; eight self-adhesive clear plastic buffers; four 2-in. 8 gauge flat head screws; adhesive; sandpaper (150-grit); finish.

The waste wood is represented by the shaded area in the diagram below.

Mark the legs. The shaded area shows the waste wood and the double lines the dovetail joint.

1 Prepare the lumber for the shelf and legs, which must be dry and stable. If you are unable to find boards wide enough, you may need to join strips together, ensuring that the grain direction is as near quarter-sawn as possible (see box top right).

2 Plane the wood's face side, face edge, width, and thickness. Test with a straightedge, winding sticks and try square. Plane all pieces true as required. Apply face-side and face-edge marks.

Making the legs

3 First, make the table legs. To determine the height of the legs, use a pencil and steel square to square two lines across the legs 18 in. apart on the face edge. Hold the material firmly in place on a pair of sawhorses and cut each leg to length using a power saw.

4 Next, mark the slots in the legs into which the shelf will fit. Square a line across the face of one leg 10 in. up from the bottom and then another 1 in. up to take the thickness of the shelf. Repeat on the other legs.

5 The shelf is held in place in dovetail dadoes, with ³⁄₁₆ in. high dovetails. Set out two more lines on the legs ³⁄₁₆ in. in from the two lines already marked out in step 4. Square all lines around the edge back to the other face.

6 Next, square a line 3¾ in. from the inside edge to mark the wood that will be removed from the bottom inside corner of the legs.

7 Now, remove the waste wood from each leg—lay them flat on a pair of sawhorses and hold firm with a C-clamp. Use a tenon saw to remove the waste from the corners.

8 Next, cut the waste away from the slots, remembering to leave ³⁄₁₆ in. at the top and bottom to make the dovetail joint marked out in step 5. Use the tenon saw and then a ½ in. chisel to remove the waste.

9 To cut the dovetails, score a line with a marking knife on the existing set-out lines on each leg. The dovetail pitch must match the router bit you are going to use to cut the dado in the shelf. Hold the leg firm on a flat surface and cut down on the waste side of the line the required

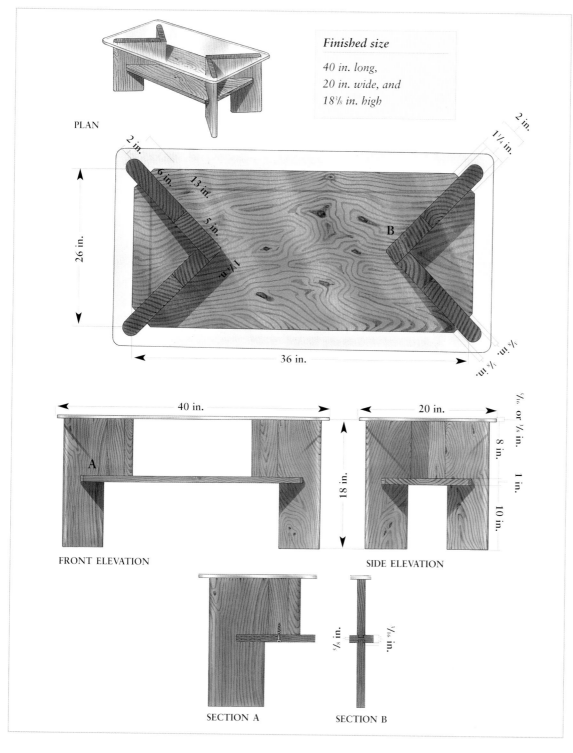

PLAN

Finished size

40 in. long,
20 in. wide, and
18⅛ in. high

2 in.

2 in.   1¼ in.

13 in.

5 in.

B

26 in.

36 in.

⅝ in.

⅝ in.

40 in.

A

18 in.

FRONT ELEVATION

20 in.

⁵⁄₁₆ or ⅜ in.

8 in.

1 in.

10 in.

SIDE ELEVATION

SECTION A

⅝ in.

³⁄₁₆ in.

SECTION B

Joining solid wood to make a wide board

It is often necessary to join several strips to make a wide board of solid wood. A suitably wide plank may not be available, or the grain direction in through and through-cut planks may make them unsuitable because of the likely movement of the wood. When joining strips, ensure that they are perfectly square, straight, and flat. It is advisable to have some form of jointing method between the faces to be glued, such as tongues in grooves or dowels. To ensure that the board stays flat, it is essential to place sash clamps on both the top and bottom faces.

depth with a tenon saw. Take care not to damage any wood on the other side of the line as this will be difficult to hide and will look unsightly. Remove the waste from the dovetail with a 1³⁄₁₆ in. chisel. Chisel at an angle in order to make the pitch of the dovetail.

Make the dovetail for each dado joint.

Making the shelf

10 Next mark, cut, and plane the shelf to size. Cut each corner at a 45-degree angle. The length of the cut is equal to the thickness of the leg—1¼ in. plus an extra ⅜ in. each side.

197

11 Now, cut the dovetail dadoes in the shelf. Make a router template (jig) from a piece of manufactured board. The slot up the center will need to match the collar and bit for your router. Set the bit to cut ³⁄₁₆ in. deep into the surface of the shelf. As always when routing, test-run a cut in scrap lumber to ensure the set-up is correct.

Make a router template or jig.

12 Fix a stop under the jig so that the router will cut the dado 11 in. long. When the jig is set correctly, lay it on the surface of the shelf and secure it at a 45-degree angle at the corner with a C-clamp. Before cutting, check it again with a miter square. Rest the router on the template. Start it up and slowly move the bit into the work. Keep the collar against the left-hand side of the slot, pushing the router forward to the end. Move the router across the end of the slot and pull it back toward you, ensuring the collar stays against the right-hand side of the slot. Repeat this on all four corners of the shelf top.

Rest the router on the template and cut the slot carefully.

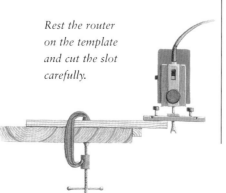

13 Adjust the stop on the template so that the router will only cut a dado 5¾ in. long. Turn the shelf over and cut the bottom dado in the same way.

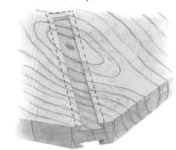

Turn the shelf over and make the dovetail dado in the other side.

14 Before you assemble the table you will need to fix the internal corners where the two pairs of legs meet. Cut 1¼ in. off one of each pair so that when they are slotted into place, the shorter leg can butt up against the longer leg.

15 Check the fit of the joints and adjust as required. Sand and apply a first coat of finish to all components, masking the joint areas.

16 To assemble, slide one long leg into its dado and apply adhesive to the edge that its matching leg will butt up against. Slide in the second leg and press together firmly. Apply adhesive to the butted edges only, not in the dovetail dado.

Slide the leg into the dado.

17 Remove any excess adhesive with a damp cloth before it is set. When dry, turn the table over and screw each leg in place from underneath the shelf. Drill a ³⁄₁₆-in. hole through the shelf followed by a ⅛-in. pilot hole into the leg. Countersink the top of the hole and insert the screw in place.

Fix the legs in place with a screw.

Use a power drill to fix the screws in place.

18 Sand the table with 150-grit sandpaper and apply the wood finish of your choice.

19 Fix two furniture glides to the bottom of each leg. At the top of the legs, position small, clear self-adhesive plastic buffers to prevent the glass top from sliding. The glass top must be manufactured from tempered glass, with all the edges ground and polished by a specialized glazier. Do not use standard glass for this purpose.

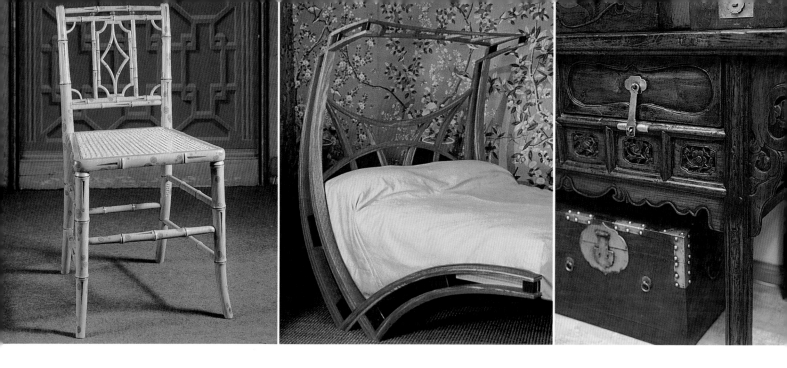

Oriental influences

The Orient has always fascinated those in the West, presumably because the culture is so very different, and Eastern furniture-making styles and techniques have often exerted an influence.

TRADE OPENS UP THE WAY

During the 16th century there was much exploration of the Far East undertaken by Western European countries. They learned about lacquerwork and took East Asian objects of art back home with them. However, it was not until the 17th century that Portugal, Holland, and England established regular trading relations with India and China. Lacquered furniture and domestic goods were imported from the East, where Asian craftsmen also created pseudo-European styles based on designs that were supplied by visiting traders. During this time there were two main styles within Indo-European furniture—Indo-Portuguese, which included furniture decorated with inlaid bone or ivory on ebony and other dark woods, and Indo-Dutch, distinguished by its production of light-colored wooden furniture with inlaid bone, incised and lacquered, as well as ebony furniture carved with flower shapes.

By the end of the 17th century Oriental decorative tastes were being widely imitated in Europe, and Chinese taste was particularly in vogue. Heavy tropical woods were also imported to Europe, which was used to fashion furniture in Oriental styles. Lacquerwork became so desirable that European craftsmen developed a technique for imitating lacquer known as japanning. During the latter part of the 17th century and the beginning of the 18th century many European countries experimented with methods of creating lacquer. None came close to the excellence of Oriental resins, but various gums and bitumens were used to create different types of varnishes.

TWISTS ON ORIENTALISM

The style reached its peak around 1750 in what could be called a craze for all things Oriental, when high-gloss lacquer and painted scenes and designs took over from marquetry, gilding, and carved work. By this time the Oriental style had evolved and rather than simply trying to imitate everything within Chinese and Indian art, including the figures, shapes, and imported lacquers, a more relaxed and playful Anglo-Chinese style emerged. This was the Rococo's twist on Chinese style—pagodas, exotic birds, and animals such as monkeys, European figures, icicles, and dripping water were all used as decoration within this style. Included in this transformation was a wide range of background colors. Whereas traditional Oriental products usually use black, brown, and gold, the European examples included scarlet, yellow, white, blue, and green.

USES OF LACQUER

The different ways that lacquer was used in Europe reflects varying tastes between the 17th and 18th centuries. In the late 17th century it was mainly used to decorate the cases of cabinets that were set upon carved Baroque bases. In the 18th century, however, lacquered secretaries, clocks, and tea tables were all fashionable in England and Germany, while in Italy and France chests of drawers and corner cabinets were also lacquered. Even whole sets of lacquer-decorated furniture existed. When there

OPPOSITE LEFT *A beechwood chair shaped and painted to imitate bamboo, from the Royal Pavilion, Brighton.* ◆ OPPOSITE CENTER *A contemporary bed design by Robin Furlong.* ◆ OPPOSITE RIGHT *An ornate 19th-century Chinese table.* ◆ ABOVE LEFT *A 19th-century Chinese armchair.* ◆ ABOVE CENTER *A carved iron lock on a Japanese cabinet.* ◆ ABOVE RIGHT *The highly polished finish enhances the smooth lines of this Japanese-style table.*

was a resurgence of enthusiasm for Oriental motifs in Britain in the mid-18th century, Thomas Chippendale (see page 173), instigated a Chinese Chippendale style—furniture with pagoda surmounts, fretwork and bamboo interlacing.

In the early 19th century the change of taste toward the plainer, classical style meant that lacquered furniture declined. However, as the Regency style took hold there was a resurgence in interest in the whole area of Chinese taste (see page 187 on the Brighton Pavilion), and it continued to survive in Victorian England with the vogue in painted tin or toleware.

JAPANESE INFLUENCES

It was in the mid-19th century that trade was opened up with Japan. This country had not developed many specialized types of furniture as its interior architecture, with the garden as the focal point, served the aesthetic and social requirements. However, its lacquering far surpassed even the best Chinese examples. Edward Godwin pioneered the Anglo-Japanese style. He combined his interest in Japanese design with 18th-century ideas, which he found to be

The simple modern cupboard combines elements of traditional Ming with European style.

complementary. His favorite materials were ebonized wood, Japanese leather paper, and bamboo, and he embraced simplicity and lightness in his work.

In the 1880s the Japanese craze of the 19th century reached its height and there were many oddities such as spindly furniture and lacquer applied to the most inappropriate pieces of furniture. During this decade and the next, Orientalism was particularly dominant in America. Near Eastern objects, as well as those from China and Japan, were chosen for smoking rooms. The "Turkish corner" became an important part of American household—this was an arrangement of pillows, Oriental rugs and a divan in a corner of a room under a canopy, with plants and exotic accessories completing the scene.

By the start of the 20th century, creating lacquer had become a part of the chemical industry, but an interest in traditional Oriental techniques nevertheless remained. The Irish born designer Eileen Gray learned the Japanese tradition of lacquer and undertook meticulous experiments, achieving extraordinary tones. Her screens and panels were widely exhibited at the time and influenced later lacquer artists and styles, such as Art Deco.

Circular plant stand   Intermediate

The elegant curves on this plant stand are produced by turning the wood on a lathe. There are two main turning methods—faceplate turning and between-center turning. This project will give you a chance to practice both because the top and bottom of the plant stand are turned on a faceplate while the connecting spindles are turned between center.

Tools

Bandsaw

Lathe with faceplate and between-center capacity

Full face shield

Set of turning tools

Smoothing plane or hand saw (optional)

Calipers

Three-jaw chuck

Lathe drill

Clamps

Skills required for project

Measuring and marking *pages 64–7*

Basic sawing *pages 68–71*

Drilling *pages 96–100*

Making dado joints *pages 110–11*

Using abrasives *pages 115–17*

Assembling projects *pages 120–7*

Using adhesives *pages 128–9*

Wood finishing *pages 130–5*

Turning *pages 142–5*

MATERIALS		
Part	**Materials and dimensions**	**No.**
	Solid wood, preferably hardwood	
Round balks	10½ in. diameter x 2 in. thick	2
Spindles	12 in. long x 5½ in. diameter	2
Connecting piece	6 in. long x 2¼ in. diameter	1
Other materials: adhesive; sandpaper; finish.		

If you purchased your wood from a specialty supplier, it may be a slice of a log where the grain travels from face to face. If you purchased it from a lumberyard it is likely to have come from a sawed board and therefore the grain will run lengthwise along the board.

Wood balks with different grain directions.

Making the top and bottom

1 First, mark out the circumference of the top and bottom of the plant stand on each balk. Use a bandsaw to shape the wood to approximately ¼ in. bigger than this circumference.

2 To make the top, select the best face of one of the balks and screw it onto the faceplate. Remember that you are going to make a rim ⅝ in. deep on the top and so ensure the screws do not project into the wood beyond ½ in.

Fix the balk face to the faceplate.

3 Mount the faceplate on the machine and adjust the tool rest just under halfway from the center.

4 Ensure that the plate runs freely and make some marks to give you a guide to the curved base and the center hole that you will be turning. Making sure that you are wearing a full face shield for protection, start the lathe and begin your cut with the roughing gouge.

5 First, follow your markings to shape the end of the balk into what will become the joint with the spindle in step 18 (see drawing opposite). Turn a flat surface in order to produce the shoulder of the joint and then turn the large hole that will accept the spindles in the center.

6 Next, turn curve A (see section on drawing opposite), placing the tool rest at an angle across the corner of the piece as you work. Since the top and bottom are the same up to this stage, turn the bottom in the same way.

Turn the curve on the stand top.

7 Next, you will need to turn the outside face of the top and bottom sections of the stand. Begin by fixing the shoulder face of the top to the faceplate. Make sure that it

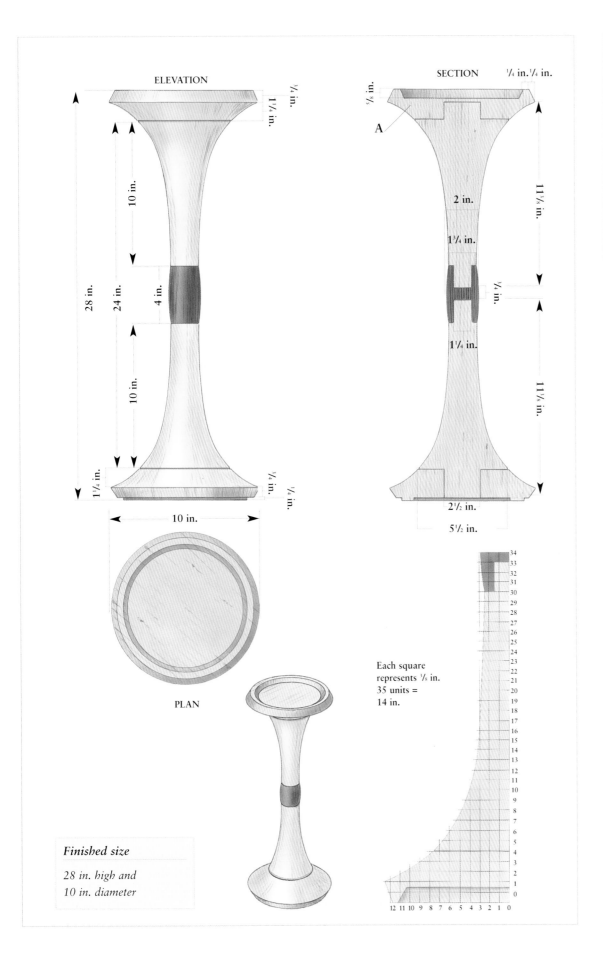

ELEVATION

¼ in.

1¼ in.

10 in.

4 in.

28 in.

24 in.

10 in.

1¼ in.

¼ in.

¼ in.

10 in.

PLAN

SECTION

¼ in. ¼ in.

⅝ in.

A

2 in.

11⅜ in.

1¾ in.

¼ in.

1¼ in.

11⅛ in.

2½ in.

5½ in.

Each square
represents ⅛ in.
35 units =
14 in.

34
33
32
31
30
29
28
27
26
25
24
23
22
21
20
19
18
17
16
15
14
13
12
11
10
9
8
7
6
5
4
3
2
1
0

12 11 10 9 8 7 6 5 4 3 2 1 0

Finished size

*28 in. high and
10 in. diameter*

Turning

*Wood turning began
with the invention
of the lathe in Egypt
some time before the
13th century AD. It
was practiced widely
by the Egyptians,
Assyrians, and Romans
and also flourished
throughout medieval
England. Turned chairs
with triangular seats
were made of
indigenous woods
from Norman times
through the 17th
century with little
change and turners
were one of the earliest
types of craftsmen.
Before the end of the
16th century, turners
had produced legs,
posts, balusters, and
spindles; turned
decoration on furniture
was widely used during
the Renaissance period.
Turners really came into
their own in the 17th
century when they
began to produce
graceful columns.
From the 19th century
onward, more complex
spiral turnings appeared
as a result of the
development in turning
tools. However, classic,
simpler styles, such as
bobbin and ball
turnings, have also
retained their popularity.*

is centered on the faceplate by checking that the overhang on the work is even all the way around. Screw into position and replace on the lathe.

8 Turn a small bevel on the outside edge of the top. Then carefully turn out the center recess, ensuring it is flat.

9 Take the top off the faceplate and fix the bottom of the plant stand in place. Turn a small bevel on the outside edge, a rim on the bottom surface, and a shallow recess, as shown below. It is better not to have a flat base because this may later distort.

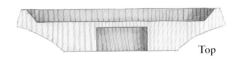

Top

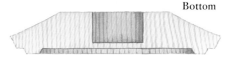

Bottom

The finished shape of the top and bottom of the stand.

Making the spindles

This stand has been designed with two upright pieces with a joint in between, in case the lathe does not have the required length to turn the center spindle in one. If your lathe has the length capacity, you can turn the centre spindle as one. If your lathe will not accept a 5½ in. diameter, the curve can be adjusted to suit.

10 Mark the center at each end of one piece. Fix one end to the driving center in the headstock, with the other end held in the tailstock with a revolving center.

11 It can be helpful, if you have the equipment, to saw or plane the square into an octagon; this means less material to remove. It is possible, however, to turn from a square shape as long as you are very careful.

It is easiest to cut the spindle to an octagon shape before turning.

12 Adjust the tool rest, making sure that the revolving wood will not be in contact with it; very carefully start initial cuts that will remove corners and make the work cylindrical.

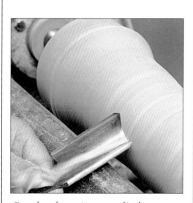

Cut the shape into a cylinder.

13 Make a template from the grid given with the drawing on page 209 so that you can measure off diameters needed at any stage easily.

14 Set the calipers to the thickest end and turn down to the correct diameter. Do the same at the thinner end. Turn along the full length until you achieve the required shape.

15 Both ends need to be turned down to fit into the holes— the thick end into the top or bottom of the stand and the thin end into the connecting piece. Repeat process on second piece.

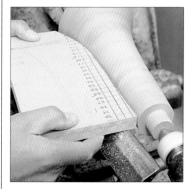

The bottom half of the spindle.

Ensure that you are cutting the right shape by using a template.

16 First, turn the connecting piece to a simple cylinder and then turn the shape of the outside.

Shape the connecting piece.

17 Hold the piece in a three-jaw chuck, and drill or turn the holes that will accept the spindles.

Assembly

18 The parts can now be assembled. Join the two spindles to the connecting piece, applying adhesive and then clamping. The top and bottom of the stand can now be fixed; glue and clamp these in place.

19 When the adhesive has cured, the whole piece can be sanded down and you can apply required finish.

Barstool Intermediate

This is a good introductory project for combining metal with more

traditional wood construction. The metal legs and wooden seat give

the stool a pleasing look and are not difficult to achieve.

Tools

Protractor

Sliding bevel

Jigsaw

Chisel

Drill and ³⁄₁₆-in., ⅛-in., ¼-in., and countersunk bits

Hacksaw

Smoothing plane

Metal file

Screwdriver

Skills required for project

Measuring and marking *pages 64–7*

Basic sawing *pages 68–71*

Planing *pages 74–81*

Chiseling *pages 86–9*

Drilling *pages 90–3*

Making half lap joints *pages 101–3*

Making mortise-and-tenon joints *pages 104–9*

Using abrasives *pages 115–17*

Assembling projects *pages 120–7*

Using adhesives *pages 128–9*

Wood finishing *pages 130–5*

Using metals and plastics *pages 146–7*

MATERIALS		
Part	Materials and dimensions	No.
Solid wood		
Side and cross-rails	16 x 3 x ¾ in.	4
Slats	16 x 2 x ½ in.	11
Footrest	12 x 2 x 1½ in.	1
V-supports	20 x 2 x ¾ in.	2

Other materials: four 24 x 1-in. diameter steel tube legs; one 12 x 1-in. diameter cross-bar; two 16 x 1¼ x ⅛ in. flat bars; thirty-six 1½-in. 6 gauge brass flat head screws; four 1¼ x ¼ in. nuts and bolts; eight 2 x ¼ in. bolts plus barrel nuts; wooden dowels; sandpaper; adhesive; finish.

1 First, make the basic seat unit. Mark out the two side rails. The sloping back is at an angle of 65 degrees; set this out with a protractor and sliding bevel. Measure along the bottom edge 13½ in. and mark a second beveled line at an angle of 85 degrees. Set out the curved shape on the top edge and cut with a jigsaw. Clean up edges with sandpaper.

Mark and cut the side rails.

2 Next, mark the front and back cross-rails, first cutting the mortises into which the side rails will fit and then the shaped ends that will receive the metal tube. Cut the shape with a jigsaw as per the drawing on the right and clean up the edges with sandpaper. Chisel from both sides.

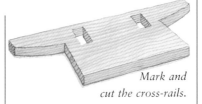

Mark and cut the cross-rails.

3 Insert the side rails through the mortises in the cross-rails. The mortises are cut so that the front of the side rail will pass through the rear mortises but each will notch into its place. Ensure that the frame is square.

Assemble the base of the seat.

4 Next, make the slats, which will go across the base to make the seat. Cut the 11 slats as shown in the drawing on the right, rounding the ends of the front slat first and shaping the

others to fit. Drill ³⁄₁₆-in screw holes through the slats and then the ⅛-in. pilot hole in the side rail. Assemble the seat dry with flat head brass screws.

Position the slats to make the seat.

Part-assembly of the seat.

5 Cut the metal legs to 24 in. long with a hacksaw. Insert wooden dowels in the tubes to prevent the bolts from crushing them. Drill holes in the top of each leg to accept the two fixing bolts. Mark from these onto the side of the cross-rails and drill them to accept the bolts and barrel nuts.

Assemble the seat unit.

16 in.

3¼ in.

3¼ in.

3 in.

2 in.

4 in.

3 in.

side rail

vertical
support

26 in.

1¼ in.

stretcher

8 in.

SIDE ELEVATION

12 in.

cross-rail

¾ in.   5 in.   ¾ in.

8 in.

footrest

FRONT ELEVATION

slat

15 in.

PLAN

Finished size

*26 in. high, 15 in. wide,
and 16 in. deep*

6 Next, turn your attention to the bottom half of the stool. Mark the holes for the stretchers in the lower legs 8 in. up and drill them, ensuring that they are in line with the holes that fix the seat.

7 Cut two metal stretchers from the flat bar to 16 in. and round the ends with a file. Mark four holes in each as shown on the drawing on page 213 and drill them. Drill corresponding ¼-in. holes through the legs. Fix the stretchers in position and secure with nuts and bolts.

8 Cut the footrest to length and plane it to shape, ensuring that the angles are correct so that it fits between the two metal side rails.

Assemble the stretchers and footrest.

9 Now, make the cross-bar, which goes across the middle between the two metal stretchers. Mark and cut the tube to fit; remember that the ends will need to be angled to fit against the stretchers. Insert wood dowels in the ends of the tube and screw the cross-bar in place.

10 Next, glue the basic seat frame together, making sure that the components are located correctly. Screw the seat slats in position one by one and then bolt the top ends of the legs to the cross-rails.

Fix the legs to the seat unit.

11 With the stool upside down, bolt the stretchers to the legs and then screw into the footrest and cross-bar.

12 Next, make the feet. You can finish the metal legs with plastic caps on the tubes. Or, you can use leftover wood to make plugs to fit inside the tube.

Use plastic leg caps or wood plugs to finish the feet.

13 Place the stool upright on a flat surface. Using a pencil on a small block of wood, mark all around the bottom of the legs to show where to angle them at the base so that the stool sits on a flat surface.

Angle the feet so that the stool will sit on a flat surface.

14 Cut to these marks and then work a small bevel around the cut edge. Sand so the edges are not damaged.

15 To ensure that the structure is rigid, make the V-support between the cross-rails and the bottom cross-bar. The two supports are different, and so measure, mark, and label each individually. With the stool assembled, mark the top angle that will connect with the inside face of the cross-rails, and mark the position of the bottom cross-bar.

16 Drill a hole in the V-support to accommodate the cross-bar. Remove the cross-bar from the stool, position both supports and replace it. Check the angled faces against the inside faces of the cross-rails and adapt as necessary.

17 Next, mark the half lap joint between the two supports as they fit over the bar. Dismantle, cut the half laps and glue the supports together.

Assemble the V-support.

18 Clean up the supports and replace them and the cross-bar on the stool. Fix the angled faces to the inside faces of the seat cross-rails with adhesive and screws.

19 Disassemble, sand and finish all wood parts; then reassemble to complete.

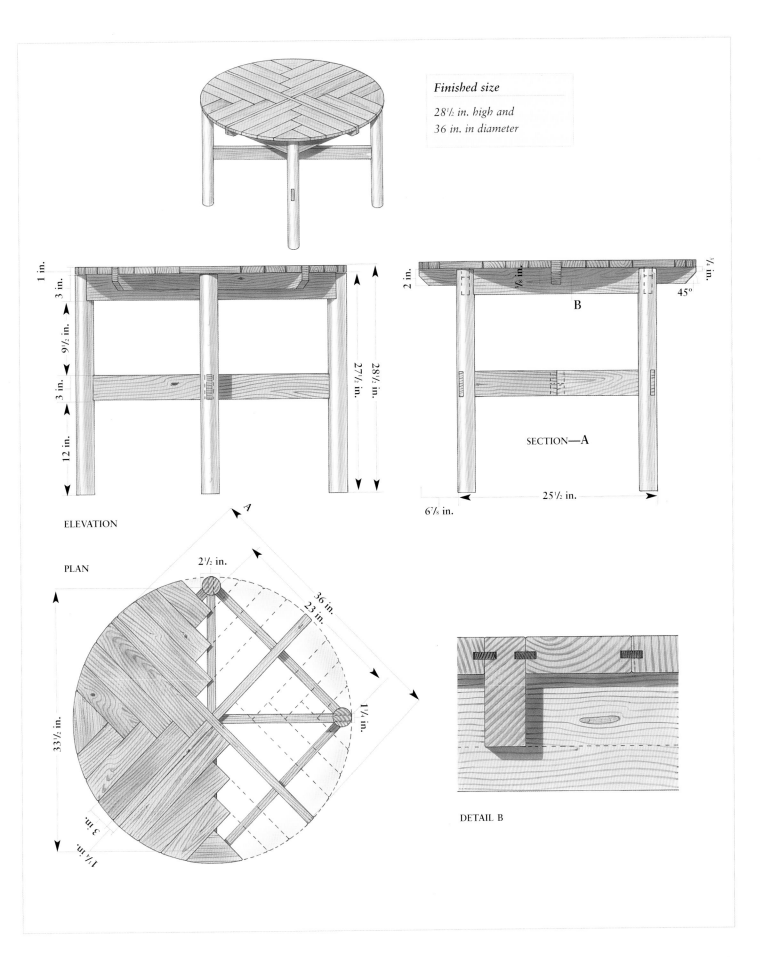

Finished size

28½ in. high and
36 in. in diameter

1 in.

3 in.

9½ in.

3 in.

12 in.

28½ in.

27½ in.

ELEVATION

PLAN

2 in.

¾ in.

⅜ in.

45°

B

SECTION—A

25½ in.

6⅞ in.

A

2½ in.

36 in.

23 in.

1¼ in.

33½ in.

3 in.

1¼ in.

DETAIL B

219

6 Now, make the legs round. If turning, you will need a lathe with a long enough bed to accept the length needed; it may make turning easier if the mortises are temporarily filled with softwood plugs inserted dry. If planing, mark the final round on each end and carefully plane the octagon round. The pencil marks on the ends will give you a good guide as to how the rounding is proceeding. Repeat the process to make the other legs round.

7 Next, prepare the four top rails by marking shoulder lengths and the stopped tenons. Square a line around the rail 1³/₁₆ in. in from one end, another 21 in. along, and then 1³/₁₆ in. for the tenon. Cut to length on the radial-arm saw. Square the shoulder lines all around the first rail with a marking knife. Set up the mortise gauge to the width of the mortise—¹/₂ in.—and ³/₈ in. in from each face. Scribe the tenon around the rail from shoulder to shoulder line. Hold vertically in a vice and cut down the sides of the tenon on the waste side to the shoulder lines.

8 Remove and lay flat against a bench hook and cut away the waste at the shoulder set-outs. Replace vertically in the vice. Pencil gauge the width of the tenon 2 in. in, and cut down the tenon to make the haunch. Remove the waste by cutting across the top edge between the shoulders. Remember to cut both haunches on the top edge. Test the fit and adjust as required. Repeat for the other top rails.

9 Cut a miter on the ends of the tenons to allow both rails to penetrate the full depth of the mortise. Measure the diagonals to check for square. Clamp the four legs and top rails together with sash clamps.

10 Prepare the two lower cross-rails. Lay each in turn across the diagonals and mark the shoulder lengths for the mortise-and-tenon joints with the legs from the dry assembled frame to ensure that the lengths are exact. Square the shoulder lines around each rail and mark the through tenons by scribing along the length with the already-set mortise gauge. Measure the distance between the shoulders and square a line around each rail ⁵/₈ in. either side of the center for the half lap joint. Use the marking gauge to scribe the center of the face between all these squared lines. Remember to gauge from the face edge on both pieces.

11 Hold each cross-rail in a vice and cut the tenons. Lay flat and cross-cut the shoulders as for the top rails. Place vertically in the vice and cut the tenon to width to suit the mortise at the bottom of the leg.

12 Cut the half lap joint in the center of both rails. Secure horizontally in a vice and cut down the shoulder lines to the required depth with a tenon saw. Remove from vice and secure flat on the bench with a C-clamp. Remove the waste with a 1-in. chisel. Take out the bulk of the waste in one or two cuts from one side, and then work back to the gauge lines from both sides. Check the fit and adjust as required. Repeat on the other rail.

The legs, top rails, and lower cross-rails.

13 Assemble the whole underframe dry and check for square.

The dry assembled underframe.

Making the top cross-rails

14 Next, make the top cross-rails, which fit across the top of the top rails and form the main support for the tabletop planks. Prepare the cross-rails by marking them 36 in. long. Set out and cut the cross half lap joint in the center of this pair of rails in the same manner as the lower rails. The only difference is that these are 2 in. in width, and so the half lap will be 1 in. Assemble the two halves and check for square.

15 Next, measure and set out a 1³/₁₆ in. wide by 1 in. deep half lap in the center of each top rail. These should still be set up dry in the clamps. Position the two assembled cross-rails over these set-outs

and make sure they are square with an even overhang.

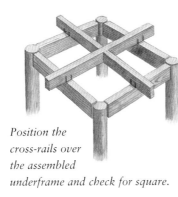

Position the cross-rails over the assembled underframe and check for square.

16 With a pencil, mark the top rail thickness on the underside of the assembled cross- rails. Square these marks up both faces at each end of the rails and use the marking gauge set at 1⁵⁄₁₆ in. to scribe the depth of the half laps from the top edge. The gauge can now scribe the depth of the half laps on the top rails ³⁄₈ in. deep. This will ensure that the top of these cross-rails sits flush with the other planks making up the tabletop. Cut the half laps as before.

Mark the thickness of the top rail on the assembled cross-rails.

17 Cut a 45-degree angle ³⁄₄ in. down from the top at each end of the cross-rails using the radial-arm saw.

18 Next, make the stopped grooves along the top of the two cross-rails, which will accept the tongues when you fit the planks for the top. Set up a ³⁄₈ x ³⁄₁₆-in. grooving bit in a router to run the groove ³⁄₈ in. down from the top edge. Disassemble the cross-rails and secure on edge in a vice so that the groove can be run on half the rail.

19 Run the groove on the rail and stop 1³⁄₁₆ in. from the end. Turn around and repeat on the other end and then repeat on the other face and on the other cross-rail.

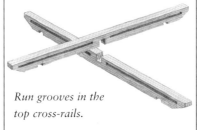

Run grooves in the top cross-rails.

20 Assemble the top cross-rails and place in position dry. Test all the work. If everything is satisfactory, disassemble, sand all the components with 120-grit sandpaper, and glue. Place in sash clamps and test for square and twist. Adjust the clamps as required to bring the frame true. Remove any excess adhesive with a damp cloth. When dry, remove any excess marks and apply a protective coat of finish.

Making the tabletop

21 Prepare the planks to the dimensions in the materials list. Take the four longest and rout grooves in the square ends and the sides from the face side to within 1³⁄₁₆ in. of the finished circular edge. Fit plywood tongues. Start to fit the planks into those rails as shown in the drawing on page 219.

Rout grooves in the tabletop planks and prepare plywood tongues.

22 Prepare and fit the remaining planks in order of descending length. The final segment over the top of the legs will have the grain running parallel with the top edge, so cut four triangles and mark them up to fit. Rout the grooves, fit the tongues, and place in position.

Slot the final triangle into place.

23 Number each board for each quadrant. Remove them and apply adhesive to the groove, edge, and end of each board. Place back into position and tap each on the end to bring up tight. If required, use a sash clamp to pull up the joint. Remove excess adhesive and check for flatness with a straightedge. Allow to dry.

24 Mark the circular shape of the tabletop with a pencil by either making a compass from a thin strip of plywood, or by using a piece of cord with a small nail tacked in the center. Trim the planks to the mark with a jigsaw.

25 True the edge with a belt sander or spokeshave. Flush the top with a try plane or orbital sander. Sand the top and apply a finish of your choice.

Breakfast tray   Intermediate

This breakfast tray will enable you to practice a traditional method, veneering by hand. It is a tricky skill at first, but if you do make mistakes, you can put them right by reheating the adhesive and relaying the veneer.

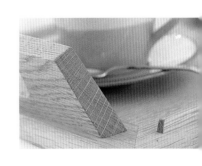

MATERIALS		
Part	Materials and dimensions	No.
	Manufactured board	
Base	20 x 15 x ¾ in.	1
	Solid wood	
Lips	20 x 1½ x 1 in.	2
	15 x 1½ x 1 in.	2
Handles	12 x 3 x 1 in.	2
Strips	16 x ⅝ x ⅜ in.	2
	Veneers	
Face	approximately 20 x 15 in.	1
Edge	the same species as the lips:	4
	2½ in. wide	
Underside	backing veneers required	1

Other materials: animal adhesive granules; glue pot and brush; adhesive (PVA); sandpaper; veneer tape; finish.

1 First, prepare the lips for all four edges of the main tray section, which will give the final size of 19 x 14 in. Plane all the lips, but leave their width over the size of the base's thickness. Trim the base to size to allow for the lips. Using a miter square, mark miters on the ends of the lips so that they fit exactly.

2 The lips are joined to the base with tongues and grooves. Cut the grooves in

Tools

Smoothing plane

Miter square

Router with ¼-in. straight bit

Tenon saw

Sash clamps

Toothing plane

Veneer hammer

Veneer knife

Electric iron

Straightedge

C-clamp

Drill and 1-in. bit

Coping saw

1-in. bevel-edged chisel

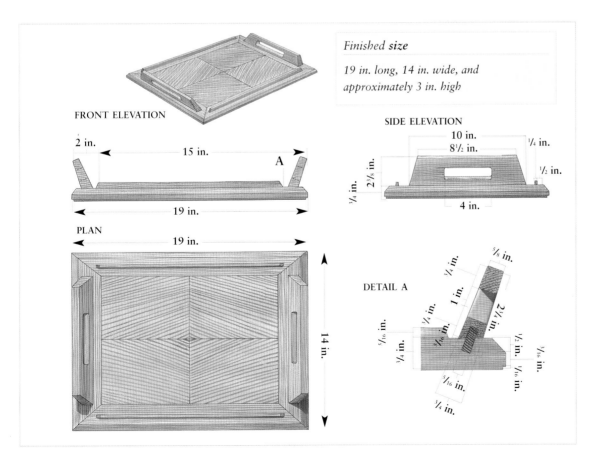

FRONT ELEVATION

2 in.   15 in.   A

19 in.

PLAN

19 in.

14 in.

Finished *size*

19 in. long, 14 in. wide, and approximately 3 in. high

SIDE ELEVATION

10 in.
8½ in.
¼ in.
½ in.
¾ in.
2⅜ in.
4 in.

DETAIL A

⅝ in.
¼ in.
1 in.
2¼ in.
¼ in.
¼ in.
⅝ in.
½ in.
³⁄₁₆ in.
³⁄₁₆ in.
⁵⁄₁₆ in.
¾ in.
⁵⁄₁₆ in.
¼ in.

Skills required for project

Measuring and marking *pages 64–7*

Planing *pages 74–81*

Fine sawing *pages 82–5*

Making grooves *pages 90–3*

Using abrasives *pages 115–17*

Using adhesives *pages 128–9*

Wood finishing *pages 130–5*

Veneering *pages 136–9*

Marquetry

This rich, decorative technique involves layering veneers in order to contrast light- and dark-colored woods to make a pictorial design. It was first developed in the 17th century in France, spread to the Low Countries, and from there to England by the 18th century. It was extremely popular until the 19th century and is still used today. Flowers and plants were popular subjects in marquetry in the late 17th century and the technique has often been combined with other forms of decoration, such as gilding (as shown in the image below). In the mid-18th century marquetry fans, shells, swags, pendant husks, and floral motifs were used on even the humblest pieces of furniture and panels of marquetry were put on more elaborate pieces. Engraved marquetry was introduced in the second half of the 18th century and consisted of cutting fine lines in the surface of veneers and filling them with a black composition.

lips and base to a depth of ¼ in. using a router with a ¼-in. straight bit. Cut the miters with a tenon saw and test the fit. Adjust as required.

3 Glue the lips, applying PVA adhesive to both surfaces, and place the tongue in the groove. Position each and hold with sash clamps if required.

4 When the adhesive has cured, use a smoothing plane to plane the excess lip flush to the surface of both sides of the board, without rounding over. Key both surfaces with a toothing plane.

5 Since veneers can exert a pull on the face of a board, you must put a backing veneer on the underside. Cut one piece for the center and some strips for a border around the edge. Lay the pieces out, slightly overlapping each other and trim to fit, including the mitered corners where the borders meet.

6 Brush some slightly thinned animal adhesive onto the board's surface to act as a size, and then apply adhesive to the veneer. Lay the veneer in position, and using the veneer hammer, work from the center and squeeze out the excess adhesive and any air pockets.

Lay the backing veneer with the veneer hammer.

7 If it is necessary to relay the veneer because of bubbles, the adhesive can be softened using an iron and damp cloth, and the veneer pushed down again with the veneer hammer. Tap the surface with a fingernail. You will hear if there are any areas that have not adhered.

8 Prepare the face veneers and board. Draw joint lines on the board where the pieces of veneer will meet. Cut the four book-matched leaves the same size to give a total rectangle of 16 x 11 in. Set this out in its location on the board over the joint lines.

9 Now lay the face veneers. Lay one of the four rectangles as described above. Then lay the second adjoining veneer with the edge to be joined overlapping the first. Using a sharp veneer knife and straightedge, cut through both veneers along the joint line. Soften the adhesive with the iron and remove the waste strips of veneer. Relay both so that the joint is perfect. Lay all four pieces in the same way. Slight movement is possible while the adhesive is wet.

Lay the first section of veneer with a veneer hammer.

10 The edge veneer can now be laid around the center. Trim the border and

prepare the four edge veneers for application. Begin by laying one strip of veneer in position, trimming the corner to the lip but overlapping at the miter. Now lay the adjacent strip of veneer, overlap the corner, and using a sharp veneer knife and metal straightedge, cut the miter at the corner where they meet. Soften the adhesive using the method explained in step 7, remove the waste pieces and press down with the veneer hammer. Repeat on the other three corners and trim the veneers to the edge.

11 Next, mark the position of the grooves on the tray—these are the two long thin grooves for the side strips and the two angled grooves for the two handles. Cut these with a router. To run the angle grooves, use a C-clamp to clamp a ¾-in. thick block 1⅜ in. in from the end, parallel to the end. Use this fence to plunge cut the groove, and set the bit to protrude ⅞ in. from the baseplate. Steady the router and cut the groove 10 in. long and 2 in. in from each edge.

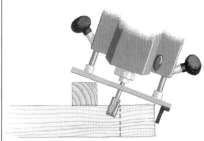

Use a router to cut the grooves.

12 Change the router bit, and with the aid of a fence, run the other two grooves ½ in. from the edge and ¼ in. wide to suit the side strips. These should be 11 in. long in the center and ¼ in. deep.

13 Plane the thin side strips to size, cut to length, and adjust them to fit the grooves.

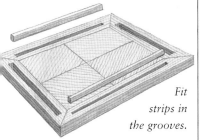

Fit strips in the grooves.

14 Plane the material for the two handles, initially keeping the pieces square. Mark the handle hole positions, drill a 1-in. hole in each end, and remove the waste from between the two holes with a coping saw. Carefully pare the edges with a chisel to true up.

15 Mark and cut the tongues that will join the handles to the tray. Run an $^5/_{16}$-in. groove in the center bottom edge of each handle $^5/_8$ in. deep.

16 To work the tapers, mark and plane the two angles on the faces, and then mark the ends; cut and plane. Plane the angle on the bottom $^5/_{16}$ in. on one side. Check the fit and adjust as required.

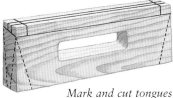

Mark and cut tongues and tapers on the handles.

17 Set up the router to run a small rabbet on the bottom edge of the tray $^1/_{16}$ x $^1/_{16}$ in. There is also a bevel on the top of the tray. Mark this on all four sides and plane.

18 Sand all components, glue the thin side strips in place and then the handles. Apply the required finish.

Arts and Crafts heritage

The rapid technological progress and industrialization that occurred in the second half of the 19th century meant that mass furniture production appeared for the first time. Some theorists reacted to this and by advocating a return to handwork.

ARTS AND CRAFTS MOVEMENT

The Arts and Crafts movement in Britain was led by the artist and social reformer, William Morris. This movement blamed the Industrial Revolution for the disintegration of society and looked back to the art and society of the Middle Ages for a more harmonious approach. Morris suggested that products would be better if they were simple and made by hand by craftsmen. He fought against machine production and sought to replace huge industrial cities with smaller communities in which craftsmanship could flourish once again. In 1861 he started the firm of Morris, Marshall and Faulkner to promote his beliefs. He discovered, however, that the sole use of handwork made most products too expensive for the mass market.

A Voysey chair designed in 1906.

However, his ideas influenced architects, designers, and makers into and through the 20th century. His ideal of a community of artists and craftsmen later became a reality with groups like the Werkstätten, which was founded at the beginning of the 20th century in Vienna. His social and ethical concerns reappeared later in the Bauhaus school (see pages 274–5).

Sidney and Ernest Barnsley and Gimson continued the movement into the 20th century in Britain. Their approach to design was based on clean lines and unadorned surfaces. They showed a fresh appreciation for the materials that they used and a respect for quality and understanding of construction.

Not all observers were anti-industrial however. In the wake of Morris's movement, the Art Furniture movement arose in the 1870s and 1880s. Charles Eastlake was its most important advocate. He warned against formal exaggeration and demanded simple lines and straightforward construction.

ART NOUVEAU

At the end of the 19th century Art Nouveau made its appearance, born out of the wish to create an entirely new style independent of traditional styles. Initially inspired by English ideas, it soon found its own language in other countries.

The first success of the movement was in Belgium with Victor Horta, who employed mahogany, maple, and pale fruitwoods with sumptuous upholstery. Henri van de Velde was more rigorous than Horta, finding a style based on the contrast between curving lines and smooth, filled planes.

In France, Emile Gallé wished to create an alliance of industrial arts, and in 1901, the School of Nancy was founded. The furniture exponents

OPPOSITE LEFT *Produced and sold by Morris, Marshall and Faulkner in 1875, this Sussex armchair has became a classic.* ◆ OPPOSITE CENTER *The beaten iron strap handles on this c1900 cabinet are a common Arts and Crafts feature.* ◆ OPPOSITE RIGHT *This oak table with two flaps is a typical Arts and Crafts style.* ◆ ABOVE LEFT *Oak armchairs with pierced side panels designed by Charles Rennie Mackintosh for the Argyle Street Tea Rooms, Glasgow in 1897.* ◆ ABOVE RIGHT *A Swedish Art Deco chair made out of birchwood c1920–30.*

of the group included Majorelle, Gallé, Gruber, and Vallin. The furniture produced there used nature, especially the flower, as its central theme.

Germany found this ornate, floral style did not sit well with new machinery. Instead, they laid the emphasis on function, not superficial decoration. One important designer, Richard Riemerschmid, made furniture in mahogany, ash, and poplar, using only the occasional scroll as decoration.

MACKINTOSH
About 1890 in Scotland, the architect Charles Rennie Mackintosh and his group began to create their own aesthetic. His furniture was slender and geometric in form, which contrasted with the rustic simplicity of the contemporary English style. His pieces were based on straight lines and rectangles combined with a gently curving, linear ornament—a style connected to the Art Nouveau movement but much simplified. His work had a great influence on European design and the angular construction of his furniture pointed the way to the future.

BEYOND MACKINTOSH
Although many designers were seduced by Art Nouveau, some eventually called for change. Otto Wagner and Adolf Loos founded the

An elegant Arts and Crafts hat stand, made of oak.

Vienna School, calling for a style that gained its expression purely from the materials used to make a piece and the construction methods employed on it. Their furniture was always simple, well proportioned, and in harmony with its surroundings.

The Arts and Crafts movement had an impact on both sides of the Atlantic, and artists began to form communities. In 1903, Josef Hoffman founded Wiener Werkstätten with Koloman Moser. He expounded Morris's theories but the movement also had upper-class clients for whom they made costly furniture with veneers of fine woods. They did, however, make simple oak furniture of pure quality. Loos and Wagner joined this group and by 1908 exotic woods combined with sharper angularity to anticipate Art Deco furniture.

LATER DEVELOPMENTS
The European Arts and Crafts and Art Nouveau movements developed during World War I into Art Deco. There was a need for rebirth after the exuberant Art Nouveau and the movement drew its inspiration from the late 18th century. Its main criteria was for form to follow function. Decoration was only to be contained within the shape itself, which meant, for example that marquetry and carving were allowed. The premier wood was ebony, which was rare and costly. Exotic veneers were employed, and there was a revival of Oriental lacquerware (see pages 206–7).

Modular storage cubes Advanced

This storage system is flexible and expandable. Two methods are outlined below: first, using preveneered MDF and secondly, using particleboard with lips. Be sure to check the sizes before you begin because you may need to alter them to suit your own storage needs.

Tools for method one

Table saw	
Router with ¼-in. straight bit	
C-clamps	
Sash clamps	
Electric iron	
Second-cut file	
Drill and ⅛-in. and ⁵⁄₁₆-in. bits	
Screwdriver	
Sanding block	
Hacksaw	

Skills required for project

Measuring and marking *pages 64–7*

Basic sawing *pages 68–71*

Making grooves *pages 90–3*

Drilling *pages 96–100*

Making dado joints *pages 110–11*

Using abrasives *pages 115–17*

Assembling projects *pages 120–7*

Using adhesives *pages 128–9*

Wood finishing *pages 130–5*

Veneering *pages 136–9*

Using metals and plastic *pages 146–7*

MATERIALS

Part	Materials and dimensions	No.
	Manufactured board—particleboard, plywood, or MDF	
Cube sides	8 x 4ft. ⅝ in.	1
	Solid wood	
Lips if required	71 x 1 x ⅝ in.	1
	Plywood sheet	
Tongues for lips	18 x 18 x ¼ in.	1

Other materials: two 1⁷⁄₁₆-in. 8 gauge flat head screws per door; pegs; adhesive (PVA); masking tape; sandpaper (120-grit); ⁷⁄₁₆-in. diameter steel rod; finish (veneer, plastic, laminate, or paint).

The desired visual finish will affect the construction sequence. If you are using the first method, with preveneered board, then you do not need to use lips. If using the second method, with manufactured particleboard, you may need to attach lips to all four edges (unless you intend to use a painted finish).

The materials listed will make three basic cubes. The most common size for manufactured board is 8 x 4 ft., giving 18 squares, plus some extra for doors and internal hardware, though more may be needed depending on your requirements.

If you use preveneered board, medium-density fiberboard (MDF) would be suitable. This can be bought cut-to-size. If all the edges are to be lipped, then you can use particleboard (chipboard), or plywood.

If cutting the board yourself, use a power saw and straight-edge, or a table saw. Cut the whole sheet to make three 16-in. wide strips. Cross-cut these to produce the squares.

Method one: construction using preveneered MDF

This method uses a system of routed edges. Wear a face mask when working with MDF as the dust can be hazardous.

1 Cut the sheets precisely to size on a table saw. Ensure that all the parts for the four sides and the back are identical.

2 The edges of the panels are joined together with routed edges. There are two types of groove (shapes A and B), which fit together. All the edges of the back panel will be shape A. Each side panel will have two B edges and one A edge—remember to leave the front edges square.

3 To make shape A, remove the shaded area shown below, either with a table saw or router. Then make the ¼-in. groove with a router—set this up so the base sits on the panel face and the fence runs along the edge. To make shape B, set the fence so that the groove is in the position shown—this time the router base needs to sit on the panel edge and the fence will run along the face.

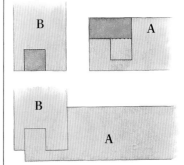

Cut grooves A and B to fit the edges together.

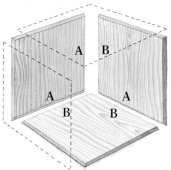

Cut the panels so that an A edge is always adjacent to a B edge.

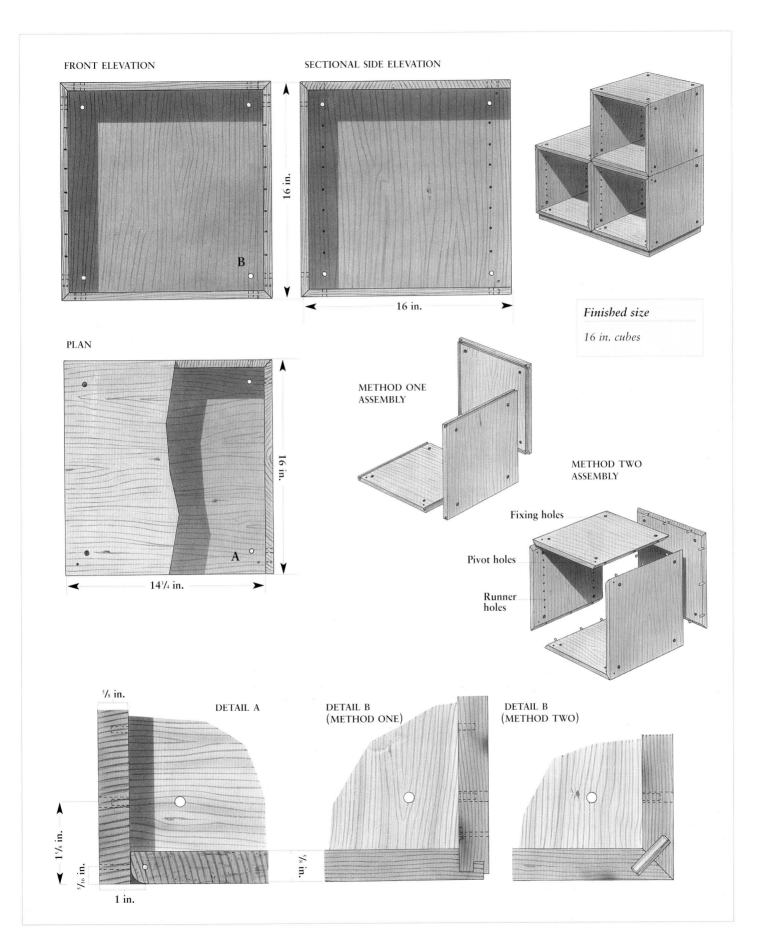

FRONT ELEVATION

SECTIONAL SIDE ELEVATION

16 in.

16 in.

B

Finished size

16 in. cubes

PLAN

16 in.

14³/₄ in.

A

METHOD ONE
ASSEMBLY

METHOD TWO
ASSEMBLY

Fixing holes

Pivot holes

Runner
holes

⁵/₈ in.

DETAIL A

DETAIL B
(METHOD ONE)

DETAIL B
(METHOD TWO)

1⁵/₈ in.

⁵/₁₆ in.

1 in.

⁵/₈ in.

4 Before assembly, sand and finish all the internal faces. Glue the four side joints and place sash clamps along each side to pull the top and bottom up.

Glue the side joints together, before fitting the back panel.

5 Apply adhesive to the back panel and push lightly down to close the joint. Additional clamps may be required if the joint does not close. Remove excess adhesive and check for square. Adjust as required.

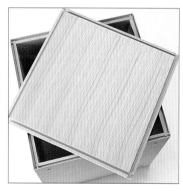

Apply adhesive to the back panel and push lightly into place.

6 Since you are using preveneered board you will need to apply a matching veneer to the front surfaces. This is best done when the cube itself has been assembled. In this case, the veneers can be mitered at the corners. Use a preglued veneer and simply iron it on. This type of veneer has a heat-sensitive adhesive, which is similar to that used

in hot glue guns. The preglued veneer has the adhesive on the back. Once melted with the iron, apply an even pressure to the surface with a sanding block, rubbing over the veneer for a few seconds until the adhesive cools enough for it to fuse.

7 Clean off any overhang with a second-cut file, and sand smooth with 120-grit sandpaper.

8 Using this method, there will be a small rabbet on the four edges and around the back where a thin edge of veneer and MDF will show. You can apply a finish or, if you want, a small strip of wood can be glued into the rabbet. Alternately, paint it black or another contrasting color. The first option is the method that has been used to make the prototype as shown. The rabbet has been finished but left unfilled, since it creates a visual line between each cube when they are joined together.

Method two: construction using particleboard with lips

1 If using this method, attach lips to each of the edges that will make up the front face of the cube. Plane the solid wood lips perfectly square to a size just over the thickness of the board. It will be easier to leave these full length—71 in.—or at least cut into two lengths of 35½ in. for planing.

2 When the lips are finished, cut the squares so that their dimension plus the width of the lip (where relevant) is slightly over the final measurement of 16 in. to allow for planing.

3 Hold each panel vertically in a vice and set up a router with a ¼-in. bit to a depth of ⅜ in. Use the fence as a guide and run the groove in the center of the front edge on four of the five pieces. Secure the edge lip onto the bench with a C-clamp and run a matching groove along its length. Make a series of tongues by cutting plywood strips ⅝ in. wide and the same thickness as the groove—¼ in.

Make tongues to fit in the grooves in the lips and sides.

4 The lips will need to be mitered at the corners before they are glued to the sides. Cut these on a radial-arm saw for accuracy.

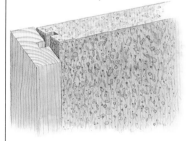

Miter the lips at the corners before fixing the joint.

5 Apply a little PVA to the face edge of the panel and edge lip, and a little into the groove. Insert the tongue into the groove and then position the lip. Align the long point of the miter with the end of the panel. Hold in position with masking tape.

6 When completely dry, use a smoothing plane to plane the lip so that it is perfectly flat with the surface of the board. Take care not to roll the surface.

7 If you want a natural wood finish, a veneer can now be applied to both top and bottom surfaces. Use a veneer with a heat-sensitive adhesive. Simply iron it down to the surface and immediately follow the iron with a sanding block or roller to push the veneer down. Trim the edges with a second-cut file and sand the surface with 120-grit sandpaper.

Plane the lips flat and then apply veneer if required.

8 Five panels are needed for each cube. The front or open face edge of each cube will be the panels that have been lipped and left square. The other edges of each panel will need to be mitered to 45 degrees. The back will need to be mitered to 45 degrees on all four edges.

9 Hold each panel upright in a vice and gauge a line parallel to the short point of the already mitered lip (see step 4). Using a smoothing plane at a 45-degree angle, plane the edge down to the gauge line to produce the miter. Repeat on the opposite and back edges, leaving the lipped edge square. Plane the miter on all four edges of the back panel.

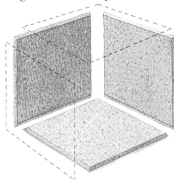

All the edges except the front four will be mitered to 45 degrees.

10 To aid in the assembly of the cubes, three locating dowels can be drilled into each miter. The dowels on the side miters need to be drilled at 90 degrees to the joint, while the dowels for the back are at 45 degrees to the joint. Position one dowel in the center and then two more dowels 2 in. in from each edge. Use a try square to mark these points along the edges. Mark the center of the dowel hole ¼ in. up from the inside face (the short side of the miter). Mark the holes on each miter face before you start to drill.

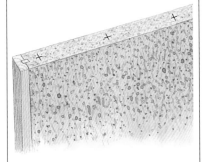

Mark the positions of the dowels.

11 Use a ¼-in. dowel bit to drill each hole ½ in. deep. Use a depth stop or masking tape to prevent drilling through the side. When drilled, place dowel centers in the holes. Position the corresponding panel in its correct alignment and push together. The dowel centers will mark the position of the holes on the other side of the joint.

12 Repeat this for all the joints around the side panels. The dowels in the back are set out the same. The only difference is the direction in which the holes are drilled; they must fit when the mitered edges are assembled.

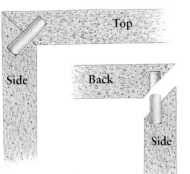

The corner joints.

13 Before assembly, sand all the surfaces and apply the finish to the internal faces. Cut the dowels to ¾-in. lengths. Dry test your work and adjust as required. Apply PVA to the miter joint and in the dowel holes, and insert the dowels in the side joints. Stand vertically on a flat surface and bring all four side panels together (see drawing on page 229). Position two web clamps around the work and apply a little pressure—just enough to close the joints. Apply adhesive to the dowel holes and miters of the back panel. Lay the back panel in position on top of the cube and tap down lightly to close the joints. Roll the cube over to one side and close the back joint with the aid of sash clamps.

14 Remove excess adhesive and check the cube is square. Loosen or apply pressure to the clamps to bring the work up true. If the back and sides were cut square and the job has no twist, it must be true.

Whichever method you have followed, you should now have one completed cube. Make additional cubes as desired. The instructions for connecting the cubes together and fitting them out with doors, shelves, and drawers are the same.

Expert tip

Use blocks between the work and clamps to prevent any marking of the surface.

Making pivots with screws

The pivots are made from modified $1^3/_{16}$-in. 8 gauge screws. Mark a 45-degree line back from each corner where the pivots are required. Drill the $^1/_8$-in. pilot holes and insert the two screws in the door or flap. Remove the screws, cut off the heads and cut another slot in the end in which a small screwdriver will fit. Place the door or flap in position with a washer in between. Use a screwdriver to insert the screws just below the surface of the cabinet.

Drilling the holes

Holes are needed to connect the cubes together, run drawers, or hold shelves. While you could just drill the holes needed for a particular application, here all the holes have been drilled so that the cubes are flexible and you can rearrange them at a later date.

1 Construct two jigs so that all the holes can be drilled in exactly the right position. On the first jig, there are four holes, one on each corner, which will be used for holding the cubes together, and two small holes on each of the front edges, which can be used for door or flap pivots. Make the first jig out of a sheet of thin plywood exactly the size of the outer face of the cubes, marking up from the holes shown on the drawing on page 229.

2 The second jig is also made from a sheet of thin plywood, which will fit the inside face of the cube and has a line of smaller holes that will hold the shelves and drawer runners. These holes will be $1^5/_8$ in. in and spaced to suit your requirements—for example, approximately $1^3/_{16}$ in. apart with a diameter of $^3/_{16}$ in.

3 Construct each jig and then position and drill the holes required.

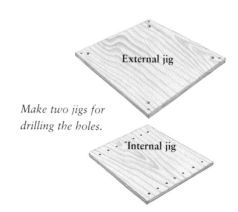

Make two jigs for drilling the holes.

Making the doors/flaps, shelves, and drawers

4 Make the doors out of manufactured board, ensuring that they are lipped and finished to complement the cubes (see steps 1–7 on pages 230–1). Finish with a $^1/_{16}$-in. clearance all around. The doors will fit the opening and be hinged on pivots (see box left), which are inserted through two of the eight small holes near the front edge, thus enabling the doors to be left- or right-handed, and flaps to hinge down from the bottom or up from the top. Plane a small round on the pivot side to enable each door to swing past the inside face.

5 The shelves are held in position with mini-wires—pieces of steel rod $^3/_{16}$ in. in diameter. The legs are inserted into a pair of interior holes, while the projecting piece runs in a groove along the side edges of the shelf. Cut the steel rod to length with a hacksaw and bend each length in a vice to suit the hole spacing. Cut the number of shelves required with a table saw and edge the front. Hold with the side up in a vice. Set the router to run a groove in the center of the shelf—the required depth for the rod. Stop the groove short of the front so that it cannot be seen. Insert the rods in the holes and check the shelves for fit.

Fit pieces of steel wire to the inside of the cube to support the shelf.

Shelf components.

6 The drawer runners follow the same principle as those used for the shelf, but are made of wood and not metal. The runners fit into grooves on the drawer sides and are held in place by the width of the drawer. The drawers are made with simple dado joints in the front and back, with the bottom grooved in. They are made from the same manufactured board with a barefaced tongue-and-groove joint on the sides. See pages 272–3 for more on making drawers.

The drawers are fixed with runners.

Two finished drawers.

Folding chair

Advanced

It is often useful to have extra chairs available for unexpected visitors. This attractive chair takes up very little room when folded away and a set of them could even be mounted on a wall if you are short of space.

Tools

- Miter square
- Radial-arm saw
- Drill and 1/8-in., 3/16-in., 1/4-in., 3/8-in., and countersink bits
- Mortise gauge
- C-clamp
- 1/2-in. and 1 3/16-in. chisel
- Marking knife
- Marking gauge
- Tenon saw
- Sash clamp
- Wrench
- Jigsaw
- Smoothing plane
- Second-cut file
- Sanding block
- Screwdriver

Skills required for project

- Measuring and marking *pages 64–7*
- Basic sawing *pages 68–71*
- Planing *pages 74–81*
- Fine sawing *pages 82–5*
- Chiseling *pages 86–9*
- Making mortise-and-tenon joints *pages 104–9*
- Using abrasives *pages 115–17*
- Assembling projects *pages 120–7*
- Using adhesives *pages 128–9*
- Wood finishing *pages 130–5*
- Using metals and plastics *pages 146–7*

MATERIALS

Part	Materials and dimensions	No.
	Hardwood	
Legs	26 x 2 x 7/8 in.	4
Cross-rail	15 x 2 3/8 x 7/8 in.	1
Hinge block	15 x 1 1/2 x 1 1/2 in.	1
Seat front rail	16 1/2 x 2 x 7/8 in.	1
Grip rail	6 x 7/8 x 7/8 in.	2
	Plywood—3/8 in. thick	
Seat	16 in. square	1
Back	12 1/2 x 14 1/2 in.	1

Other materials: two 1/4 x 2 in. domed nuts with bolts and washers; eight 1/2-in. 6 gauge nuts with countersunk bolts and washers; fourteen 1 1/4-in. 8 gauge flat head screws; four 1-in. 6 gauge flat head screws; two 2-in. 8 gauge round-head screws; one 2-in. barrel bolt; two pairs of narrow butt hinges; adhesive (PVA); sandpaper (120-grit); finish.

Making the legs and cross-rail

1 Prepare the material for the four legs, face side, face edge, width, and thickness. There are two pairs of legs—the outside pair (A) and the inside pair (B). They need to be marked left- and righthanded (see drawing opposite).

2 First, make the angles on the top and bottom of each leg. The first pair (A) are marked 24 in. long. Square a line around the leg at this length. Mark the center point across the squared line at each end. From this point, use a miter square and pencil to mark a 45-degree line back to the edge. Turn the miter square over and mark a second 45-degree line toward the opposite edge to create the point. Square this line around the edges. Repeat to complete the marking on both ends of the (A) legs. Cut these ends on the set-out lines (45 degrees) with a tenon saw. Set out the other pair of legs (B) 20 1/2 in. long. Mark out the 45-degree points and cut as before.

3 Next, mark the positions toward the middle of the legs where the pair will cross and be joined. Measure up 12 in. from the bottom on all four legs. Square a line across the face and mark the center 1 in. in from the edge. Drill a 1/4-in. hole through each leg at this location.

4 Next, mark the positions where the cross-rail will be joined to the two (B) legs—this is held in place with through mortise-and-tenon joints. Lay the 20 1/2-in. pair of legs side by side on a flat surface. Measure up 1 in. past the drilled hole, and then another 2 3/8 in. Square a mortise line back in 1/8 in. Return this line around to the opposite side. Use a mortise gauge to scribe the width of the mortise 1/2 in. in the center face of each leg. Remember to gauge from the face side.

5 Secure the work on a firm, flat surface with a C-clamp. Take care to keep the sides of the mortise straight and square. Drill out the bulk of the waste in the mortise. Finish by working from both sides and paring back to the set-out lines at the ends with a 1/2-in. chisel, and a wider 1 3/16-in. chisel on the sides. Repeat on the other leg.

6 Next, cut the cross-rail to length—14 1/4 in. Measure in 3/4 in. from each end. Square this around the wood with a marking knife. This is the shoulder line for the tenon. Set a marking gauge to 1/8 in. and scribe a line from the shoulder line on the face side back to the end, and then across the end and back down the other side to the opposite shoulder line. Repeat from face edge to face edge and then mark the tenon on the other end of the rail in the same way.

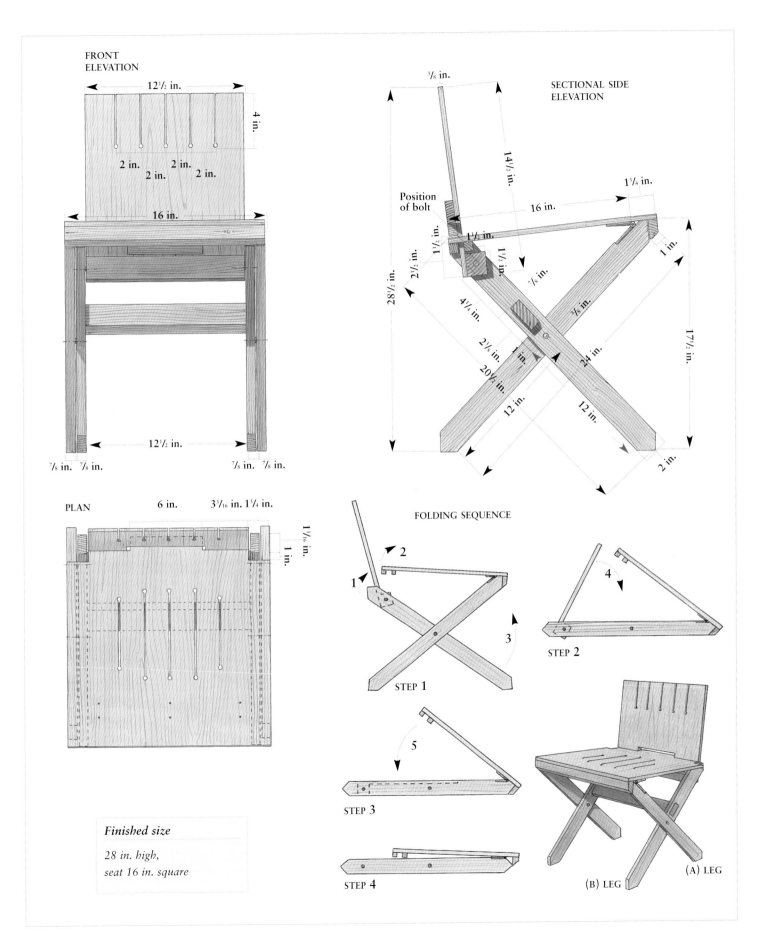

FRONT
ELEVATION

12½ in.

4 in.

2 in.   2 in.
  2 in.   2 in.

16 in.

12½ in.

⅞ in.   ⅞ in.   ⅞ in.   ⅞ in.

PLAN   6 in.   3³⁄₁₆ in. 1¾ in.

1⁷⁄₁₆ in.
1 in.

Finished size

28 in. high,
seat 16 in. square

⅜ in.

SECTIONAL SIDE
ELEVATION

14½ in.

1¾ in.

16 in.

Position
of bolt

1½ in.

1½ in.

1 in.

2½ in.

7⁄8 in.

28½ in.

4¼ in.

⅜ in.

17½ in.

2⅛ in.

1 in.

24 in.

20½ in.

12 in.

12 in.

2 in.

FOLDING SEQUENCE

1

2

3

STEP 1

4

STEP 2

5

STEP 3

STEP 4

(A) LEG

(B) LEG

235

7 Stand the rail vertically in a vice and saw down on the waste side of the gauge lines to the shoulder line. Lay flat against a bench hook and cut the shoulders with a tenon saw. Clean the faces of the tenon with a sharp chisel. Test the fit and adjust as required.

8 Next, set out the pivot position where the (B) legs will be joined to the chair back. Set out a point in the center of each leg—another 4¼ in. up from the cross-rail. Drill a ³⁄₁₆-in. hole through each leg.

The two sets of legs and the cross-rail.

9 Apply adhesive to the tenons on the cross-rail and glue to the (B) legs. Place in a sash clamp and make sure that the frame is square. Wipe off the excess adhesive and allow to dry.

10 Join the legs together with the domed nuts and bolts. Tighten with a wrench, placing a washer each side and between the legs.

The completed underframe.

Making the seat

Make the seat initially as a separate component.

11 Cut the seat to the outside shape 16 x 16 in. Mark the clearance cutouts in the two back corners 1¾ in. square across from the edges and 2³⁄₁₆ in. in from the back. Cut away the waste with a tenon saw or jigsaw. Mark a second cutout for the grip rail another 3³⁄₁₆ in. across and 1³⁄₁₆ in. wide. This will leave a 6 x 1³⁄₁₆-in. tongue on the underside of the seat. Mark the position of the front rail across the full width and the rear gripping rails 6 in. in the center of the back edge. Do not put the seat slits in yet.

12 Cut the front rail to match the width of the seat. Drill four holes of ³⁄₁₆ in. diameter across the front of the seat, making sure that they are evenly spaced and ⅜ in. in from the edge. Countersink the top. Hold the rail in position and drill a ⅛-in. pilot hole through each clearance hole into the top edge of the rail. Apply the adhesive to the edge and fix in place with 1¼-in. 8 gauge flat head screws. Turn the seat over and plane a 45-degree angle on the bottom edge of the front section to match the angle on the leg.

13 Cut two ⅞ x ⅞-in. grip rails 6 in. long. The first rail should be fixed 1¼ in. in, and the second rail should be flush with the back. Fix these in the same manner as for the front rail with three screws in each.

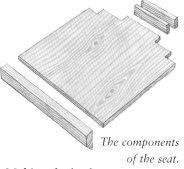

The components of the seat.

Making the back

Make the back initially as a separate component.

14 Cut the backboard 14½ in. high x 12½ in. wide. Use a try square and marking gauge to mark out the cutout for the tongue slot in the center 2½ in. up from the bottom edge, 1⁵⁄₁₆ in. high and 6 in. long. Hold firm on a flat surface with the set-out overhanging the surface. Drill a ⅜-in. hole through the back within the set-out. Place a jigsaw through the hole and cut around the set-out to remove the slot. Clean all the edges up with a second-cut file and 120-grit sandpaper.

15 The back is fixed to the legs with a hinge block, measuring 2½ x 1½ in. Fit it so that it finishes flush with the outside edges and the bottom of the chair back. Glue and screw in place as you did with the front rail in step 12.

Fit the hinge block to the back.

Making the bed rails and cleats

The main structural supports for the bed are the two large bed rails that connect the head and footboards. The bed rails are attached to the legs with two dowels and a bolt (see detail on drawing on page 240). On the inside of these are square cleats that support the mattress slats.

12 Prepare the two rails and mark the length. To be sure the holes connecting the bed rails and legs are the correct size, you will need to have the bolt and barrel nut at hand. On the inside face of each leg, cut a small flat to allow the end of the bed rail to sit flat. Measure up 6¾ in. and 12⅝ in. from the bottom. Square these lines across the leg with a box square and pencil. Mark two lines along the leg 1³⁄₁₆ in. apart, ensuring they are in the center of the leg. Cut across the top and bottom lines with a tenon saw to a depth of ³⁄₁₆ in., and pare away the surface with a 1-in. chisel to produce a flat surface.

13 In the end of the bed rails, set out the dowel location 1 in. from each edge on the center line. Drill the holes 1 in. deep with an ⁵⁄₁₆-in. dowel bit. Insert a pair of dowels and bring the joint together. The centers will mark the correct location for the matching holes in the leg. Drill these 1 in. deep.

14 On the outside of the leg 9 in. up, drill a ⁵⁄₁₆ in. diameter hole through the leg for the bolt. Hold the bed rail in position and place the drill back in the bolthole to mark the position on the

end of the rail. Remove the leg and drill the hole in the rail to a depth of 2⅜ in. Mark the barrel nut hole on the inside face 3 in. up from the bottom edge and 1¼ in. in from the end. Drill a ½-in. hole ¾ in. deep to accept the nut. On the outside of the leg, you can counterbore the bolt head, if required.

Drill holes in the bed rails for the bolt and nut.

15 Next, mark the location of the cleats on the inside face of the bed rails. Scribe a line parallel to the top edge, ¾ in. down. Cut two 1½ x 1½ in. cleats ¾ in. shorter than the length of the bed rails. Fix in place—⅜ in. in from each end with 2-in. 8 gauge flat head screws at approximately 6-in. spacings. Drill a ³⁄₁₆-in. countersunk hole in the center of the cleat. Apply adhesive, hold in position and drill the ⅛-in. pilot holes. Insert the screws and tighten.

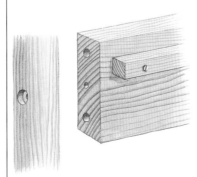

Fix the cleat in place on the inside face of the bed rail.

Assembly

16 Assemble the two bed rails on the head and footboards with locating dowels. Put the ⁵⁄₁₆-in. bolt in its hole. Secure the barrel nut in its hole, and the screw, so that the joint is brought up tight. Repeat on the other three corners.

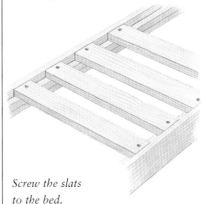

Secure the barrel nut and screw.

17 Cut 14 slats to length to fit between the bed rails on the cleats. Drill a ³⁄₁₆-in. hole, countersunk at each end of the slats. Remove any sharp edges with a smoothing plane and sandpaper.

18 Place each slat in position—evenly spaced along the bed. Drill the ⅛-in. pilot holes through the slats into the cleats and fix with 1-in. 8 gauge screws.

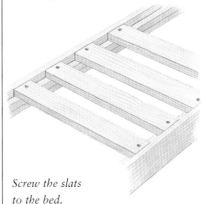

Screw the slats to the bed.

19 Disassemble the bed and apply your chosen finish before final assembly.

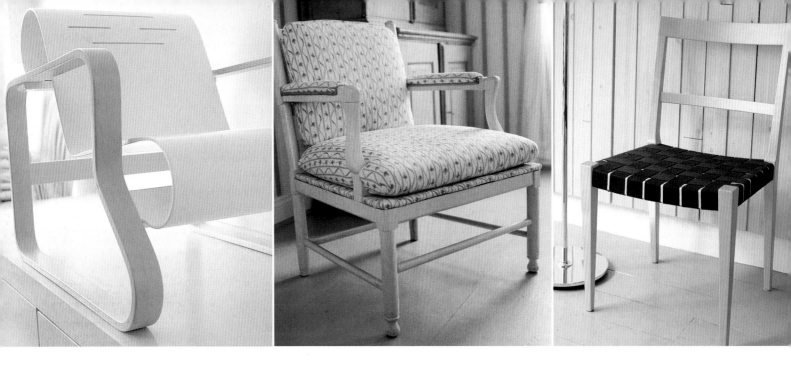

Scandinavian design

Scandinavian design conjures up ideas of simplicity and the use of natural materials, based on the culture and weather of the various countries. Scandinavia enjoyed long periods of peace during the 19th and early 20th centuries. The style of living there was based on a peasant tradition. The comparatively late industrialization and low population density gave the countries a feeling of stability so they didn't feel the need for new forms of housing or furnishing and kept to their traditional values. After World War II, however, liberal socialism and rapid industrialization swept across Scandinavia and changed the social structure. This, inevitably, had an impact on furnishings.

Scandinavian designers held the Vienna School as their ideal (see page 227), and while the Bauhaus movement was taking Europe by storm in the 1920s and 1930s, they remained true to it. They finished industrial products by hand, giving the furniture a personal quality, which was one of the reasons it became so famous after World War II. Scandinavia was relatively unscathed during the war, while other European countries had witnessed the terrible things that technology could do. As such, the traditional craftsmanship and warm, natural materials used in Scandinavian design became popular throughout Europe after the war. The simple but classic designs that emerged at this time show how designers in Scandinavia have maintained an interesting but functional look to pieces made out of natural solid woods, laminates, or preforms and later metals and plastics. The desire for well-designed and beautiful homes has led to a clean and honest approach that is applied to both structure and furnishings.

SWEDEN

One of the fathers of modern Swedish furniture was Carl Malmsten. He was influenced by the Arts and Crafts movement, nature, and traditional Swedish design. He believed it was his duty to furnish people's homes in a way that combined utility with beauty. He mapped out the path that most Scandinavian furniture design has followed since—cultivated craftsmanship in conjunction with functional correctness. This traditional approach nevertheless made use of modern manufacturing processes. At the same time, one young designer, Bruno Mathsson, was building chairs made of wooden frames that rested on flexible plywood legs. Josef Frank moved to Stockholm from Vienna in 1934 and took the playful lightness of his design with him.

FINLAND

At the beginning of the 20th century, Finland was battling for political independence. The peasant culture began to fascinate young craftsmen and a new Finnish style was born—National Romanticism. Alvar Aalto was one such craftsman and his work is dealt with in depth on page 267.

DENMARK

Architect Kaare Klint was one of the founders of modern Danish furniture design. Rather than turning away from the influences of earlier centuries he drew upon other periods and "renewed" them in his own unique way. He took elements from late 18th-century English furniture, Chinese, and Egyptian designs and eliminated the stylistic characteristics in order to create timeless forms. His designs do not show a craving for

◆ OPPOSITE LEFT *Alvar Aalto's "Paimio" armchair (designed in 1924) was made out of birch plywood.* ◆ OPPOSITE CENTER *A Swedish Gripsholm Gustavian armchair made c1930 after a 1780s style.* ◆ OPPOSITE RIGHT *A 1932 "Monat" chair, designed by Bruno Mathsson, who had been inspired by Aalto's designs.* ◆ ABOVE LEFT *Alvar Aalto's "Chair 43" (designed in 1936–7) made from steamed birch bentwood.* ◆ ABOVE CENTER *Solid oak book shelf, designed by Lloyd Schwan.* ◆ ABOVE RIGHT *The "Ant" stacking chairs, designed by Arne Jacobsen in 1955.*

newness but are a restatement of classic solutions that combine comfort and dignified simplicity.

The country was particularly interested in the Thonet process of manufacturing bentwood parts (see page 266). A company founded by Fritz Hansen was one of the major organizations that worked on its development. His son Soren Hansen brought out a new chair made of laminated wood in 1950. In 1952, Arne Jacobsen produced the famous "Ant" chair—the seat and back were made of one piece of plywood and it had steel legs. This was probably one of the first Danish chairs to be designed expressly with mass production in mind.

The architect Borge Mogensen developed inexpensive, practical furniture based on a system of dimensions that he devised himself. His mastery of materials was very like Klint's. Finn Juhl's style was accepted abroad as well as being popular at home. His 1945–55 style dissolved the traditional chair into two separate, defined components— the frame and the seat.

The "Wishbone" chair, made from beech, was designed by Hans J. Wegner in 1950.

Hans Wegner's style falls somewhere between Klint's discipline of form and Johl's temperament. His designs were amenable to mass production—so much so that five factories merged under the name of Salesco to devote themselves to manufacturing his furniture. The standard of design in Denmark was high, as illustrated by the work of Hans Wegner, along with his master cabinetmaker Johannes Hansen. Much of Wegner's furniture from the 1940s and 1950s shows how machinery and handwork could be combined to give the most elegant designs. The components are shaped or bent to exquisite forms and joined in such a way as to enable the form of the piece to flow without undue interruption. Machinery was used initially to ensure the most precise joints, and handwork was used for the final shaping and finishing.

The export of Danish furniture began in the early 1950s—many talented designers including Borge Mogensen, Ole Wanscher, Hans Wegner, Grete Jalk, Poul Kjarholm, and Arne Jacobsen took up the challenge of form and material to create rare syntheses of precision construction, imagination, and truth to materials that has earned Danish furniture its international reputation.

Octagonal birdhouse | *Advanced*

This design has been sized for small garden birds. It has individual

compartments and stands on its own central support. The base is

attached with dowels that can be removed for cleaning purposes.

Tools

Try plane

Compass

Marking gauge

1-in. chisel

Hand saw or power saw

Smoothing plane

Hammer

Nail punch

Drill press with ¼-in. and 1³/₁₆-in. drill bits

Hole saw

Jigsaw or coping saw

Sliding bevel

Skills required for project

Measuring and marking
pages 64–7

Basic sawing *pages 68–71*

Planing *pages 74–81*

Fine sawing *pages 82–5*

Drilling *pages 96–100*

Using abrasives
pages 115–17

Assembling projects
pages 120–7

Using adhesives
pages 128–9

Wood finishing
pages 130–5

MATERIALS		
Part	Materials and dimensions	No.
	Softwood or **hardwood** (exterior grade)	
Support pole	6 ft. x 1⁵/₈ in. or adjust to suit requirements	1
	Plywood (exterior grade)	
Roof	10 x 4 x ¼ in.	8
Walls	4³/₁₆ x 4 x ¼ in.	8
Internal partitions	10 x 4 x ⅜ in.	8
Base	8 x 8 x ½ in.	1

Other materials: eight 3 x ¼-in. diameter dowels; ¾-in. nails (exterior grade); adhesive (exterior grade); masking tape; sandpaper (120-grit), finish (exterior grade).

1 With the try plane, plane the upright support pole to 1⁵/₈ in. square. Then, mark an octagon on one end of the pole. Draw diagonals from corner to corner. To find the equal 45-degree lines across the corners, place the point of a compass on one of the corners, and rotate from the center point to the outside edge. Mark a line across the corner to the opposite edge. Repeat the measuring process to mark the 45-degree lines across the other corners. Next, set a marking gauge and scribe the points along the length of the pole.

2 Secure the wood on a flat surface or in a vice and plane the octagon to shape using the try plane. At each point of the octagon, plane a ⅜-in. flat edge, along 12 in. from the top. The bottom of this flat-edged length of pole can be finished with a chisel to give a square-stopped end.

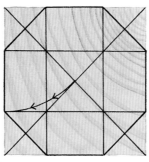

Setting out an octagon.

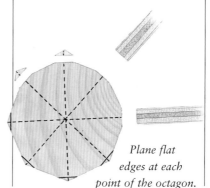

Plane flat edges at each point of the octagon.

3 Cut the internal partitions to a shape of 9⅝ in. long by 3⅛ in. wide. Taper the top by measuring up 3⅜ in. along the outside edge and drawing a line up to the top of the opposite edge. Use a hand saw or power saw and true the edges with a smoothing plane.

4 Plane a bevel along the side and top edges and taper to 22.5 degrees off each face. This is best set out with a sliding bevel. Mark the bevel on the top edge and pencil gauge a line along the inside face to represent the amount to be removed. Hold on edge in a vice and plane to the line. Check with the bevel as you go.

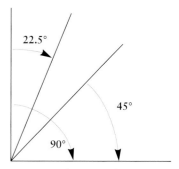

Bisect a 45-degree angle to produce a 22.5-degree angle.

5 Use adhesive to position the partitions on the small flat edges of the support pole with the bottom of each resting on the 12 in. stopped end. Secure them in place with ¾ in. nails. To prevent movement while the adhesive dries, wrap masking tape around the outside, making sure the partitions are evenly spaced.

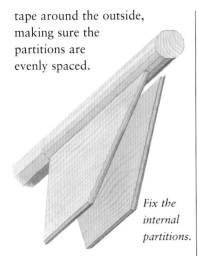

Fix the internal partitions.

6 Cut the eight walls to 3⅜ in. wide and to 4⅛ in. long. Measure the positions of the two holes in each wall at 9/16 in. and 2 in. up from the middle of the bottom. Mark these and use a drill press to drill the ¼-in. bottom hole. Use a 1³/16-in. hole saw to make the top hole.

7 Next, bevel the side edges of each wall to 22.5 degrees (see step 4). Plane one wall and then fit the rest individually by measuring them against the finished edge of the first.

8 In contrast, the bottom edge of each wall is slightly curved. Mark a pencil line along the length in the center of each wall. Measure up 2³/16 in. from the bottom. Place the point of a compass on this spot and scribe the curve along the bottom edge. Cut this curve with a jigsaw or coping saw, and smooth with 120-grit sandpaper.

Make the eight walls.

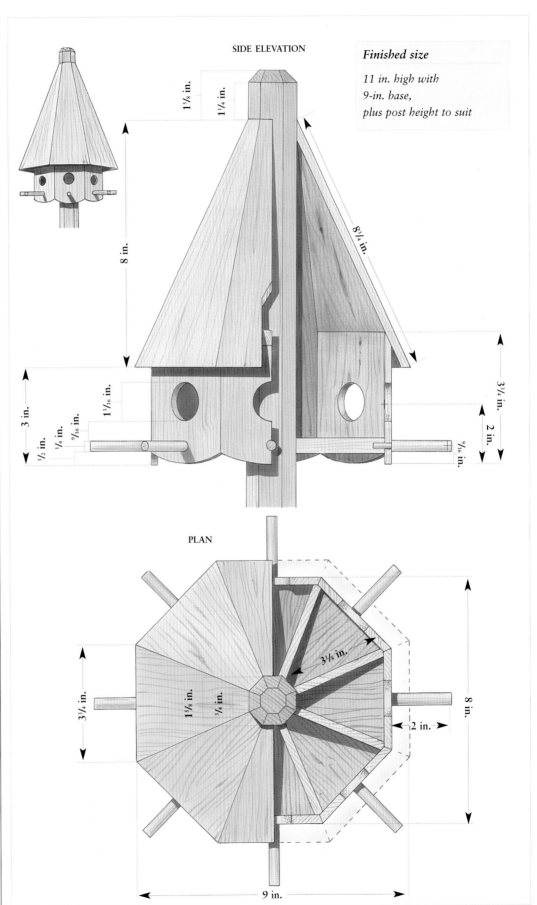

SIDE ELEVATION

Finished size

11 in. high with 9-in. base, plus post height to suit

PLAN

9 Next, mark and cut the base. Set out the octagon in the center of an 8-in. square board. Drill and chisel the octagonal hole for the upright from both sides. Slide this up the pole from the bottom and mark the point at which it meets the outside edge of the partitions. Remove from the upright. Adjust the shape with a hand or power saw. Test fit and adjust as required.

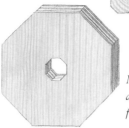

Make the base and check it for size.

10 Next, fit the walls to the partitions. Lay one wall piece on top of its two partitions so that the beveled edges of each match up. Plane to fit if necessary and fix in place with adhesive and pins.

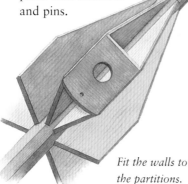

Fit the walls to the partitions.

11 With the structure lying flat, plane the bevel at the top of each wall to match the bevel on top of the partition. Make the eight roof sections in the same way that you made the walls in step 6. Cut the basic pieces to 8⅞ x 3¾ in. and plane an angled bevel on the top of each section so that it will sit against the upright pole.

12 Position one of the roof sections on top of its wall and two partitions. Check the fit at the top and adjust the bevel as required. Mark the tapering sides on the underneath by tracing along the right-hand partition with a pencil. Cut and plane the bevel on this right-hand edge only. Repeat this on a second roof section but bevel the left-hand edge. Lay the two sections together in their adjacent locations and test their fit against one another. Plane and adjust as required.

13 Once a neat fit has been obtained, set the sliding bevel to the edge. Mark the width at the top and bottom of the first section. Hold the timber in the vise and plane it to match the sliding bevel. Fix that completed roof section in place with adhesive and pins.

14 Place the second section in position and mark it out. Plane to shape, but do not fix this yet as it will be used for a template for the remaining pieces.

15 Trace the shape of the second roof section onto the remaining pieces of timber. Cut these to shape, making sure that they are slightly oversized.

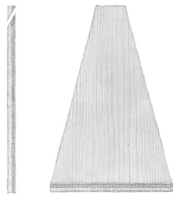

Make and fit the roof sections.

Plane the bevel on all the right-hand edges. Working counterclockwise, position each in turn, and check and mark the width, top and bottom. Plane the bevel along this edge to suit the sliding bevel and then fix as before. The last section may need a little extra fitting before you fix it in place.

16 The base of the birdhouse is held in position by dowels. Cut the dowels to 3 x ¼ in. Put the base in position and drill through the ¼-in. hole in each wall. Drill 1 in. into the edge of each face of the base. Fix the base in place with the dowels. The dowels can be removed and the base taken away for cleaning.

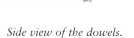

Side view of the dowels.

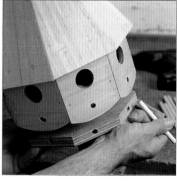

Insert the dowels to hold the base in position.

17 Plane a ⅜-in. chamfer around the top of the upright support pole. Sand all the surfaces in order to remove any set-out lines and marks that may be left, and apply an exterior finish to all the outside faces. Leave the inside of the birdhouse in natural timber.

36 Mark out the curve across the top of slats. Disassemble and cut on bandsaw. Sand and apply first finish coat.

Final assembly

Assemble the chair before adding the buttons and the leather arms.

37 Sand all components to remove any marks. Glue up the two side frames first by applying the adhesive to the tenons on each end of the side rails and in the holes for the ³⁄₄-in. dowels. Place each side frame in sash cramps and tighten. Check for square and ensure that it is free of wind. Remove excess adhesive, and leave to dry.

38 Remove from the cramps and complete the assembly by applying the adhesive to the tenons on the other rails. Position each rail and cramp up the whole frame. Check for square and wind. Remove excess adhesive and leave to dry.

39 Remove from the cramps and sand off any marks. Apply the final finish to the frame, seat and back slats.

40 Refit the seat and back slats with the brass screws on the lower back rail. The other ends will be 'floating' over the front and top back rails. It would be possible to screw through the outside face into these rails – however this would show. Therefore make 'buttons' to hold the slats in place. The buttons are made with a flat face so that they can be screwed under or behind the slats and will locate in holes drilled into the rail (see main photograph, page 255).

41 Take the 1 x ³⁄₄ in. strip and mark the eleven buttons, each 1³⁄₁₆ in. long. Mark the position of the screw holes in the center and then drill and countersink using a ³⁄₁₆-in. bit and a countersink bit. Cut the buttons to length and drill the holes to accept ¹⁄₄-in. dowels in the end, ³⁄₈ in. down.

42 Cut the dowels to length and glue into the holes. Shape the top either round, or chamfer the edge and end on the face.

Make the buttons and cut the dowels to length.

43 Using one button as a pattern, mark where the dowel will enter the rails on the bottom edge of the top rail for the back and behind the front rail for the seat. Fix the slats with the buttons by inserting the dowel into the hole. Mark with a bradawl where the screw will be positioned. Drill a pilot hole and fix into place with 1³⁄₁₆-in., 8-gauge steel screws.

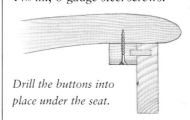

Drill the buttons into place under the seat.

Making the leather strap arms

The chair is very comfortable without any upholstery but, rather than using solid arms, use leather straps as a contrast to what is otherwise an all-wooden piece.

44 Make the strap supports/ tensioners by cutting four pieces of ³⁄₄-in. dowel to the same length as the width of the straps, and mark and drill a ⁵⁄₁₆-in. clearance hole at right angles in the center of each rod to accept the threaded studding. Drill the same size holes in the four legs at heights to suit. T-nuts are used to hold the threaded studding to the dowel, and a hexagonal (Allen key) nut that shows on the outside of the legs is used to tighten and stretch the straps. For the screw or bolt, use four short lengths of ¹⁄₄-in.-threaded studding.

45 Mark the leather straps to length and ensure they are long enough to fold over to make the 'eye' for the dowel and be secured beneath.

46 Determine the length between the eyes and fold the strap over, marking the end of the overlaps. Take the straps to your local boot maker or upholsterer to have the overlaps sewn. Cut a slot in the end of the eye so that the bolt can be screwed through the dowel and T-nut. Fit the straps and tension as required.

Fit the leather straps in place.

Garden bench Advanced

The design for this garden bench provides a strong basic frame with a comfortably shaped seat. There are three different options given for the back of the seat: a back with curved top rails, three cross-rail panels, and a cross-weave effect. This bench is a two-seater, but it is possible to modify the dimensions and extend the length slightly if you wish.

Tools

Jack plane

Marking gauge

Try plane

Mortise gauge

C-clamp

Drill and ³/₈-in., ⁵/₈-in., and ³/₄-in. bits

¹/₂-in. mortise and 1-in. bevel-edged firmer chisel

Marking knife

Tenon saw

Ripsaw

Sliding bevel

Brace and ³/₄-in. auger bit

Hand saw

Sanding block

Sash clamps

Hammer

Nail punch

MATERIALS

Part	Materials and dimensions	No.
	Any hardwood with resistance to weathering, such as oak, elm, or teak; if you use a softwood, make sure that it is treated	
Legs	25 x 2¹/₂ x 2¹/₂ in.	4
Side rails	28 x 4 x 1 in.	2
Longitudinal rails	56 x 4 x 1 in.	2
Arms	31 x 4 x 1 in.	2
Back rail	57 x 4 x 1 in.	1
Seat bearers	19⁵/₈ x 4 x 1¹/₄ in.	2
Seat slats	49 x 4 x 1 in.	
Option 1: back with curved top rails		
Curved back rails	17³/₄ x 6 x 1 in.	2
	29¹/₂ x 6 x 1 in.	1
Vertical uprights	17³/₄ x 1³/₄ x 1 in.	2
Angled uprights	15³/₄ x 1³/₄ x 1 in.	2
Back rail	47 x 2³/₄ x 1¹/₈ in.	1
Dowels	17³/₄ x ⁵/₈ in.	5
	12 x ⁵/₈ in.	6
Sheet of plywood or particleboard for set-out		
Option 2: back with three cross-rail panels		
Horizontal rails	47 x 2³/₄ x 2³/₄ in.	2
Outside vertical stiles	23¹/₂ x 2 x 2 in.	2
Inside vertical stiles	15 x 1⁷/₈ x 1⁷/₈ in.	2
Cross-rails	18 x 2¹/₂ x 2¹/₂ in.	6
Option 3: back with cross-weave effect		
Horizontal rails	47 x 2 x 2 in.	2
Outside vertical stiles	23¹/₂ x 1³/₄ x 1³/₄ in.	2
Inside vertical stile	16 x 1³/₁₆ x 1³/₁₆ in.	1
Vertical strips	16 x ⁵/₈ x ⁵/₈ in.	14
Horizontal strips	45 x ⁵/₈ x ⁵/₈ in.	5

Other materials: 2 x ¹/₈-in. 500 gauge galvanized jolt head nails; adhesive (exterior grade); sandpaper (120-grit); finish (exterior grade).

Making the main frame

1 Plane all the components with a jack plane to the finished size. Your lumberyard may do this for you, which will save time and effort.

2 First, make the legs. Mark the height of the legs 23¹/₂ in. for the front and 24¹/₄ in. for the back. Square a line around and cut to length with a tenon saw. Mark out an octagon on one end of one leg (see page 246) and then set a pencil gauge to scribe the points along the leg length. Secure the wood and plane the octagon to shape with the try plane. Repeat to make the other legs.

3 Next, make the two end frames—the two side rails are fixed to the legs with stopped mortise-and-tenon joints. Begin by making the mortises in the legs—square two lines across the face edge 8¹/₂ in. and 12¹/₂ in. up from the bottom. Use a mortise gauge to scribe the width of the mortise ¹/₂ in. in the center of the leg between the squared lines.

4 Lay flat and secure with a C-clamp on a firm surface. Use a drill with a ³/₈-in. bit to

Skills required for project

Measuring and marking *pages 64–7*

Basic sawing *pages 68–71*

Planing *pages 74–81*

Chiseling *pages 86–9*

Making grooves *pages 90–3*

Drilling *pages 96–100*

Making half lap joints *pages 101–3*

Making mortise-and-tenon joints *pages 104–9*

Using abrasives *pages 115–17*

Assembling projects *pages 120–7*

Using adhesives *pages 128–9*

Wood finishing *pages 130–5*

Finished size

Approximately 24 in. high,
55 in. long, and 30 in. deep

FRONT ELEVATION

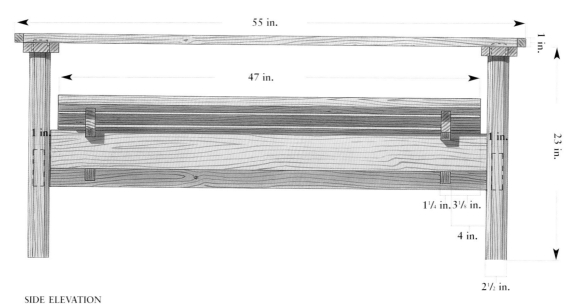

55 in.

1 in.

1 in.

47 in.

23 in.

1 in.

1 in.

1¼ in. 3⅛ in.

4 in.

2½ in.

SIDE ELEVATION

30 in.

1 in.

1 in.

11 in.

4 in.

23 in.

4 in.

75°

1 in.

18 in.

16½ in.

9 in.

1 in.

8 in.

6¼ in.

14½ in.

22 in.

2 in.

2½ in.

2½ in.

1 in.

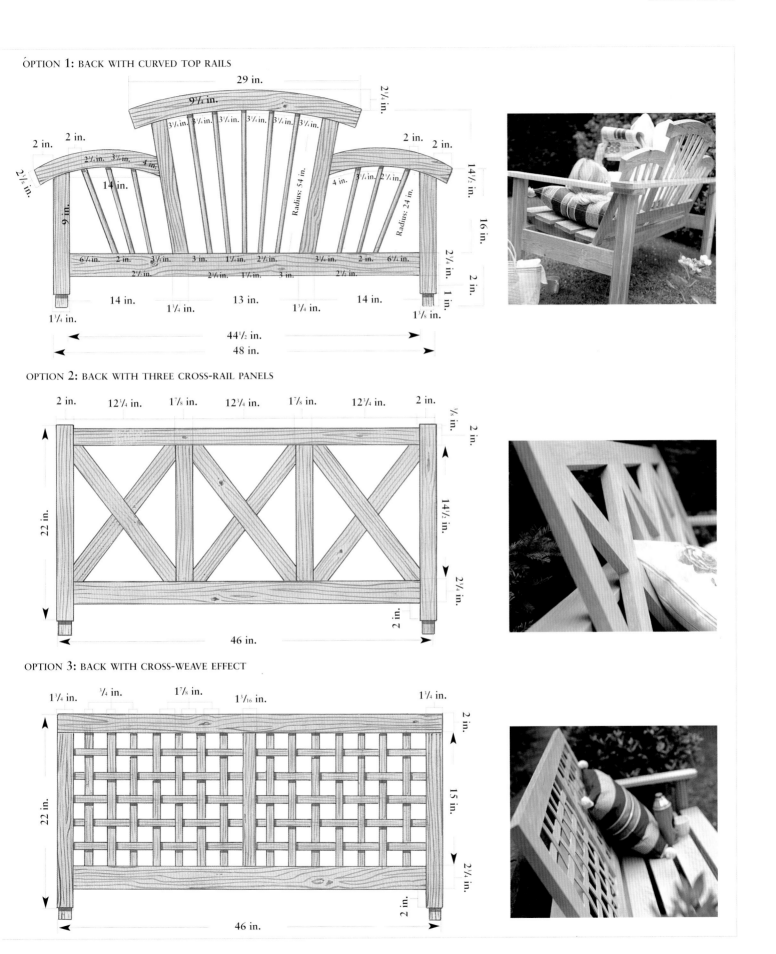

OPTION 1: BACK WITH CURVED TOP RAILS

OPTION 2: BACK WITH THREE CROSS-RAIL PANELS

OPTION 3: BACK WITH CROSS-WEAVE EFFECT

drill the bulk of the waste out of the set-out mortise to a depth of 1⅝ in. Use a depth stop or place masking tape around the bit to maintain the correct depth. Remove the waste from the mortise with a ½-in. mortise chisel to the squared lines.

5 Finish the width with a 1-in. bevel-edged firmer chisel, paring back to the gauged lines. Be sure you chisel straight to keep the mortise true.

6 Next, cut the side rails 25¼ in. long. Set out the shoulder lines 1⅝ in. in from each end. Square these around the rails with a marking knife. Scribe the tenons ½ in. thick. Place vertically in a vice and cut down to the shoulder lines with a tenon saw. Remove and lay flat against a bench hook. Cut on the waste side of the shoulder line to remove the waste on both sides. Stand upright again and cut ¼ in. off the width on each edge. Cut across the shoulder lines to reveal the tenon. Test for fit and adjust as required.

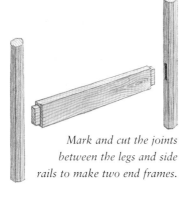

Mark and cut the joints between the legs and side rails to make two end frames.

7 Now, mark the mortise-and-tenon joints for the front longitudinal rail. The rail is 9 in. up and 4 in. high. Set out and cut the mortises in the front legs, 1⅝ in. deep. Cut the rail 53½ in. long and set out and cut the tenons.

8 Now, cut the bottom longitudinal rail 52⅜ in. long. Square a shoulder line 1⅛ in. in from each end. Set the marking gauge to 1 in. and mark the double tenon on each end. Scribe a line off each edge from the shoulder line to the end, across the end, and back down to the shoulder line. Hold flat on a sawhorse and cut down the waste side to the shoulders with a ripsaw. Remove the center with a 1-in. chisel from both sides. Maintain a square cut to ensure the rail fits against the side rail.

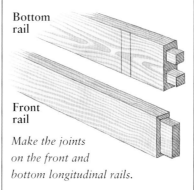

Bottom
rail

Front
rail

Make the joints on the front and bottom longitudinal rails.

9 Next, mark and cut the through mortises on the side rails, which will accommodate the bottom longitudinal rail. These will need to be cut at an angle so that the rail sits in the correct position. Measure 6⅜ in. across from the back leg on the bottom edge. Square this across the bottom edge, sloping up to the back. Mark a 75-degree bevel up each face with a sliding bevel and pencil. Mark a second line 1 in. parallel. Lay the side rail on a flat surface and stand the back rail on end between these beveled lines. Keep the bottom corner flush with the bottom of the side rail. Trace the tenon width onto the rail to mark the mortise sizes. Mark the mortises on both sides of the side rails. Bore a hole in the center of each mortise with a ¾-in. auger

bit in a brace. Chisel the mortises square from both sides with a 1-in. chisel. Test the fit and adjust as required.

10 Next, set out a square stub tenon at the top of both the front and back legs. The measurement from the bottom of each leg is 22½ in., giving a larger tenon on the two longer back legs. Set a marking gauge to ½ in. and scribe the width of the tenon. Lay flat and cut on the waste side of the shoulder line down to the gauge line on all four sides. Hold the leg vertically in a vice and cut the sides with the tenon saw.

11 Now, make the arms of the bench. Cut them to a length of 28¾ in. Set out the stopped mortises that match the stub tenons on the top of the front legs—1⁷⁄₁₆ in. square x ¾ in. deep. Square the first line across at 2½ in. along from one end. Square the second line another 1⁷⁄₁₆ in. along. Gauge the width with a marking gauge set at 1¼ in. from both edges.

12 The front stopped mortise is cut with a 1-in. chisel. First cut a small mortise the size of the chisel down to the required depth of ¾ in., and then work back to the set-out lines.

13 Set out the through mortises of the same size for the back legs in the underside of the arms—½ in. in from the end. Transfer the mortise set-out on the bottom to the top. Drill this mortise right through the arm and chisel square to the set-out.

14 The front end of the bench arm can be shaped: In this case, a beveled 45-degree corner has been cut, which echoes the angles in the octagonal legs.

Cut a mortise in the shaped arm and fit it to the tenon on the leg.

15 Assemble the end frames dry. If all is well, sand all marks off with 120-grit sandpaper and glue with exterior grade adhesive. Check the frame for square and twist. Apply pressure with sash clamps until the adhesive has set. Remember to remove any excess with a damp cloth before it dries.

The completed end frame.

16 Next, cut the upper back rail square and to a length of 55 in. Set out a stopped mortise on each end to fit over the tenon that protrudes through the arm. The mortise is 1¼ in. in from each end and only ⁵⁄₁₆ in. deep. Cut this in the same way as you did before. The ends of the back rail can also be shaped with a 45-degree corner.

17 Cut the mortises in the bottom longitudinal rail. First, set out a mortise ½ in. wide and 4⅞ in. on the face side along from the shoulder line at each end. Scribe a line ⅜ in. down and 3³⁄₁₆ in. down from the top edge to give a 2¾ in. long mortise. Cut these mortises ¾ in. deep in the same manner as before. On the top of this rail, set out a mortise 1½ in. in from each shoulder line, 1⁵⁄₁₆ in. long and ½ in. wide. Hold the rail securely in a vice, and drill and chisel the mortise out in a similar manner as the other mortises.

Cut two mortises in either end of the back rail to fit onto each arm.

18 Assemble the glued end frames, two longitudinal rails, and back rail dry. Keep them clamped and check for fit and square. Adjust as required.

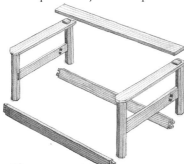

The components of the main frame.

19 Disassemble and glue the main frame together. Place in clamps again and be sure the frame is square and true. When dry, remove from clamps and clean all surfaces with sandpaper. You now have a strong frame to which you will add the seat and back.

Making the seat

20 Mark out the two seat bearers 18½ in. long. Set out and cut the 2¾ in. wide x ½ in. thick tenons at one end to fit the ¾ in. deep mortises in the face of the back rail.

Fit each seat bearer into the back longitudinal rail.

21 Mark the position of the bearer on the front rail. Square these marks down the inside face of the front rail. Scribe a line across this squared line 1 in. down. Measure the distance between this scribed line and the inside of the bottom edge of the back rail. Square a line across the bottom of the bearer this distance from the shoulder. Mark the beveled line on the face side at a 75° angle. Mark a second parallel line 1 in. farther forward. Measure up 1 in. on the inside bevel. Square a line off the bevel between the two. Remove the center by cutting down to the line and chiseling away the waste to create the groove.

Using a trammel

A trammel is used to draw large circles. It works like a protractor, enabling you to mark out accurate curves. A trammel has a pair of points that are attached to a timber arm. Each point is adjustable along the arm to provide varying centers. One point can usually be replaced with a pencil.

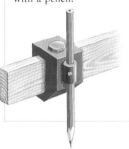

Additional tools for back option 1

Trammel

Jigsaw

The shaped bearers in position on the end frame.

22 The top edge of the bearer has a shape cut for the seat slats to sit on, which makes it more comfortable. Square lines across the top edge from the front at 3³/₁₆ in., 7 in., 11½ in., and 15¾ in. At the front end, measure down ½ in. from the 11½-in. mark to create the shape. Cut to shape with a hand saw and clean up with abrasive paper. Position the bearers in the mortises and over the front rail.

23 Check the fit and adjust as required. Apply adhesive and fix in place with a 2-in. galvanized nail through the back of the front rail to hold the bearer in place.

24 Mark and cut the four seat slats 47 in. long. After giving the slats a light sand, apply a little adhesive to the back of each slat and hold in place ensuring the overhang at each end is equal. Fix through the top of the slats with two 2 x ¹/₈ in. jolt-head galvanized nails into each bearer. Remember to angle each nail to increase the holding power. Punch the nails below the surface.

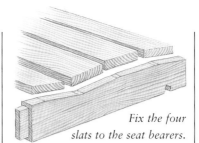

Fix the four slats to the seat bearers.

The drawing on page 259 shows the seat back with three alternative backs.

Option 1: back with curved top rails

The curved effect of the top rails is marked out with a tool called a trammel (see box, left).

1 First, mark and cut the tenons on the lower end of the vertical uprights 1 in. long, 1³/₈ in. wide, and ½ in. thick. Test the fit in the top of the back longitudinal rail.

2 Next, cut the back rail 46 in. long. Set out a 1-in. tenon at each end – 1½ in. thick and 2 in. wide. Cut these in the usual manner.

3 Mark out and cut a matching mortise in each upright 2½ in. up from the shoulder line of the tenon, for the bottom rail. Cut these in the usual manner.

Cut the joints between the back and the bottom rail.

4 Next, set out and draw a full scale drawing (set-out) of the back on a sheet of plywood or particle board (see drawings on pages 258–9 for measurements). This will help you to set out the curved rails and angled uprights.

5 Lay the bottom rail over the set-out and mark the position of the two angled uprights on the top edge. Be careful to keep the shoulder lines at each end in the correct location and set out the mortises on the top of the rail. Chisel the two mortises 1 in. deep, ½ in. wide, and 1³/₈ in. long. Chisel out and check for fit.

6 Next, prepare the timber pieces from which you are going to cut the curved rails. Position one of the lower curved rail pieces over the top of the set-out. Set a trammel to a 24-in. radius. Place the base of the trammel arm on the top edge of the bottom rail position on the set-out and use the trammel to trace the curve of the lower edge of the rail on the timber piece.

Mark the curve on the timber with a trammel.

7 Fix the rail over the saw stool and hold firm with a G-cramp. Cut the curve with a jigsaw. True the cut edge with abrasive paper. Lay over the set-out and check the shape. If all is right, change the radius on the trammel to 26 in. and scribe the top curve. Cut as before. Repeat this for all three curved back rails, using the measurements given on the drawings on pages 258–9. Clean up the curves with abrasive paper.

8 Next, mark and cut the mortises and tenons on the curved rails. Position each of the three curved rails in its correct location over the set-out and transfer the shoulder lines from all the upright pieces onto the edge of the rails. The two lower curved rails have a tenon on the inside end while the other end is cut at an angle. A mortise is also cut in from the outside end to match the tenon on the vertical upright. The top curved rail has a mortise cut in at each end and the ends cut at a bevel.

9 Set a sliding bevel to the angles the mortises are to be cut and mark the bevels down the face. Gauge the width of the mortises on the edges and at the ends for the tenons. Hold each in a vice and drill out and cut the mortises as before. Note all these mortises are at an angle.

10 Stand each lower rail in the vice and cut the tenons in the ends. Cramp horizontally to a flat surface and cut the shoulder lines. Cut the tenon 1 in. long and parallel to the shoulder. Cut it 2 in. wide and trim the waste.

11 Next, mark the shoulders for the tenons on the uprights from the set-out – there should be one at the top of each vertical upright and one at the top of each angled upright. Note the shoulders are at an angle. Cut these tenons as before. Test each for accuracy.

12 Fit the angled uprights to the back rail and to the top curved back. Check for an accurate fit

over the set-out and mark the mortises in the outside edges. Cut as before.

13 Dry assemble the whole frame in cramps and check for fit. Adjust as required. Mark the position of the centers of the splayed dowels on the inside edges of the back rail, top curved rail and lower curved rails. Lay the dowel across from top to bottom to find the splay. Mark each angle on the face. Mark the length of each dowel to fit $\frac{5}{8}$ in. into each rail (see the drawing on pages 258–9). Number each dowel as the lengths vary, and cut to length with a tenon saw.

14 You can now disassemble the frame. Drill each dowel hole $\frac{3}{4}$ in. deep in the center of each edge. Hold the drill with the lead screw of the auger on the center line. Tilt the drill and bore the hole at the angle marked on the face. Test that each of the dowels fits and is leaning at the angle required.

Splay out the dowels and fix to the curved rails.

15 At this stage carry out a dry assembly of the complete back frame and, if all is well, disassemble, apply adhesive and cramp. Ensure the frame is square and free of wind. Remove all excess adhesive and leave to dry.

16 After a final sand, the back frame can now be fitted to the main frame. Apply the adhesive to the tenons at the bottom of the uprights. Insert the frame and push it onto the back rail. Fix each upright to the rail with two nails.

Finished bench with back in place.

Option 2: back with three cross-rail panels

1 Start by making a back frame consisting of two horizontal rails, two external vertical stiles and two internal vertical rails. First, make the two external vertical stiles: cut them to 22 in. in length and set out the tenons at one end of each, which will fit into the back longitudinal rail (see step 1, option 1). Set out two mortises on each stile 2 in. up from the shoulder line and

¾ in. down from the top – to accommodate each horizontal rail. The mortises are 1 in. deep, 2 in. long, and ½ in. wide in the center of the edge.

2 Make the two horizontal rails by cutting to 46 in. in length and set out the tenons at each end. These are 1 in. long, 2 in. wide, and ½ in. thick. Cut the tenons. Test the fit and adjust as required.

3 Set out the mortises, which will accommodate the internal vertical stiles. Square a line across the edge of each rail 13⅜ in. along from each shoulder. Square a second line the width of the internal stiles – 1¾ in. As with the other mortises, gauge a line ½ in. wide in the center. Cut each mortise in the usual manner, 1 in. deep.

4 Cut the two internal vertical stiles 16½ in. long, and set out 1-in. tenons at each end to suit the mortises.

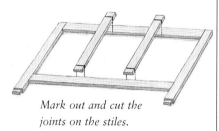

Mark out and cut the joints on the stiles.

5 Test the frame dry. Adjust as required and glue up. Ensure the frame is square and free of wind.

6 Now, make the cross-rails, which will fit into the back frame. Set out a halving joint on each pair of cross-rails 17¾ in. long. The halvings are in the center of each rail. Mark the width of the timber and

square it around the rail. Set a marking gauge to half the thickness and then scribe a line in between the set-out lines.

7 Lay flat against a bench hook and hold with a G-cramp. Cut with a tenon saw to the line. Place several other cuts across the timber between the set-out lines. Remove the waste with a chisel. Check the bottom for flatness. Repeat on the other rails. Test the fit of the three pairs and adjust the components as required.

8 Mark a center line down the length on the face of each end with a pencil. Hold the assembled cross-rail under the back frame so that the pencil lines align with the intersections of the vertical and horizontal rails. Trace the shapes onto the face of the cross-rail.

9 Cut the cross-rails to length. Square the corner marks down each edge of the rails. Hold flat and cut the ends of the rails to produce pointed ends. Cut, test the fit and adjust as required. Repeat for all three crosses.

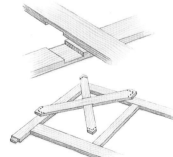

Cut and fix the halving joints where the two cross-rails meet.

10 Apply a little adhesive to the halving and the pointed ends. Insert the crosses into the back frame so that the faces are flush. Tap a 2-in. nail at each end of the cross-rails

into the back frame. Leave to dry. Sand all surfaces flat. Remove any sharp edges and fit the back to the seat and main frame.

Option 3: Back with cross-weave effect

This third option is made up of three vertical stiles and two horizontal rails. Plywood strips are interwoven within this frame to create the cross-weave effect.

1 Follow the step instructions given for option 2 to cut three vertical stiles and the horizontal rails to length. Fix stiles and rails together to make the basic frame as before with mortise and tenon joints.

2 Next, rout a ⅛-in groove along the inside edge of each of the frame members to accommodate the cross-weave strips.

3 Now, cut two vertical and two horizontal beech strips to length about 15¼ in. long and 45¼ in. long respectively and have a trial weaving of the strips. Remember to allow for the amount that will sit in the grooves. Check the length and trim as required. Once the correct length is obtained, cut the remaining strips.

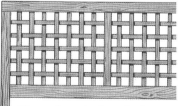

Weave the strips into the frame.

4 Put some adhesive in the grooves and reweave the strips. Ensure they fit all the way into the grooves.

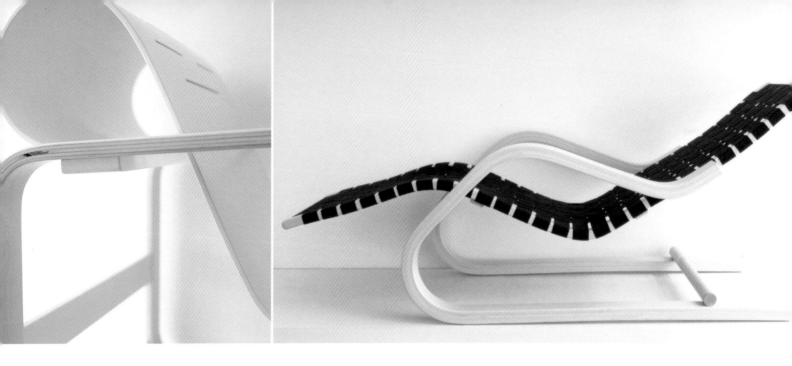

Bentwood and laminated furniture

The human body is not made up of straight lines and corners, and even though early chairs were rectilinear, it was realized that curved shapes were better suited to the human body. So during the early 19th century craftsmen set out to find a method by which wood could be shaped in different ways to make comfortable furniture.

BENTWOOD

The suppleness of wet wood had been utilized for centuries. The chair makers (Bodgers) in the English Chiltern woodlands used to make the bent backs from green ash or beech and even used the branches of small trees to drive their pole lathes. The "Windsor" chairs they made were ecological because components were cut, split, and turned to size and shape before leaving the forest. All waste would remain where the wood was worked and rot and so contribute to the growing cycle.

Later it was found that if wood is steamed, bent on a mold, and allowed to dry thoroughly, the shape would be permanent. Furniture made from this method is known as bentwood. The most successful early company to use the technique for large production runs was owned by Michael

Thonet's classic chair with a solid bentwood frame and cane seat.

Thonet, who came from a line of craftsmen. From about 1830 he began experimenting with wood bending as a way of making parts of his Biedermeier-style furniture. He began with chair backs and rungs, gluing together strips of thick veneer and clamping them in forms made of wood. He experimented with lamination and bending by steam by 1840, and by 1850, he had perfected a method for bending birch rods into fanciful shapes. The curvilinear shapes he employed followed the Rococo tradition. Bentwood chairs were technically innovative and cheap to produce—they became the model of furniture for a mass society and an ideal for furniture designers up to the present day. Thonet's classic chair that came to be called the "café chair" was produced in vast numbers and exported around the world. However, many of the chairs exported to South America were damaged by the humid climate, so the use of laminated parts was discontinued. It was a logical step to use solid wood but this caused great difficulties because it split at points of tension. So he developed the idea of using steel inlays and screwing or bolting wooden elements to them.

266

OPPOSITE LEFT *Alvar Aalto armchair in laminated birch and preformed plywood, designed in 1924.* ◆ OPPOSITE RIGHT *Alvar Aalto's laminated birch "Chair 43," designed in 1936–7.* ◆ ABOVE LEFT *Alvar Aalto stacking stools designed in 1932–3.* ◆ ABOVE CENTER *"Wishbone Chair" designed by Hans J. Wegner in 1950.* ◆ ABOVE RIGHT *Sori Yanagi's "Butterfly" stools, designed in 1956, made out of laminated birch bentwood.*

DEVELOPERS OF LAMINATION

The principle of laminating and preforming is different from steam bending. The wood is cut into thin sheets or strips and kept dry. Adhesive is applied to the faces and this parcel of strips is placed in a shaped mold. When the adhesive has cured the shape is thus captured. There were experiments during the 19th century by Thonet and others but it was not until adhesive technology developed from natural to synthetic resins that the technique became successful and widely used.

The master designer of laminations was the Finnish architect Alvar Aalto. He made use of wood in dramatically new ways. His most original idea was to make use of the natural moisture in woods such as birch, rather than bending by steam alone, which is what Thonet had done. In 1932 he produced a chair with a seat and back made up of one continuous piece of bent plywood resting on frames of tubular style. He made furniture entirely of wood and made use of solid wood, laminated wood, and combinations of the two. His tables, desks, cabinets, and chairs rest on solid wood legs that separate at the knee into laminated curves and run either partway or connect horizontally with the opposite leg. This unusual construction gives a light, strong knee joint and greater stability. He worked entirely in laminated wood, taking advantage of the resilience, strength, and lightness inherent in the wood. The material was abundant in Finland at the time.

Before World War II the architects Charles Eames and Eero Saarinen (see also page 282) entered a competition in New York for "Organic Design in Home Furnishings" and both won first prizes. Their designs for chairs were revolutionary—united seat, back, and armrests in a single shell form made of strips of veneer, laminated in a cast-iron mold. The war stopped the development of such designs but Eames and his wife Ray helped the war effort by developing their techniques to make splints and other aids for wounded soldiers. Eames continued after the war with superb furniture, which again was very simple and classic. In 1956 he produced his famous "Lounge Chair" and "Ottoman 670/671," which used preform plywood shells with an outside facing of rosewood veneer and black leather down cushions on a cast-aluminum base.

Eames's classic "Lounge Chair" designed in 1956.

267

Linen cupboard *Advanced*

This linen cupboard is very versatile, and features two different cupboard doors and two drawers. If necessary, the dimensions of the linen cupboard can be adjusted to suit your own particular storage requirements.

Tools

- Smoothing plane
- Radial-arm saw
- C-clamp
- Sanding block
- Router with 1/4-in straight cutter
- Sash clamps
- Sliding bevel
- Dovetail saw
- Coping saw
- 1/4-in. bevel-edged and 1/2-in. paring chisels
- Marking knife
- Marking gauge
- Tenon saw
- Bradawl
- Drill and 1/8-in., 5/32-in., 3/16-in., and countersink bits
- Screwdriver
- Hand saw
- Drill press and 1 5/8-in. Forstner bit or hole saw

Skills required for project

- Measuring and marking *pages 64–7*
- Basic sawing *pages 68–71*
- Planing *pages 74–81*
- Fine sawing *pages 82–5*
- Making grooves *pages 90–3*
- Drilling *pages 96–100*
- Making mortise-and-tenon joints *pages 104–9*
- Making dovetail joints *pages 112–14*
- Assembling projects *pages 120–7*
- Using adhesives *pages 128–9*

MATERIALS

Part	Materials and dimensions	No.
	Solid wood, hardwood to suit (light-colored advised):	
Legs	40 x 2 x 3/4 in.	4
Sides	30 x 12 1/2 x 3/4 in.	2
Top	21 x 16 x 1 in.	1
Top cross-rails	16 x 3 3/8 x 1 in.	2
Bottom rails	16 x 2 x 1 in.	1
	16 x 1 3/4 x 1 in.	1
Inside cross-rails	16 x 2 x 3/4 in.	4
Door fronts	13 x 6 x 3/4 cutout	1
Cupboard fall	13 x 12 x 3/4 cutout	1
False top drawer front	13 x 5 x 3/4 cutout	1
Top drawer front	13 x 3 1/2 x 1/2 cutout	1
Top drawer sides	13 x 3 1/2 x 1/2 cutout	2
Top drawer back	13 x 3 x 3/8 in.	1
False bottom drawer front	13 x 6 x 3/4 in.	1
Bottom drawer front	13 x 5 x 1/2 in.	1
Bottom drawer sides	13 x 5 x 1/2 in.	2
Bottom drawer back	13 x 3 3/4 x 3/8 in.	1
Drawer runners	12 1/2 x 1 1/2 x 5/8 in.	4
	Plywood	
Cabinet back	28 1/2 x 12 1/2 x 1/4 in.	1
Drawer bottoms	12 1/4 x 11 1/2 x 1/4 in.	2
Shelves	14 1/2 x 9 1/2 x 1/4 in.	2
Tongues	30 x 3/8 x 1/4 in.	4

Other materials: fourteen 1/2-in. 5 gauge flat head screws; three 3/4-in. 6 gauge flat head screws; twelve 1 1/4-in. 8 gauge flat head screws; one pair of 2-in. broad butt hinges with screws; two pairs of 2-in. butt hinges with screws; double-sided tape (thin); adhesive (PVA); sandpaper (120-grit); finish.

Making the cabinet

1 The cabinet sides may need to be made from two or more pieces of wood in order to obtain the required width (see box, page 197). Cut and plane the sides to 2 x 3/4-in. Cut and plane the four legs to size—28 1/2 x 12 1/2-in. Cut them to a length of 38 3/4 in. on a radial-arm saw.

2 The bottom of each leg is shaped. Square a line around each leg at 8 7/8 in. up from the bottom to represent the top of the cut-out shape. Pencil gauge a line 3/4 in. in from the face edge, from the bottom to this line. Set out a curve between the set-out lines. You can do this by simply tracing around a can or jar. Repeat the shaping on each leg. Clamp each leg down on a flat surface with a C-clamp and cut along the set-out on the waste side. Clean up the sawed edge with 120-grit sandpaper.

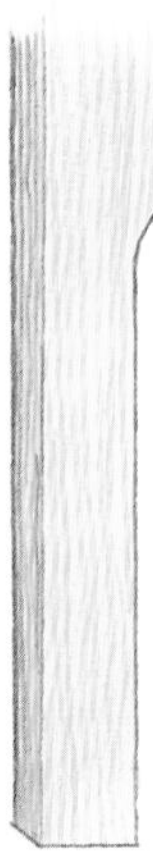

Cut the curved legs to shape.

3 Make the grooves that will accept the sides on the inside face of each leg. Remember to set out in pairs. Square a line 1 in. up from the curve on the inside face of each leg. Set up the router with a 1/4-in. straight cutter and the fence to run a groove 1/4 in. deep and 5/16 in. in from the face. Hold the leg on a firm, flat surface with a C-clamp, and run the router from the top along the length to the squared set-out lines.

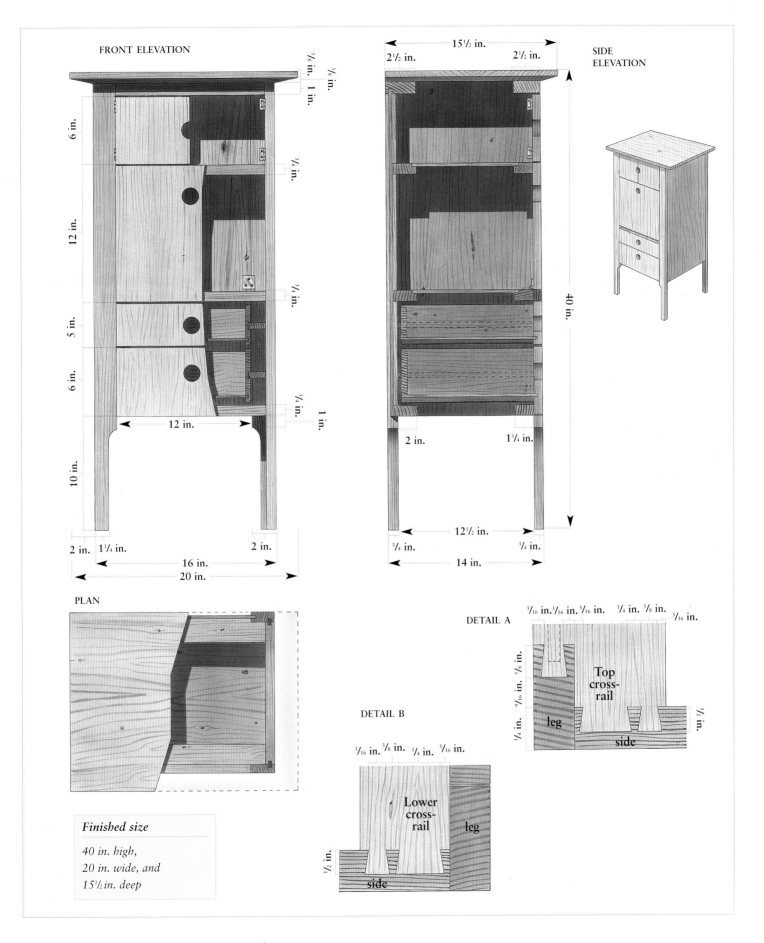

FRONT ELEVATION

⅝ in.
⅜ in.
1 in.

6 in.

12 in.

5 in.

6 in.

¾ in.

¾ in.

¾ in.

1 in.

12 in.

10 in.

2 in. 1¼ in. 2 in.

16 in.

20 in.

15½ in.

2½ in. 2½ in.

SIDE
ELEVATION

40 in.

2 in. 1¾ in.

12½ in.

¾ in. ¾ in.

14 in.

PLAN

Finished size

*40 in. high,
20 in. wide, and
15½ in. deep*

DETAIL A

3/16 in. 3/16 in. 3/16 in.   ¼ in. ⅜ in.   3/16 in.

⅝ in.

9/16 in.

¾ in.

leg

Top
cross-
rail

side

½ in.

DETAIL B

3/16 in. ⅜ in. ¾ in. 3/16 in.

Lower
cross-
rail

leg

½ in.

side

269

Linenfold panels

Linenfold panels

These are stylized representations of linen arranged in vertical folds, and were first made in the late 15th century, probably by Flemish carvers. Regional variations appeared in France, England, and Germany by the end of that century. Linenfold was used on chests, presses, wall paneling, and chimneypieces and was the commonest form of furniture decoration in the late 15th and 16th centuries, although it lost favor after about 1570. Some authorities have suggested that the panels were originally intended to indicate the storing place of bed linen, but there is no evidence for this. The term linenfold was given to the decoration much later, probably in the 19th century. Despite its origin, linenfold is now regarded as the trademark of the English carver.

4 A second groove is required in the inside face edge of the back legs to accept the plywood backing. This groove is routed with the same set-up. Hold each leg on edge in the vice and run the groove. The same grooves can be run along both edges of the side panels to match. Repeat on the other legs.

Cut a groove in the inside face of each leg for the panel sides.

5 Cut a ³⁄₈ in. wide plywood tongue for each side panel joint. Glue the legs onto the sides, applying PVA adhesive to each groove, and insert the tongue. Make sure that the outsides are flush and each leg is flush on the top edge. Place in a pair of sash clamps and remove any excess adhesive with a damp cloth. Check that the panel unit is flat and flush across the surface. Let dry. Make the second panel unit in the same way.

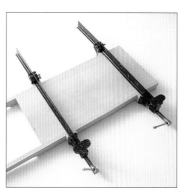

Clamp the frames together and allow to dry.

6 Next, make the top cross-rails, which will dovetail into the top of the legs and sides. Cut the rails 15¹⁄₈ in. long. Square a line around each end for the shoulders and mark the

spacing for the dovetails on the rails, as shown in detail A on page 269, at a pitch of 1:6. Note the top rails are 3³⁄₈ in. wide and have two shoulder lines. Mark the dovetails with a sliding bevel down the face to the shoulder lines. Square these across the end and then return the set-out bevels to the opposite side.

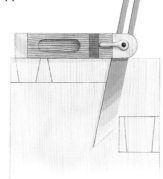

Mark the dovetails on the cross-rails.

7 Hold vertically in a vice and cut the sides of the dovetails on the waste side to the shoulders with a dovetail saw. Turn the piece in the vice horizontally and accurately cut the half pin sockets to the line with the dovetail saw. Remove the bulk of the waste from the full pin sockets using a coping saw and cutting approximately ¹⁄₈ in. on the waste side of the line. Hold the wood firmly on a flat surface and trim the socket back to the shoulder line with a sharp ¹⁄₄-in. bevel-edged paring chisel. Cut only half way through and then turn the piece over and pare the remaining waste to the shoulder line.

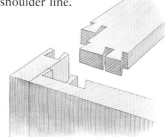

Dovetail the top rails into the sides and legs.

8 The two bottom cross-rails are similar, but are only dovetailed in the sides, not the legs (see detail B on page 269).

Dovetail the lower rails into the sides.

9 Place each completed rail in position on the appropriate end of the cabinet sides. Number the end of each rail and side panel for ease of matching later. Accurately align the shoulders and edges. Cut around the shape of the tails to set out the sockets, using a sharp marking knife. Square the set-out back down the inside face. Set a marking gauge to the thickness of the rail and scribe the depth on the inside face.

10 Hold the side firmly and cut at an angle with the dovetail saw on the waste side of the sockets. The cut will extend from the depth line on the end grain down to the shoulder line on the face. Lay flat and remove the waste from the socket with a sharp chisel. Use the chisel to remove the bulk of the waste by cutting straight down—in from the shoulder line and then along the grain—splitting out the waste to approximately ¹⁄₈ in. from each set-out line. Trim the shoulder and depth lines with a sharp paring chisel. Assemble the parts and adjust as necessary by carefully paring with a chisel.

11 With the top and bottom rails in position, the cabinet should now stand. The four inside cross-rails will be stub-tenoned into the sides, and so these joints need to be marked and cut. The shoulder lengths are the same as for the top and bottom rails. The tenons are also the same length as the dovetails—$\frac{1}{2}$ in. at each end. Cut the four rails to length and square the shoulder lines around each end. The tenon is 1 in. wide. Set a marking gauge to $\frac{1}{2}$ in. and scribe the tenon from each edge. Cut the tenons with a tenon or dovetail saw down the gauge line and then across the shoulder line. The two back rails will require the same cutout at each end as the bottom rail—$\frac{5}{16}$ x $1\frac{3}{16}$ in. Check the fit of the cross-rails in the carcass and adjust as required.

Check that the cross-rails are cut to the correct length.

12 Set out the mortises on the inside face of the side panels. The first rail is 6 in. down from under the top rail. Measure down another 12 in. for the second. Mark the thickness of each rail below these points. Hold the rails in position between the set-outs and mark the tenon width with a pencil. Hold firmly on a flat surface and chisel the mortise to a depth of $\frac{1}{2}$ in. Cut down the required depth, and then work back to the shoulder lines. Check the fit and adjust as required.

Mark the positions of the mortises on the inside face of the carcass.

13 With the router set as before, run a groove on the underside of the back top rail to accept the plywood backing. Move the fence on the router and run a $\frac{1}{4}$ x $\frac{1}{4}$-in. rabbet along the top inside edge of each inside cross-rail.

14 Assemble the cabinet dry to check all is correct. When you are satisfied, sand all the components to remove the set-out lines and marks with 120-grit sandpaper. Apply the first finish coat on the inside faces. Assemble the carcass using PVA glue and sash clamps. Check the cabinet is square and free of twist. Any correction may be made by moving the clamps a little. Clean off excess adhesive. Let to dry.

15 Cut the plywood to size. Check that it will fit in the grooves in the back legs, and will slide up from the bottom to the top groove. Finish both sides of this panel, slide it in position and fix to the bottom rear rail with three $\frac{3}{4}$-in. screws.

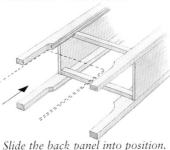

Slide the back panel into position.

The completed carcass.

Making the top

16 Plane the top all round to 20 x $15\frac{1}{2}$ in., and be sure the surface is flat and the edges true.

17 Mark the bevel with a pencil. Gauge one line $\frac{5}{8}$ in. down from the top and another 2 in. inside the three edges on the bottom. This will be the bevel that needs to be planed off on the two ends and front while the back is left square. Hold upright in a vice or clamp down on a flat surface, and plane the bevels on the end grain first. Plane at a slight angle to prevent breakout. Plane with the grain along the front edge.

Plane the underside bevel on the cabinet top.

18 The cabinet top will be fastened in place with screws inserted from underneath the top rails. Drill and countersink four $\frac{3}{16}$ in. clearance holes in these rails. Place the top in position and mark the holes with a bradawl.

Fitting doors

There are two ways of fastening doors to the linen cupboard. Here, the top doors are held in place with two hinges in each side. The bottom door is a fall, which is held secure with a pivot hinge in the bottom.

Door on side hinges.

Door as a fall.

19 The top can be removed and ⅛-in. pilot holes drilled, and then secured temporarily with 1¼-in. 8 gauge screws.

Screw the top in place.

Fitting out the cabinet

20 Take the two plywood shelves and cut to fit neatly in place between the rabbets on the inside rails. Cut slightly oversize with a hand saw and trim to fit with a smoothing plane. Secure with a little adhesive in each rabbet.

Fit the plywood shelves.

21 Now gather the pieces that will make the two top doors, the fall, and the two bottom drawer fronts. The grain should run horizontally through all of these. Each piece can be cut approximately to its vertical size and planed to fit between the front legs with a ⅛-in. clearance. Now mark the positions of the centers of the handle cutouts and drill with a Forstner bit or a hole saw using a drill press.

22 The top two doors are cut from the one piece already fitted. Crosscut this through the center vertically and plane precisely to fit. Fasten the top doors to the cabinet with hinges on the sides and the bottom one as a fall (see box left and pages 120–7).

23 Because the legs form a recess within the cabinet sides, normal drawer-running methods cannot be used. Here the drawer runners are fixed to the inside of the cabinet, projecting from the line of the legs as shown in the drawing on page 269. Prepare, mark, and cut the runners. Fit each with two 1³/₁₆-in. 8 gauge flat head screws through the side panel. Be sure that the screw heads are well below the surface.

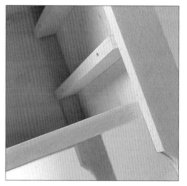

Fit the drawer runners.

Making the drawers

24 The two drawers are joined at the corners with dovetail joints. Cut the wood to length. The sides are 12 in. long, and the back and front are cut to the distance between the runners, plus ½ in. for the side grooves. Note the width of the material for the back is smaller than that of the sides and front to fit the plywood bottom.

25 Mark the thickness of the material on the ends of all the pieces. Square this around each. Determine the number of dovetails required. The side pieces will have the tails cut on each end. Measure ½ in. across from the left-hand edge on the squared line. Divide the remaining width up into even parts equal to the number of tails required.

26 Mark the width of each tail—½ in.—to the left of each division. Set a sliding bevel to a pitch of 1:6 as before. Mark the sides of each dovetail using the sliding bevel. Square the tails across the end and bevel down the other side to match. Clearly mark the waste in the pin sockets.

27 Cut the sides of the dovetails with a dove-tail saw and remove the waste using a coping saw. Then pare back to the shoulder lines with a chisel. Cut the pins as shown on pages 182–3.

28 With the router, run a ¼ in. wide groove ¼ in. deep. Run the top edge of the groove to line up with the bottom edge of the back, but set inside the bottom edge on the side pieces and front. Apply adhesive to the contact surfaces and assemble the drawer. Clamp if required and allow to dry, ensuring the drawer is square and free of twist.

29 Remove from clamps and clean up the joints. Cut the drawer bottom and slide into the groove. Check for square and fix in place through the bottom of the drawer into the edge of the back with three ½-in. 5 gauge flat head screws. Make the other drawer.

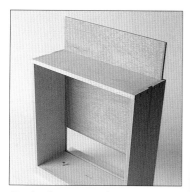

Fit the drawer together.

30 Running the drawers requires a groove along each side of the drawer. Adjust the router to cut a groove wide enough for the runner in the center of the side. The depth is already set to ¼ in. Adjust the fence to run the groove. This will need to have several passes along the drawer, adjusting each time until a width of ¾ in. is obtained. Clean groove with a chisel and sandpaper.

31 False decorative fronts are attached to the drawers. Place each drawer in the cabinet and apply two small pieces of thin double-sided tape on the front. Push all the way in. Hold the false front in position and bring the drawer forward to meet the back of the false front. The tape will hold the two together. Remove and place face down on a flat, smooth surface. Drill four ½-in. screws through the inside of the drawer into the decorative front. Replace drawer to check alignment and adjust as required. Repeat for the other drawer, leaving enough room for the fall above to operate.

Finishing

32 Sand and apply required finish. A strap or flap stay can be added to the fall to prevent straining the hinges.

Modernism and beyond

The transition from the 19th to 20th century was marked by many social, political, and technological changes. In the arts the old ways were questioned and new ideas brought different approaches to all manner of problems. New technologies were established that, by the end of the 20th century, caused very great changes. This evolution was both interrupted and quickened by World War I between 1914 and 1918. Mobilization and the resulting carnage meant the loss to some countries of a whole generation, but it also forced progress in technology, changed social attitudes, and gave art and design new practical, visual, and aesthetic aims. The 1920s and 1930s were times of very varied experiences, none more so than in art and design. The cataclysm of war marked the turning point because what came out of it was not only disillusionment and poverty but a desire to experiment.

DE STIJL AND BAUHAUS
Although occupied by German forces, Holland had avoided much of the fighting and been largely spared by the war, so it was in a better position to lead the way. Gerrit Reitveld had worked during the war years on radical designs that discarded any reference to the past, drawing exclusively upon rectangular and cubic forms. He was a constructionist and a member of a group that explained its theories in a magazine called de Stijl, and the name has since been used to refer to the group itself. Their ideals valued abstract, rectangular forms that used only the primary colors of red, blue, and yellow.

The design of this chair by Le Corbusier has the ergonomics of the human form in mind.

274

OPPOSITE LEFT *A child's chair, designed in 1928 by Erick Dieckmann, a member of the Bauhaus school.* ◆ OPPOSITE CENTRE *Designed by Charlotte Perriand, working with Le Corbusier, Le Petit Confort chair is made out of chromed, bent tubular steel with dark leather upholstery.* ◆ OPPOSITE RIGHT *Designers used minimal materials for maximum style as shown in this table, made in 1929–33.* ◆ ABOVE LEFT *Classic tubular steel chairs with red leather seats and backs, called "Basculant" and designed by Le Corbusier.* ◆ ABOVE CENTER *Mies van der Rohe's "Daybed," designed in 1929.* ◆ ABOVE RIGHT *A glass and steel table designed by Eileen Gray in 1927.*

They felt their choice of geometric forms had a higher spiritual level and believed that, through total simplification and abstraction, the art and design world could transform individual, selfish civilization into a spiritual, idealistic one.

The basic ideas of the de Stijl group were developed by the Bauhaus in the 1920s. In Germany this was the focal point for a new movement after the war. Started in Weimar in 1919 by the architect Walter Gropius, it approached the education of architects, artists, designers, and makers in a new way. The most progressive practitioners were invited to become lecturers, the studio and workshops were linked and the subjects ranged from architecture, design, and graphics to the performing arts. Newness and invention were paramount to this movement— students were taught to probe and seek out a solution that was both a rational result of the tools and materials that they were using and an exact fulfillment of its function. This approach was so right for the time that its influence was felt across the world.

INTRODUCTION OF METAL

Bauhaus designers often used furniture materials other than wood, and it was at this time that Marcel Breuer first experimented with metal furniture. In 1924–5 he used non-resilient chrome tubing to construct a number of totally new designs, notably an armchair that was related in formal structure to Rietveld's work. It emphasized the angular form, but instead of upholstery Breuer used canvas, and the frame was made of metal. Architect Mies van de Rohe also began working in metal, creating work in steel strip. In 1928,

Breuer designed a tubular steel chair, which was later manufactured by Thonet. This became the accepted prototype for many chairs to come. It combined maximum comfort with minimum materials—one piece of continuously curved metal tubing—eliminating the need for costly joints. It fueled the urge to reduce form to its minimum, then referred to as "functional" design. Some resulting furniture was crude, but done well, this approach led to extreme elegance in design. Breuer designed chairs, tables, cabinets, and beds using this method.

In 1929, Mies designed the Barcelona chair, which was named after the international exhibition for which he designed the German Pavilion, where his chair was an integral element. The chair's frame consisted of two crossing curves of steel bars. This has become a classic piece of 20th- century furniture design.

Many other architects and designers also used metal in their designs including the famous French architect, Le Corbusier. Initially he used simple Thonet bentwood chairs in his interiors. Then, along with his associate Charlotte Perriand, he designed metal furniture that was closely related to Bauhaus work. However, while the German interest lay in the individual design of pieces, Le Corbusier saw design as a technical, social, and economic problem for which a general solution could be found. He reduced all furniture to three categories—tables, chairs, and open or enclosed shelves—and then set about designing standard forms for each. Another designer who experimented with new materials and processes was Eileen Gray (see also page 207).

Dining chair *Advanced*

This chair has simple classic but modern lines. Dining chairs are normally made without arms, but there are often two chairs in a set called carvers, which are versions with arms. Instructions and measurements are given for both.

Tools

- Radial-arm saw
- Smoothing plane
- Box square
- Marking gauge
- C-clamps
- Drill press and 1-in. Forstner bit
- $\frac{3}{8}$-in.mortise
- $\frac{1}{2}$-in. and 1-in. paring chisels
- Drill and $\frac{5}{16}$-in. and $\frac{3}{8}$-in. bits
- Sliding bevel
- Tenon saw
- Jigsaw
- Coping saw
- Router with $\frac{5}{16}$-in. straight bit
- Smoothing plane
- Screwdriver

Skills required for project

- Measuring and marking *pages 64–7*
- Basic sawing *pages 68–71*
- Planing *pages 74–81*
- Fine sawing *pages 82–5*
- Making grooves *pages 90–3*
- Shaping *pages 94–5*
- Drilling *pages 96–100*
- Making mortise-and-tenon joints *pages 104–9*
- Using abrasives *pages 115–17*
- Assembling projects *pages 120–7*
- Using adhesives *pages 128–9*
- Wood finishing *pages 130–5*

MATERIALS

Part	Materials and dimensions	No.
	Hardwood	
Front legs	18 x $1\frac{3}{8}$ in. diameter	2
Back legs	$33\frac{1}{2}$ x $1\frac{3}{8}$ in. diameter	2
Front rail	16 x $2\frac{1}{2}$ x $\frac{3}{4}$ in.	1
Back rail	16 x $2\frac{1}{2}$ x $\frac{3}{4}$ in.	1
Top rail	13 x $1\frac{1}{2}$ x $\frac{3}{4}$ in.	1
Cross-rails	$16\frac{1}{2}$ x $3\frac{1}{4}$ x $\frac{3}{4}$ in.	2
Arms for carver	16 x $3\frac{1}{2}$ x $\frac{7}{8}$ in.	4
	Bending plywood	
Chair seat	18 x 16 x $\frac{1}{16}$ in.	5
Chair back	22 x 18 x $\frac{1}{16}$ in.	5
	Manufactured board	
Two preform molds	$17\frac{3}{4}$ x 2 x $\frac{3}{4}$ in. $23\frac{5}{8}$ x 4 x $\frac{3}{4}$ in.	28 16

Other materials: six 1-in. 8 gauge brass flat head screws; adhesive (PVA); sandpaper (120-grit); finish.

Making the underframe

The underframe is made up of four legs, a front rail, a back rail, two cross-rails, and a backrest top rail.

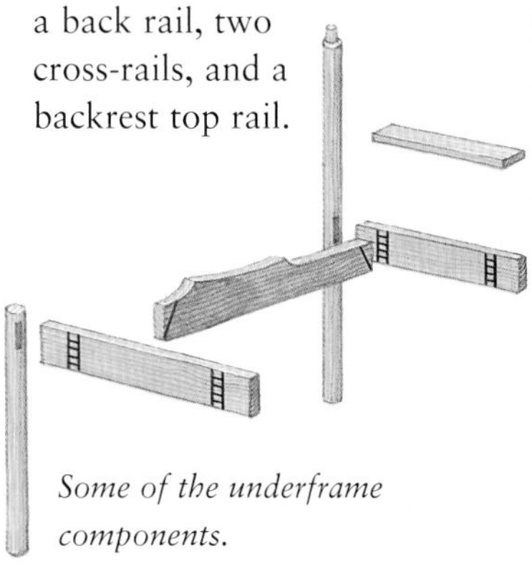

Some of the underframe components.

1 Prepare the two back and two front legs. Saw these square with a radial-arm saw, leaving a little extra on the length. You will make these round later either by turning or planing. Plane each to an octagonal shape in order to make marking and cutting the joints easier (see page 246). Mark the length and the position of the rail joints using a box square. Measure up $12\frac{1}{4}$ in. on the back legs and $13\frac{5}{8}$ in. on the front legs.

2 Then mark a mortise on each leg $2\frac{3}{16}$ in. farther up. Set a marking gauge and mark the mortise between the lines. Hold the leg on a solid surface with a C-clamp and drill out the bulk of the waste from the mortise to a depth of 1 in. Use a depth stop or masking tape to prevent drilling all the way through. Chisel the mortise to the set-out lines with a $\frac{3}{8}$-in. mortise chisel. Clean up the sides of the mortise with a 1-in. paring chisel. Take care to chisel true to the set-out.

3 Next, prepare the front rail. Cut to $14\frac{5}{8}$ in. long on a radial-arm saw. Square a line across the bottom edge at both ends—1 in. in from each end, leaving $12\frac{5}{8}$ in. in between. Set a sliding bevel to a pitch of 1:6 and mark the shoulder across both faces. Return the squared line across the top edge.

4 Cut the tenons on the ends of the rail to match the mortises in the front legs. Hold vertically in a vice and cut down to the shoulder line on the waste side of the line with a tenon saw.

5 Remove from the vice and lay flat on the bench. Hold in place with a C-clamp and cut the shoulder line to remove the waste. With the marking gauge already set, scribe a line down each side of the tenon and then saw away the sides so that the tenon is $2\frac{3}{16}$ in. wide. The end of the tenon will also be beveled parallel to the shoulders. Cut this with the tenon saw and check the fit. Adjust the components as required.

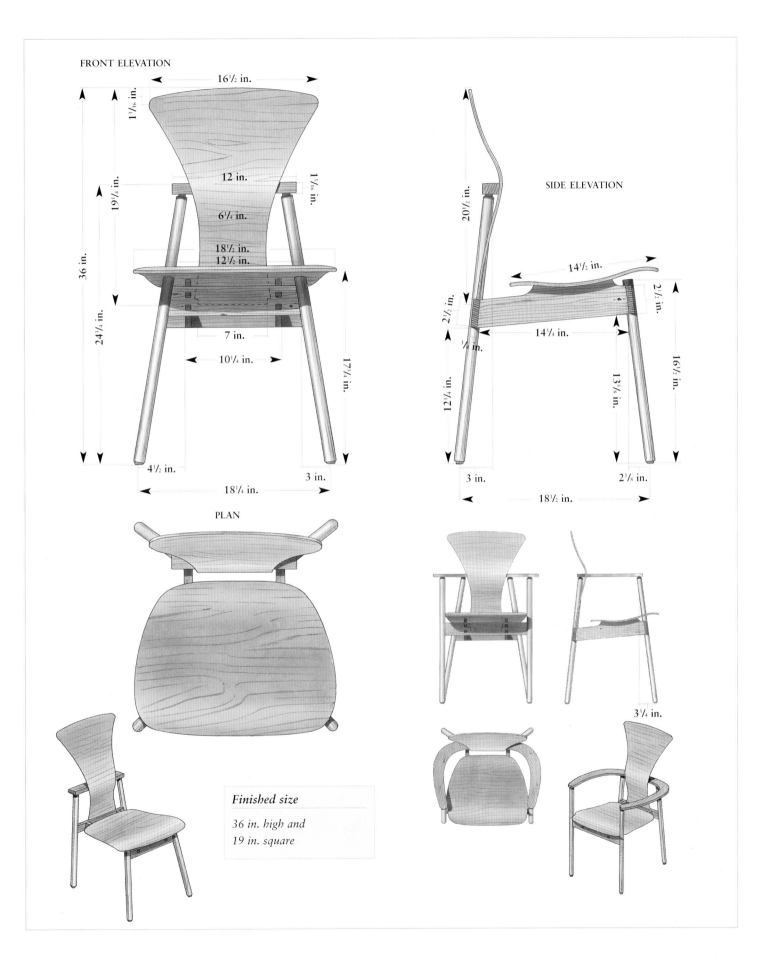

FRONT ELEVATION

16½ in.

1³⁄₁₆ in.

12 in.

1³⁄₁₆ in.

6¼ in.

18½ in.

12½ in.

19¼ in.

36 in.

24¾ in.

7 in.

10¼ in.

17¼ in.

4½ in.

3 in.

18¼ in.

SIDE ELEVATION

20½ in.

14½ in.

2½ in.

2½ in.

14¾ in.

¾ in.

12¼ in.

13⅝ in.

16½ in.

3 in.

2³⁄₈ in.

18½ in.

PLAN

3¼ in.

Finished size

36 in. high and
19 in. square

6 The back rail is set out the same as the front with one exception—it needs to be slightly longer as it is lower down the legs. To find the length, assemble the front rail and legs. Lay the back legs on top of the front ones with the bottoms flush. Mark the back legs at the top and bottom edge of the rail $^3/_{16}$ in. below these points, giving the shoulder lines. Set this out on the bottom edge of the back rail. Mark the bevels on the face and complete the set-out. Cut the tenon in the same manner as for the front rail.

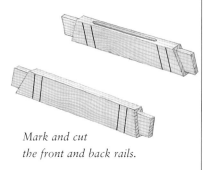

Mark and cut the front and back rails.

7 Set out the two cross-rails of the seat frame by marking the bevel across the face at one end at a pitch of 1:85. Mark the shoulder line— parallel to the bevel 1$^3/_{16}$ in. along. Measure up this line 1$^1/_8$ in. from the bottom edge. This represents the distance that the back rail is lower than the front rail. Measure a 14$^3/_4$-in. line perpendicular to the bevel from this point to the bottom edge— this indicates the length between the shoulders on the bottom edge. Mark the other shoulder line at a pitch of 1:7, and then the tenon length of $^3/_4$ in.

Carefully mark out all the cut lines on the cross-rails.

8 Set out the cutouts for the cross-rails. Measure up the front of each shoulder line 2$^5/_8$ in., and mark a line along the length from shoulder to shoulder. From the front shoulder, measure back 2 in., and then another 8 in. on the top edge. Make a curve from this point back toward each end down to the previous line along the length. Cut these with a jigsaw, and clean up with a plane or chisel.

9 Cut the cross-rails slightly over length. They will be cleaned up when assembled.

10 The width of the double tenons on the cross-rails is $^1/_2$ in. Divide the 2$^5/_8$-in. shoulder line into five equal spaces. Cut these down on the waste side to the shoulder lines and crosscut away the waste on the outside. Remove the waste between the tenons with a coping saw, and then pare back to the shoulder line with a chisel.

Cut the tenons on the cross-rail.

11 To set out the double mortises in the front and back rails, find the center of the bottom edge of both rails and measure 4$^3/_8$ in. on each side, plus the thickness of the wood. Square a line across the faces of both rails. Measure up five spaces of $^1/_2$ in. from the bottom edge. The second and fourth are the through mortises. Set these out on all four faces. Cut the mortises with a $^3/_8$-in. drill bit and then a chisel. Check the fit and adjust as necessary.

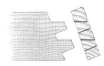

Mark and cut the double mortises for the front and back rails.

12 Dry-assemble the chair frame and check the shoulders of the rails. It will be necessary to adjust the shoulders with a chisel in order to achieve neat fitting joints.

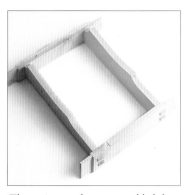

The main seat frame assembled dry.

13 It is at this stage that the octagonal legs should be planed or turned to a round shape. At the top of the back legs, turn a 1-in. diameter dowel $^5/_{16}$ in. long.

14 Mark out the top rail. Here the tops of the back legs are rounded to fit the holes in the rail. Mark the rail and these angled holes by holding the rail behind the legs and marking the positions of the dowel tops. Square the lines across the face and mark the centers for the holes. Drill the holes in the center on this set-out. These holes will also be at an angle in order to match the marks on the edge. This is best achieved on a drill press with a Forstner bit. Cut the rail to an approximate length of 12 in. on a radial-arm saw.

Fit the legs to the top rail.

15 Set up a router with an ⁵⁄₁₆-in. straight bit and cut a groove 6⅜ in. long and ⁵⁄₁₆ in. deep in the center of the top edge of the lower back rail.

Assembling the underframe

You should now be able to assemble the whole underframe dry, before securing the components with adhesive.

16 The cross-rail joints are wedged through mortise and tenons, so disassemble and cut the slots for the wedges. Cut the wedges from any piece of scrap. Sand off any set-out marks.

17 Assemble the seat frame, cross, front, and back rails by gluing and clamping the joints. Insert the wedges. Be sure the frame is completely square and free of twist.

18 When the adhesive has cured, plane off the excess tenons and wedges on the outside face.

19 Fix the four legs to this frame by gluing the tenons and clamping. Pull the joints tight with the clamps. Check that each pair of legs is in line with the other and that there is no twist in the frame.

20 Finally, fit the top rail over the dowels and wedge these joints into

place. Skim any projection with a smoothing plane and sand as necessary.

Fit the legs and cross-rails together.

Using preforms to mold the seat and back to shape

The interesting feature of this chair is the preformed seat and back. If produced in a factory these would be made from sheets of constructional veneer, but for our purposes it is better to make them from thin plywood. First, it is necessary to make the molds that will form these individual sheets of plywood into the required shape. The seat is a single curvature, while the back has a single curve but also wings that are slightly curved at the top of the central shape. Very precise work is necessary to make these molds.

21 First, determine the availability of suitable plywood, particularly as to the thicknesses that are available. The final form does not need to be any thicker than ⅜ in., and so if you use ⅛-in. plywood you will need three layers. If you use ¹⁄₁₆-in. plywood, you would get a thinner form using five layers, resulting in a thickness of ⁵⁄₁₆ in. Since it is desirable for the grain direction on both outside faces to run the same

way, particularly on the back preform, you will need an uneven number of layers.

22 Now, make the seat mold. First, make the sides of the mold by setting out a curve on the piece of manufactured board to suit grid shape on the right. Set out another line parallel, equal to the thickness of the form. Cut both lines with a jigsaw. This will give two matching sides (top and bottom) with a space for the form to go between.

23 Next, cut the lateral strips to length and fix them into the sides as shown below. Make sure that the top edges are flush. Check fit and finish by shaping or sanding to the correct curvature.

24 Cut and fix the two end pieces, which stabilize the mold when pressure is applied. Finally, cut the top of the mold and glue in place.

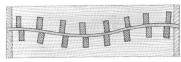

Make the seat mold.

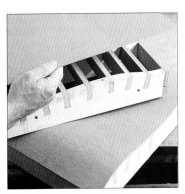

Fix the top of the seat mold.

25 Try the mold dry with the pieces you have cut for one seat form. Clamp the jig together to press the sheets to the shape.

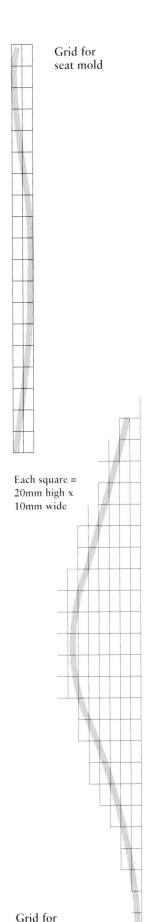

Grid for
seat mold

Each square =
20mm high x
10mm wide

Grid for
back mold

279

Expert tip

Place paper or poly-ethylene sheets between the mold and the work to keep any adhesive that may seep out between the laminated pieces from gluing the work to the form.

26 If all is well, apply adhesive to the faces to be glued and clamp the mold, leaving it clamped long enough for the adhesive to cure. Remove from the mold, mark the shape from the grid on page 279, trim with a jigsaw, and sand the edges.

Clamp the plywood in the mold.

27 The back mold is made in a similar way as the seat, except that at the top there is a slight curve on each side (see drawing on page 277). Make the center of the mold in the same way as you made the seat mold (see page 279 for grid). In addition, make a second mold for the wings of the back—this takes in the curve of the first mold along its side edges. Cut and fit into the first mold as shown below.

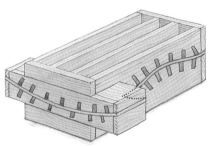

Make the back mold.

28 When this mold is finished, follow the above procedure to produce the preform, and when it is complete, cut the correct shape and finish the edges.

Final assembly

29 Sand and apply the required finish to all components and then set the preforms in position. The bottom of the back will need to be trimmed to fit into the groove on the top edge of the back rail. A ³/₈ in. wide x ⁵/₁₆ in. high cutout in each corner is required.

30 The back will be glued at the bottom into the groove and held in position with two 1-in. 8 gauge brass flat head screws into the top rail. Drill the two ³/₁₆-in. holes through the back, followed by ¹/₈-in. pilot holes. Countersink the top of the holes to let the heads of the screws sit just below the surface.

Screw the back in position.

31 The seat will be held on the cross-rails with four screws. Check the fit of the seat on the cross-rails. Plane the top edge of these for a neat fit. Drill holes through the seat, as for the back. Apply adhesive to the cross-rails and screw in place. Sand and apply required finish.

Making the Carver chair

The Carver chair is based on the standard chair described above, with just a few changes.

1 The seat frame is the same except that the front legs are straight and extend up past the seat to support the arms. The front rail is longer and the tenons are square.

The front rail is longer on the carver.

2 The front legs are also longer—mark and cut to length. Cut a dowel top in the front legs as you did for the back legs in step 14. Fit the back legs and top rail as before, and then fit the longer front legs in position. The back will be the same, as will the seat, except for slight shaping around the legs.

3 Make and fit the arms. They are made in pairs with ⁷/₈-in. wood. The arms are made from two pieces that are joined together with half lap joints on the sharp back curve. Join the two pieces together before marking and cutting the shape.

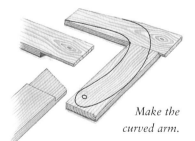

Make the curved arm.

4 When the arms are ready, drill the hole that will accept the top of the leg. Place in position and check that each fits on the top of the top rail. Mark and cut so that they join in the center of the back. Glue in place. The top of the leg can be wedged, while the back parts can be glued to the top of the top rail. Sand and finish.

The swinging avant-garde

In the second half of the 20th century, technological advances dramatically changed many aspects of everyday life and furniture design also began to develop in previously unknown directions. Advances made due to the exigencies of World War II led to the development of more modern manufacturing processes and materials, which were enthusiastically embraced by designers. For example, Du Pont created nylon in 1939 and a new lightweight plastic—polyethylene—was first used commercially by the Tupper Corporation. The new materials gave designers more scope and had a dramatic effect on the forms of furniture.

THE UNITED STATES

In the United States, Charles and Ray Eames completely rejected right angles and entered a new sphere of "sculpted" furniture based on the latest technology. They designed the first mass-produced molded fiberglass shell chair, the "DAR" chair, in 1950. They also combined steel and aluminum, in conjunction with leather or fabric, for the "Aluminum group" chair of 1958 and the "GRP la Chaise." David Rowland's "GF 40/4" stacking chairs made use of steel rods with laminated plywood. A rounded womb-like shape was one of the most distinctive to emerge for chairs. Eero Saarinen's "Womb" chair was constructed of latex foam on a molded plastic shell, reinforced with fiberglass on chromium-plated steel supports. He had envisioned an enveloping chair when he designed it—one where the sitter could draw their legs up but still be supported elsewhere. It employed very generous, wide proportions and was covered in foam-rubber padding and fabric. The aim of his

design was to reduce the number of parts and minimize the manufacturing process. George Nelson's "Coconut" chair of 1956 was manufactured by Herman Miller, of which Nelson was the design director from 1946. This company devoted much of its time to studying the process for molding plywood, as well as solving the problems of attaching metal legs to plywood seats and molded plywood parts to one another. The company also paid particular attention to the new plastics that were used in the aircraft-manufacturing field.

GREAT BRITAIN

Britain's industrial capacity suffered greatly in World War II and rationing of wood and steel was in place as early as 1940. The 1950s heralded a new era in design in Britain, with inspiration from Italy, Scandinavia, and the U.S. Light, spacious interiors and vivid colors marked this period, and motifs such as molecular patterns and space imagery were popular. Ernest Race won justifiable acclaim with the medal-winning "BA aluminum chair." This was the result of real ingenuity—he used aluminum taken from scrapped war planes. This innovative technical spirit was carried forward by Robin Day, who created the "Polyprop" chair in 1963, a stackable chair that had a strong polypropylene one-piece shell and was the first that could be injection molded. This is a truly modern classic and can still be seen everywhere—in offices, schools, etc. It perfectly suited the furniture production of the time, since it was light and cheap to produce. Another influential designer of the decade, Vernon Panton, created the first single molded-fiberglass form with his "Stacking" chairs of the 1960s, which had no need for any embellishment.

In the 1960s, Britain was swinging with new ideas, attitudes, and trends. This change of attitude was apparent in many aspects of popular design. And furniture was no exception, reflecting the upbeat mood of the age with the introduction of fun pieces—the "Series Up" polyurethane foam chairs popped out of the packing containers that compressed them and Peter Murdock's "Polka Dot" children's chair was made of bright laminated paperboard that could be packed flat. These were some of the first examples of successful mass-produced furniture.

SCANDINAVIAN DESIGN
Scandinavian design of the 20th century was characterized by classic lines that resulted in high-quality furniture. Designers were sympathetic to natural materials but not afraid to take advantage of machine production, which they employed to create bold shapes and curves. When one thinks of Scandinavian design, beautiful wooden pieces spring to mind, but in the second half of the century many designers turned to new materials and proved that a similar feeling could be evoked without wood. Chairs with molded-fiberglass forms and metal frames were characteristic of this period. Arne Jaacobsen's innovative "Swan" and

Pesce's Donna chair, designed in 1969.

"Egg" chairs show how latex-foam padding can be applied over the top of a fiberglass shell to create simple, inviting curved shapes that swivel on cast-aluminum star-shaped bases. The "Egg" chair, which has been in production since 1957, has a sense of comfort and stability and is also strongly sculptural.

ITALIAN DESIGN
In Italy designers produced some classic modern pieces. Earlier pieces were based on more traditional shapes but Italian design quickly took a lead in innovation with Magistretti's 1961 stackable chair "Selene" and Joe Colombo's 1967 "Colombo" chair, which was the first all-plastic chair to be made by injection molding.

There was an explosion of ideas around the world during the 1970s and 1980s. Two major groups were Studio Alchmia under Alessandro Mendini and the Memphis group, led by Ettore Sottsass. Kukkapuro, who designed the "Karuselli" chair in 1964 became associated with the Memphis group during the 1980s. They rejected ascetic modernism and were radical, inventive, and over the top. Anything went, as long as it was modern, progressive, and decorative.

283

Display shelves

Advanced

The design of this display-shelf unit looks both modern and attractive. It provides plenty of display space and includes a small drawer within one of the shelves. The back piece (inserted as six separate panels of plywood) is optional—if you do want to add it, then follow the instructions on page 288. If not, then follow the drawing opposite.

Tools

- Smoothing plane
- Sliding bevel
- Marking knife
- Tenon saw
- Panel saw
- C-clamps
- Router with ¼-in. and ½-in. straight bit and ½-in. rabbet cutter with a ball race
- Marking gauge
- 1-in. paring chisel
- Drill and ⅛-in., 3/16-in., countersink, and ⅜-in. dowel bits
- Screwdriver
- Sash clamps
- Dovetail saw

Skills required for project

- Measuring and marking *pages 64–7*
- Basic sawing *pages 68–71*
- Planing *pages 74–81*
- Fine sawing *pages 82–5*
- Making grooves *pages 90–3*
- Drilling *pages 96–100*
- Making dado joints *pages 110–11*
- Making dovetail joints *pages 112–14*
- Using abrasives *pages 115–17*
- Assembling projects *pages 120–7*
- Using adhesives *pages 128–9*
- Wood finishing *pages 130–5*

MATERIALS

Part	Materials and dimensions	No.
	Solid wood—hardwood	
Triangle		
Long sides	82 x 12½ x 1 in.	2
Bottom short side	60 x 12½ x 1 in.	1
Plinth	59 x 2 x 1 in.	2
	12 x 2 x 1 in.	2
Shelves		
Top	86 x 8 x 1 in.	1
Second	81 x 8¾ x 1 in.	1
Third	75 x 9½ x 1 in.	1
Fifth	63 x 10¼ x 1 in.	1
Shelf/drawer	71 x 10½ x 1 in.	1
Build-up	71 x 6 x 1 in.	1
Thickness	71 x 3 x 1 in.	1
battens	16¾ x 2 x 1 in.	4
Dowels	2 in. x ⅜ in. diameter	30
Support battens	71 x 3 x ¾ in.	2
	82 x 3 x ¾ in.	2
	94½ x 3 x ¾ in.	1
Drawer		
Sides	16 x 2 x ⅝ in.	2
Back	32 x 2 x ⅝ in.	1
Drawer runner	16 x 5/16 x 5/16 in.	2
	Plywood—the approximate sized triangles will be base x height x ¼ in. thick; do not cut these until the carcass is assembled	
Top back	14 ½ x 12 in.	1
Second back	21 x 9 in.	1
Third back	29 x 8 ¼ in.	1
Fourth back	37½ x 8¼ in.	1
Fifth back	47 x 10¼ in.	1
Sixth back	56 x 12½ in.	1
Drawer bottom	32 x 16 x ¼ in.	1

Other materials: forty 1 1/16-in. 8 gauge flat head screws; fifty ½-in. 6 gauge flat head screws; six 2-in. 8 gauge flat head screws; adhesive (PVA); sandpaper; finish.

Making the triangular carcass

1 First, make the slanting front face of the two long sides of the triangle (see drawing opposite, side elevation)—the sides measure 12 in. at the base tapering to 8 in. at the top. Cut and plane both sides to shape. Apply a face-edge and face-side mark to the opposite side. Do all the setting out from this back edge.

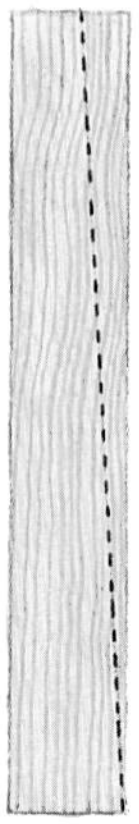

Taper the front edge of the sides.

2 On a piece of manufactured board, make a set-out, either full-sized or scaled, for the miters on each corner. Remember that the top one is a more acute angle than the two at the bottom. Set up a sliding bevel to the miter joint.

3 The overall measurements of the two sides are 80½ in. long and the bottom is 59 in. long. Mark these lengths with the miter joints on the side faces. Mark the joints across each face.

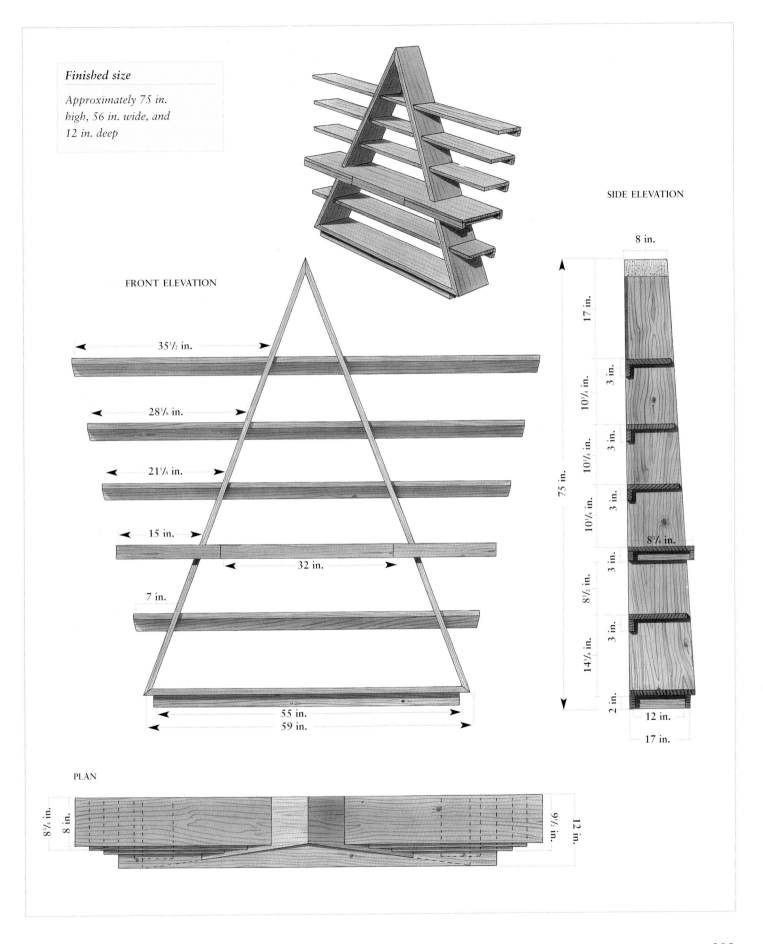

Finished size

Approximately 75 in.
high, 56 in. wide, and
12 in. deep

SIDE ELEVATION

8 in.

17 in.

3 in.

10¼ in.

3 in.

10¼ in.

3 in.

10¼ in.

3 in.

8½ in.

3 in.

14¼ in.

2 in.

75 in.

8¾ in.

12 in.

17 in.

FRONT ELEVATION

35½ in.

28⅛ in.

21⅝ in.

15 in.

32 in.

7 in.

55 in.

59 in.

PLAN

8¾ in.

8 in.

12 in.

9½ in.

4 These miters should be cut first with a marking knife and then sawed on the waste side with a tenon saw—a power saw will not tilt over the required angle. Hold each side on edge in a vice and cut the miter down the waste side of the line, stopping periodically to check the cut. Remove from the vice and lay flat on a firm surface. Hold with a C-clamp.

5 Plane the miter true with a finely set, sharp smoothing plane. Hold the plane at an angle and plane across the miter from side to side. Test the surface with the sliding bevel and then place a metal straightedge on the planed surface to check that it is flat. Plane off any highs down to the knife lines. Repeat on all the miter joints.

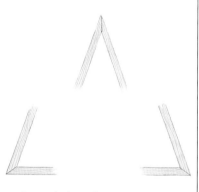

Cut and plane the miters to make the triangular corners.

6 Next, cut a bevel on the edge of six softwood clamping blocks, which give parallel faces to the miter surface so that the clamps will pull the miter joint together securely and precisely as well as protecting the surface of the project during clamping. When a block is cut along its length on the bevel, the scrap will form the clamping block for the opposite side of that miter. The beveled edge must be cut to produce a 90-degree surface off the face of the joint, with the outside edge parallel to that of the joint.

7 Glue the blocks to the outside faces at the three miters. Apply PVA adhesive to all the surfaces, align the top edge of the block to the end of the miter and allow to dry completely.

Glue softwood clamping blocks to each miter.

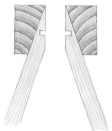

8 Set up a router with a ¼-in. straight bit to run a ¼-in. deep groove in the face of each miter for a loose tongue. Run the router fence off the block. The groove must be set across the face of the joint, taking care not to cut through to the outside of the work. Run the groove on all six faces. Cut three ½ x 12¼ in. tongues from ¼ in. thick plywood. Test the fit of each joint and then dry-assemble the three pieces in clamps. Adjust as required.

9 Do not glue these mitered corners together yet. Leave them in the clamps face down on a flat surface.

10 On the edge of the sides of the triangular carcass, mark the position of the shelves, ensuring that they will be parallel with the base. Use a scrap piece of wood as a sample—the same thickness as the shelf material. Lay this on top of the assembled carcass and measure the spacing required at each end from the bottom to ensure that they are parallel. Mark both ends of the sample on the carcass with a pencil and square across each face. Repeat for all the shelves.

11 Now, mark the positions of the support battens that go under the rear edge of the shelves. The battens are 3 in. high x ¾ in. thick. Measure 3 in. below each shelf mark on the carcass. Mark this across the back edge parallel to the shelf and square down each face. Set a marking gauge to the thickness of ¾ in., and scribe the line back to the shelf. These slots will be cut later in step 17. Take the carcass out of the clamps.

12 Cut the dado joints in the sides of the carcass to accommodate the shelves. Mark the depth of the dado ¼ in. between the set-out shelf lines on the back edge. Square a line from the top of the shelf across to the depth line. Repeat this on the bottom inside shelf line.

13 Construct a router jig to cut the dado. Note that one shoulder is square to the face while the other is angled. The router needs to cut the dado to the width at the bottom ¼ in. line. Use a ½ in. straight bit and a template collar fixed to the baseplate. Make the jig and test on a piece of scrap wood before cutting the work. Make a stop to fit to the jig that can be adjusted for each different shelf width. Set up the jig and machine each dado.

Set up a router jig, ready to pare away the waste.

14 Use a sharp chisel to cut the angled shoulder on one side of each housing. Pare away the waste and square up the ends with a chisel. Reassemble dry in the clamps.

Chisel the angled edge of the housing.

Making the shelves

Prepare the materials for the five shelves to their full lengths (see drawing on page 285). The instructions are virtually the same for each shelf but, of course, each is a different length. The center portions of these shelves will be fitted to the inside of the carcass on the rear battens first and the outside extensions will be fitted later. The ends of the shelves will fit into dadoes on both the inside and outside faces of the triangle sides and have dowels fitted within for added strength.

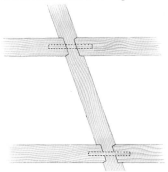

The shelves are held in place with dado joints and dowels.

15 When preparing the shelves, mark each to the final length so that the grain will match. First, mark the part of the shelf that will fit inside the carcass and the outside parts to match up later. Cut the center part of each shelf to length with a panel saw, shaping a bevel in each end to match the angle of the triangle side. Plane this true. Note that the bottom edge of the bevel will require a matching angle planed on it to fit the dado. Fit the three top shelves and the bottom shelf. Be sure that they will fit into the dadoes. It is always best to work on one shelf at a time.

16 Next, construct drilling jigs to match the angles of the shelf and the sides. Use the jigs to drill the holes in the ends of the shelves and in the sides, right through to a depth of ¾ in. for the dowels.

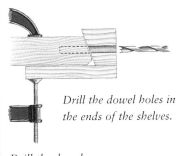

Drill the dowel holes in the ends of the shelves.

Drill the dowel holes in the sides.

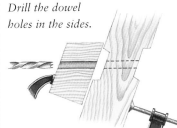

17 Next, check the positions of the slots for the rear battens, which you marked out in step 11. Ensure that they are all level with each other and the back. Then cut these slots into the carcass sides with a tenon saw.

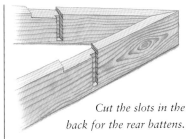

Cut the slots in the back for the rear battens.

18 Prepare to assemble the three top shelves and the bottom shelf. Assemble the triangle and shelves dry to check fit and then apply adhesive to the joints on the inside faces of the shelves. Insert dowels through the sides into the ends of the shelves, leaving them protruding on the outside of the carcass.

Glue the shelves into place. The grooves will be cut in step 28.

19 Next, apply adhesive to the mitered corners and insert the tongues at the joints. C-clamp the miters and check the work for true.

Clamp the mitered bottom corners of the triangular carcass.

Clamp the top miters together.

Fixing the rear battens

20 Next, prepare the five rear battens that support the shelves. Check that they all fit into the slots already cut in step 17, that they are the correct length and that when positioned they are all parallel with each other and the base.

Check the rear battens are parallel.

21 Glue and screw them into place through the back using 1³/₁₆ in. 8 gauge flat head screws. You will now have a triangular cabinet with four inside shelves in place and with five extending battens to support the outside shelves.

Making the back and plinth

22 Prepare the plywood backs for fitting. Since the back will not be one whole piece, rabbets need to be made around each opening in the

sides and in the rear battens into which the plywood backs will fit. Use a ¹/₂ in. rabbet cutter with a ball race, and cut the rabbets ¹/₄ in. deep and ¹/₂ in. wide.

Cut rabbets for the back panels.

23 Now mark each of the six back pieces of wood—because of the angled ends you will be able to cut economically from a single sheet of plywood. Cut and fit each back into the rabbets and fix with ¹/₂ in. 6 gauge flat head screws.

Screw the back panels in position.

24 Now fit the bottom plinth. Prepare the wood and mark and cut the dovetails in the corners. Glue the four sections of the plinth together. When dry, sand the surface.

25 Fix the plinth in place by pocket screwing through the bottom

edge, using three 2 in. 8 gauge flat head screws along each long edge.

Screw the plinth into place on the bottom of the unit.

26 Now, prepare the outer shelf extensions. You will already have these pieces from when you measured them before step 15. Using the jig as shown in step 16, drill the holes for the dowels and offer up to the unit so that you can ensure that the shelf ends fit into the dadoes.

27 When the outside ends are finished, the shelves can be placed into position. The rear battens and the shelves can be pocket screwed together. Drill pocket holes ⁵/₁₆ in. in diameter and a clearance hole of ³/₁₆ in. Check that all fits well, apply the adhesive, and clamp and screw the shelves into place.

Check the fit and then fix the outer shelves into position.

Metabo UK Ltd
25 Majestic Road
Nursling Industrial Estate
Southampton SO16 0YT
(for machinery)

Purves & Purves
80–81 Tottenham Court Road
London W1T 9QE
Tel: + 44 (0)20 7580 8223
for suede square
footstools (chessboard
project), ivory Phoenix
chairs (dining table
project) and Zen rug
(home office project)

Record Power Ltd
Parkway Works
Sheffield S9 3BL

Smee Timber Ltd
Smokehall Lane
Winsford
Cheshire
(for timber)

**For providing images
for us to use:**

Axminster Power Tools Centre,
for permission to use images
of machine tools (for address,
see tools suppliers).

Batheaston
20 Leafield Way
Leafield Industrial Estate
Corsham
Wiltshire SN13 9SW
Tel: + 44 (0)1225 811 295

Stewart Linford Furniture Maker
High Wycombe

**For allowing us permission
to photograph on site:**

The Antique Trader
at The Millinery Works
85/87 Southgate Road
Islington
London N1 3JS
Tel: + 44 (0)20 7359 2019
Fax. + 44 (0)20 7359 5792
www.millineryworks.co.uk

Didier Aaron
21 Ryder Street
St James'
London
Tel: + 44 (0)20 7839 4716
Fax: + 44 (0)20 7930 6699

Eltham Palace Court Yard
Eltham
London SE9 5QE
Tel: + 44 (0)20 8294 2548
Fax: + 44 (0)20 8294 2621

The Fine Art Society Plc
148 New Bond Street
London W1Y 0JT
Tel: + 44 (0)20 7629 5116
Fax: + 44 (0)20 7491 9454
www.the-fine-art-society.co.uk

Geffrye Museum
Kingsland Road
London E2 8EA
Tel: + 44 (0)20 7739 9893
Fax: + 44 (0)20 7729 5647

Indigo
275 New Kings Road
London SW6 4RD
Tel: + 44 (0)20 7384 3101
Fax: + 44 (0)20 7384 3102

Ki UK Ltd
Commonwealth House
148-153 High Holborn
London W61V 6PJ
Tel: + 44 (0)20 7404 7441
Fax: + 44 (0)20 7404 7442

Norman Adams
10 Hans Road
London SW3 1RX
Tel: + 44 (0)20 7589 5266
Fax: + 44 (0)20 7589 1968

Rupert Cavendish Antiques
610 King's Road
London SW6 2DX
Tel: + 44 (0)20 7731 7041
Fax: + 44 (0)20 7731 8302
www.rupertcavendish.co.uk

SCP Ltd
135–139 Curtain Road
London
Tel: + 44 (0)20 7739 1869
Fax: + 44 (0)20 7729 4224
www.scp.co.uk

Skandium
72 Wigmore Street
London W18 9DL
Tel: + 44 (0)20 7935 2088
Fax: + 44 (0)20 7224 2099
www.skandium.com

Shaker Ltd
72–3 Marylebone High Street
London W1M 3AR
Tel: + 44 (0)20 7935 9461
Fax: + 44 (0)20 7935 4157
www.shaker.co.uk

Twentytwentyone
Shop:
274 Upper Street
London N1 2UA
Tel/Fax: + 44 (0)20 7288 1996
Office/warehouse:
18c River Street
London EC1R 1XN
Tel: + 44 (0)20 7837 1900
Fax: + 44 (0)20 7837 1908
www.twentytwentyone.com

Index

Entries in italic refer to
photographs or illustrations.